access to history

Br GB

access to history

Britain 1945–2007

Michael Lynch

HODDER
EDUCATION
PART OF HACHETTE LIVRE UK

Study guides revised and updated, 2008, by Sally Waller (AQA), Angela Leonard (Edexcel) and Martin Jones (OCR A and B).

The publishers would like to thank the following individuals, institutions and companies for permission to reproduce copyright illustrations in this book: AFP/Getty Images, page 91; © Bettmann/Corbis, page 44; Churchill Archives Centre, Thatcher Papers, THCR 8/2/33 (White House Press photograph) page 162; Michael Cummings, *Daily Express*, 10th November 1969/British Cartoon Archive, University of Kent, page 225; © Sergio Gaudent/Kipa/Corbis, page 118; Getty Images, pages 94, 108, 110; Charles Griffin, *Daily Mirror*, 12th May 1988/British Cartoon Archive, University of Kent, page 157; © Hulton-Deutsch Collection/Corbis, page 6; By permission of Llyfrgell Genedlaethol Cymru/National Library of Wales/Solo Syndication, page 19; Mac (Stan McMurtry), *Daily Mail*, 12th February 1975/British Cartoon Archive, University of Kent, page 119; Paul Popper/Popperfoto/Getty Images, page 84; Punch Ltd, pages 14, 31; *The Scotsman*/Corbis Sygma, page 172; Trog (Wally Fawkes), *The Observer*, 20th February 1972/British Cartoon Archive, University of Kent, page 99; Vicky (Victor Weisz), *Evening Standard*, 6th November 1958/British Cartoon Archive, University of Kent, page 45; Vicky (Victor Weisz), *Evening Standard*, 19th May 1959/British Cartoon Archive, University of Kent, page 56; Vicky (Victor Weisz), *Evening Standard*, 3rd March 1960/British Cartoon Archive, University of Kent, page 68; George Whitelaw, *Daily Herald*, 2nd December 1941/British Cartoon Archive, University of Kent, page 9; George Whitelaw, *Daily Herald*, 26th November 1944/British Cartoon Archive, University of Kent, page 8.

The publishers would like to acknowledge use of the following extracts: Arrow Books Ltd. for extracts from *The Benn Diaries* by Tony Benn, 1994; Collins Educational for an extract from *Britain 1914–2000* by Derrick Murphy, 2000; The Daily Telegraph for an extract from *The British Century* by John Keegan, 1999; HarperCollins Publishers Ltd. for extracts from *The Downing Street Years* by Margaret Thatcher, 1993; Longman for an extract from *Britain Under Thatcher* by A. Seldon and D. Collings, 2000; Penguin Books Ltd. For extracts from *Hope and Glory Britain* by Peter Clarke, 1990; Poolbeg Press for an extract from *INLA: Deadly Divisions* by Jack Holland and Henry MacDonald, 1996; Weidenfeld & Nicholson for extracts from *As It Seemed to Me* by John Cole, 1995.

Every effort has been made to trace all copyright holders, but if any have been inadvertently overlooked the Publishers will be pleased to make the necessary arrangements at the first opportunity.

Hachette Livre UK's policy is to use papers that are natural, renewable and recyclable products and made from wood grown in sustainable forests. The logging and manufacturing processes are expected to conform to the environmental regulations of the country of origin.

Orders: please contact Bookpoint Ltd, 130 Milton Park, Abingdon, Oxon OX14 4SB. Telephone: (44) 01235 827720. Fax: (44) 01235 400454. Lines are open 9.00–5.00, Monday to Saturday, with a 24-hour message answering service. Visit our website at www.hoddereducation.co.uk

© Michael Lynch 2008
First published in 2008 by
Hodder Education,
Part of Hachette Livre UK
338 Euston Road
London NW1 3BH

Impression number   5 4 3 2 1
Year   2012 2011 2010 2009 2008

Cover photo shows the then Prime Minister, Margaret Thatcher, after her closing speech at the Conservative Party Conference in Brighton in 1984, © Bettmann/Corbis
Typeset in 10/12pt Baskerville and produced by Gray Publishing, Tunbridge Wells
Printed in Malta

A catalogue record for this title is available from the British Library

ISBN: 978 0340 965 955

Contents

Dedication

Keith Randell (1943–2002)

The *Access to History* series was conceived and developed by Keith, who created a series to 'cater for students as they are, not as we might wish them to be'. He leaves a living legacy of a series that for over 20 years has provided a trusted, stimulating and well-loved accompaniment to post-16 study. Our aim with these new editions is to continue to offer students the best possible support for their studies.

For Lily May Lynch, born 2007

1 The Labour Party in Power 1945–51

POINTS TO CONSIDER

The period 1945–51 was one of the most formative in the whole century. Labour came into power with a large majority following an impressive victory in the 1945 election. During the next six years it introduced the welfare state and nationalised a significant part of the industrial economy. In doing so, the Labour government set a pattern that was largely followed by all succeeding governments before 1979. This chapter describes the domestic achievements of Clement Attlee's post-war governments and examines the historical debate over those achievements:

- Labour's victory in 1945
- Clement Attlee and his ministers
- Labour's creation of the welfare state
- Nationalisation
- Labour's economic problems
- Labour's defeat in 1951
- The legacy of the Attlee years

Key dates

1945	Overwhelming election victory for Labour
	Family Allowances Act
1946	National Insurance Act
	Industrial Injuries Act
	Nationalisation of coal, civil aviation, Cable and Wireless, Bank of England
1946–7	A severe winter intensified the government's austerity measures
1947	Government undertook to develop Britain's independent nuclear deterrent
	Nationalisation of road transport and electricity services
	Independence of India
1948	NHS began
	National Assistance Act
	Britain began to receive Marshall Plan aid
1949	Nationalisation of iron and steel
	Government forced to devalue the pound

1950   Start of Korean War
       Election reduced Labour majority to five seats
1951   Bevanite rebellion over prescription charges
       Election success for Conservatives, but Labour
          gained highest popular vote yet

1 | Labour's Victory in 1945

The scale of the Labour Party's victory in 1945 surprised even the party itself. It had gained a massive majority of 180 over the Conservatives and one of 148 overall.

Key question
What was the scale of Labour's success in the 1945 election?

Overwhelming election victory for Labour: 1945

Key date

Table 1.1: Election results July 1945

Political party	No. of votes	No. of seats	Percentage of vote
Labour	11,995,152	393	47.8
Conservative	9,988,306	213	39.8
Liberal	2,248,226	12	9.0
Communist	102,780	2	0.4
Others	751,514	20	3.0

In proportional terms, the victory is less impressive; Labour was two per cent short of winning half the total vote, and the opposition parties collectively polled more votes and had a greater percentage of popular support. Despite its overwhelming number of seats, Labour was a minority government. The disparity that the '**first past the post system**' electoral system had produced is evident in the following figures:

- for each seat Labour won, it had polled 30,522 votes
- for each seat the Conservative Party won, it had polled 46,893 votes
- for each seat the Liberal Party won, it had polled 187,352.

However, the observations made above apply to all the governments elected between 1945 and 2005; none of them came to power with the majority of the electorate having voted for them. In all their future election victories, the Conservatives would similarly gain from the inbuilt imbalance of the system which does not operate according to the principle of **proportional representation**. It was only the Liberals who missed out because they could not convert their popular following into seats in Parliament. Political commentators are fond of talking, as in regard to 1945, of landslides and crushing defeats, but these things simply do not happen. What does occur is a marginal shift in a range of closely fought constituencies, sufficient to give the winning party the edge over its opponents.

With that said, it is undeniable that Labour had performed extraordinarily well. In the previous election in 1935, it had gained 37.9 per cent of the overall vote, but had won only 154 seats. In 1945 it gained 10 per cent more of the vote, increased its support by three and half million, and won 393 seats.

First past the post system
The candidate with more votes than his nearest rival wins the seat, irrespective of whether he has an overall majority of the votes cast.

Proportional representation
The allocation of seats to parties according to the number of votes they gain overall.

Key terms

Key question
Why did the Labour Party win a large-scale victory in the 1945 election?

Key terms

Depression
The period of industrial decline that had witnessed high unemployment and social distress in many areas of Britain in the 1930s.

'Land fit for heroes'
Term used by Lloyd George's wartime government of 1916–18 when promising to reward the British people for their heroic efforts.

Gestapo
The notorious Nazi secret police that had terrorised Germany under Adolf Hitler, between 1933 and 1945.

In hindsight, the reasons for this are not difficult to find. Churchill's great popularity as a wartime leader did not carry over into peacetime. In the minds of a good part of the electorate his Conservative Party was associated with the grim **depression** of the 1930s and with the failure either to prevent war or to prepare for it adequately.

In 1945 there was also a widespread feeling in Britain that effective post-war social and economic reconstruction was both vital and deserved, and that the tired old Conservative establishment that had dominated the inter-war years would be incapable of providing it. People could remember clearly how a generation earlier the Lloyd George Coalition and the Conservative governments of the 1920s had failed to deliver the **'land fit for heroes'** that the nation had been promised. It was not so much that Labour won the election as that the Conservatives lost it.

Another important factor was the Conservatives' poor electioneering. Confident of victory, Churchill misread the mood of the nation. On one notorious occasion he suggested that the Labour Party's proposed reform programme would require 'a *Gestapo*' to enforce it. He also failed to appreciate the reputation that had been gained by the leading Labour figures who had served in his own wartime Coalition. The ministerial record of such men as Attlee, Cripps, Bevin, Dalton and Morrison had destroyed any doubts there might have been about their ability or loyalty.

It used to be claimed that the size of Labour's victory was due to the pro-Labour teaching in the education services of the armed forces. The argument was that the teachers conscripted into the education corps during the war were predominantly left-wing and gave slanted talks and instruction in the classes they put on for the troops. When the soldiers cast their vote in the election, therefore, they had already been indoctrinated into supporting Labour.

It is a difficult claim to sustain. Even if one could know precisely how the armed services voted, it would still not be possible to know their motives. The personnel in education may indeed have leaned to the left, but to ascribe Labour's victory to their efforts would be an exaggeration. What is more likely to have had an impact on voters' attitudes was the work of the government's wartime propaganda department. The documentary films that it put on regularly in the cinemas were not simply anti-German. A recurring theme was the need for the people to look beyond the war and think in terms of acting together to reconstruct a better nation. Such films were not overtly supportive of the Labour Party, and were probably not deliberately intended to be, but their message was much more in tune with the ideas of Labour than any of the other parties.

Reasons for Labour's large-scale victory in 1945
Conservative handicaps
- A broad feeling that the inter-war governments which had been largely dominated by the Conservatives had not understood the needs of ordinary people.
- Churchill's inability to carry his wartime popularity into peacetime. While he was deeply admired for his wartime leadership, Churchill was unable to convince the British people that he could be relied upon as a domestic politician in peacetime.
- The inability of Conservative politicians to manage the economy and deal with unemployment during the 1930s.
- The inglorious **appeasement** policy of the Conservative-dominated National Government that had failed to prevent war occurring.
- The memories of the failure of the inter-war governments to provide 'a land fit for heroes'.
- The Conservative Party's ill-judged and unconvincing election campaign.

Labour's advantages
- The attractive image of the Labour Party as representing the progressive *zeitgeist* that encouraged reform and reconstruction.
- Even the Conservatives had accepted the need for post-war construction, but the general view was that Labour was better fitted to carry it out.
- The leading Labour figures had gained invaluable experience as ministers in the wartime Coalition and had gained the respect of the electorate.
- A willingness among voters to overlook Labour's own failings in 1924 and 1929–31 or to put them down to Labour's difficulties as a minority government.
- In 1945 the imbalance in the electoral system worked in Labour's favour.

The leading members of Attlee's governments
In forming his government, Clement Attlee could call on the services of a remarkable set of politicians, most of whom had already proved themselves in public office as loyal and successful members of Churchill's wartime Coalition.

Ernest Bevin
Bevin ranks alongside Churchill and Attlee as one of the most influential British statesman of the age. Between the wars, as a right-wing Labour Party member and trade unionist, he fought against the Communist infiltration of the unions and the party. He held ministerial office continuously for over 10 years after 1940, playing a critical role as Minister of Labour under Churchill in organising the war effort. As Foreign Secretary between 1945 and 1950, in a critical period of **Cold War** diplomacy, he established the basic lines of British foreign policy for the next

Key terms

Appeasement
The policy followed by the British government between 1935 and 1939 of trying to avoid war by accepting German and Italian territorial demands.

Zeitgeist
Spirit of the times, i.e. the dominant prevailing attitude.

Cold War
The period of strained relations over the period 1945–91 between the Soviet Union and its allies and the Western nations led by the USA.

Key question
What qualities distinguished the members of Attlee's government?

Key term

Austerity
Describes the hard times the British experienced in the late 1940s. In addition to the restrictions and rationing imposed on them, people had to endure a particularly severe winter in 1946–7 which exhausted coal stocks and led to fuel shortages and regular and dispiriting cuts in domestic and industrial electricity supplies.

half century. His pro-American and anti-Soviet stance was the essential position adopted by Britain throughout the Cold War.

Stafford Cripps

Cripps was regarded as the most intellectually gifted member of Attlee's government. His strong pro-Communist leanings became more acceptable after the USSR entered the war in 1941. He took the post of Minister of Aircraft Production between 1942 and 1945. Cripps was sent on special missions to India in 1942 and 1946 and helped prepare the way to Indian independence (see page 22). His lean features and joyless manner seemed perfectly fitted to his role as Chancellor of the Exchequer during the period of **austerity** after 1947, calling on the nation to make sacrifices and put up with shortages and restrictions. In an unfortunate, but not altogether inappropriate, slip of the tongue, a BBC radio announcer once introduced him as 'Sir Stifford Craps'.

Herbert Morrison

Morrison served with distinction as Home Secretary throughout the war and showed the same dedication as Attlee's second in command after 1945. However, at a personal level Morrison was not an easy man to get on with. He had a running feud with Aneurin Bevan, whose left-wing views he regarded as dangerous. Morrison also clashed with Ernest Bevin. On hearing someone describe Morrison as being his own worst enemy, Bevin growled, 'Not while I'm alive, he ain't.' Having lost to Attlee in the leadership election in 1935, Morrison seemed to be permanently sidelined within the party. He served as Deputy Prime Minister between 1945 and 1951 and, after a brief spell as Foreign Secretary in 1951, as deputy leader of the party between 1951 and 1955.

Hugh Dalton

Dalton had been Minister of Economic Warfare and President of the Board of Trade under Churchill. He made a major contribution to the planning of Labour's nationalisation programme. A loud, self-opinionated academic whom Attlee tolerated only because of his talents, Dalton had to resign as Chancellor of the Exchequer in 1947 after incautiously leaking some of his budget plans.

Key date

A severe winter intensified the government's austerity measures: 1946–7

Aneurin Bevan

Bevan was the dominant figure on the left of the Labour Party in Attlee's time. He came from a Welsh mining background and represented the Ebbw Vale constituency continuously from 1929 to his death in 1960. Like Churchill, he overcame a speech impediment to become an outstanding parliamentary orator. His greatest achievement as a minister was the creation of the National Health Service (NHS), which came into operation in 1948 (see page 12). He was defeated for the leadership of the party after Attlee's retirement in 1955 by Hugh Gaitskell.

History now suggests that Attlee himself may be regarded as the outstanding figure in his government.

Profile: Clement Attlee 1883–1967

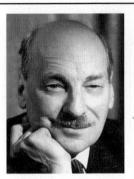

1883	–	Born in London into a comfortable middle-class family
1901–4	–	Studied law at Oxford
1907	–	Became the manager of a boys' settlement in London's East End
1914–18	–	Served as an officer in the First World War
1919	–	Became Mayor of Stepney
1922	–	Elected Labour MP for Limehouse
1930–1	–	Served in Ramsay MacDonald's Labour government
1935–55	–	Leader of the Labour Party
1940–5	–	Deputy Prime Minister in Churchill's wartime Coalition government
1945–51	–	Prime Minister
1955	–	Retired as Labour leader and went to the House of Lords
1967	–	Died

In his own time and for years afterwards, Clement Attlee tended to be underrated. He suffered by comparison with Winston Churchill. Attlee's unprepossessing physical presence and limited skills as a public speaker did not create the grand image.

However, in the 1970s, Attlee began to be reassessed. Stress was laid upon his skill in surviving six years of one of the most difficult periods of twentieth-century government. Nor was it merely survival. His record as Prime Minister was truly remarkable. Nationalisation, the welfare state, NATO, Indian independence: these were the striking successes of this unassuming man. His ordinariness was, indeed, a positive virtue in that he came to typify the very people whose well-being he did so much to advance. Attlee's achievements would have been impressive at any time, but when it is appreciated that they were accomplished in a post-war period dominated by the most demanding of domestic and international crises they appear even more striking.

In an interview in 1960, Attlee summed up his own practical, down-to-earth style of conducting government business:

> A Prime Minister has to know when to ask for an opinion. He can't always stop ministers offering theirs; you always have some people who'll talk on everything. But he can make sure to extract the opinion of those he wants when he needs them. The job of the Prime Minister is to get the general feeling – collect the voices. And then, when everything reasonable has been said, to get on with the job and say. 'Well, I think the decision of the Cabinet is this, that or the other. Any objections?' Usually there aren't.
>
> (*A Prime Minister on Prime Ministers* by Harold Wilson, 1977)

Stories are often told of Churchill's withering comments on Attlee's lack of personality. The stories are apocryphal; Churchill always denied them. Despite their party differences, Churchill had the deepest respect for the talent and integrity of the man who had been his committed and loyal wartime deputy, describing him as 'a gallant English gentleman'.

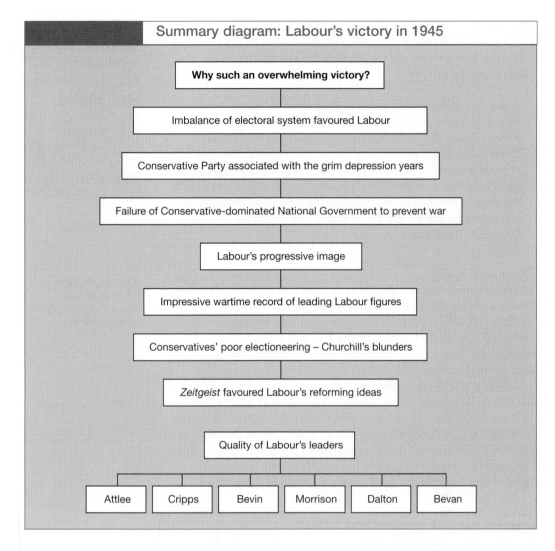

Summary diagram: Labour's victory in 1945

Why such an overwhelming victory?

Imbalance of electoral system favoured Labour

Conservative Party associated with the grim depression years

Failure of Conservative-dominated National Government to prevent war

Labour's progressive image

Impressive wartime record of leading Labour figures

Conservatives' poor electioneering – Churchill's blunders

Zeitgeist favoured Labour's reforming ideas

Quality of Labour's leaders

| Attlee | Cripps | Bevin | Morrison | Dalton | Bevan |

Key question
How had the
Beveridge Report
prepared the ground
for Labour's
introduction of the
welfare state?

2 | Labour's Creation of the Welfare State

The Beveridge Report

In late 1940, although Britain was in the throes of a war that it was not certain of winning, Winston Churchill had asked his officials to consider the preliminary steps that ought to be taken towards post-war reorganisation. The outcome was the setting up in June 1941 of an Interdepartmental Committee to study the existing schemes of social insurance and make recommendations for their improvement. **William Beveridge** (see page 8) was appointed Chairman of this Committee of senior civil servants. Taking his remit very seriously, Beveridge immersed himself totally in his work. His role in the drafting of the Report containing the Committee's proposals was so central that it was considered appropriate that he alone should sign the document which bore his name and which was presented to the House of Commons in November 1942.

The Report has come to be regarded as singly the most significant social policy document of the twentieth century. The following is a key passage expressing the vision that inspired Beveridge's proposals:

> This is first and foremost a plan of insurance – of giving, in return for contributions, benefits up to a subsistence level, as of right and without means test, so that individuals may build freely upon it. Organisation of social insurance should be treated as one part only of a comprehensive policy of social progress. Social insurance fully developed may provide income security; it is an attack upon Want. But Want is only one of five giants on the road of reconstruction, and in some ways the easiest to attack. The others are Disease, Ignorance, Squalor and Idleness.

Beveridge's aims

Beveridge aimed at the abolition of material want. He believed that it was possible to establish a national minimum level of welfare without recourse to extreme methods. He proposed a universal scheme of insurance which would provide protection against the distress that invariably accompanied sickness, injury and unemployment.

Additionally, there would be grants to ease the financial hardships that came with maternity, parenthood and bereavement. The term 'protection from the cradle to the grave', although not Beveridge's own, was an appropriate description of the envisaged scale of welfare provision. The plan was to replace the current unsystematic pattern of welfare with a centrally funded and regulated system. Since it would be based on

Key figure

William Beveridge 1879–1963
Beveridge had a long experience as a civil servant specialising in social security provision that dated back to the Liberal welfare reforms of 1908–14; he was a Liberal MP 1944–5.

Key question
What were the Report's basic social principles?

A 1944 *Daily Herald* newspaper cartoon, welcoming the Beveridge Report, but suggesting that, like the proverbial curate's egg, it might be good only in parts. Why should the *Daily Herald*, a pro-Labour newspaper, have had reservations about the Beveridge plan?

Key terms

Means test
In the pre-war period, to qualify for dole or relief, individuals or families had to give precise details of all the money they had coming in.

'Five giants'
A representation of the major ills afflicting post-war Britain. *Want*, to be ended by national insurance. *Disease*, to be ended by a comprehensive health service. *Ignorance*, to be ended by an effective education system. *Squalor*, to be ended by slum clearance and rehousing. *Idleness*, to be ended by full employment.

insurance, it would avoid being associated with the hated **means test**.

Insurance was to form the base with welfare organisations providing the superstructure. Beveridge's **'five giants'** to be defeated on the road to reconstruction were a figurative representation of the major ills afflicting society.

Beveridge's scheme pointed toward 'the welfare state', a term which pre-dated the Report by some 10 years but which began to be widely used during the war years. Hardly any of Beveridge's proposals were new. What made them significant in 1942 was their integration into a comprehensive scheme. Beveridge had laid the theoretical foundations for all subsequent developments in the field of social-welfare provision.

Beveridge proposed to take the best aspects of the existing welfare systems and integrate them into a universal plan. It was no mere coincidence that as a younger man Beveridge had been directly involved in the introduction of the social service programme when, between 1908 and 1914, the Liberal government of the day had introduced a set of important social reforms that included the introduction of old-age pensions and national insurance.

In his proposals Beveridge, true to his Liberal background, insisted on the principle of insurance. He specifically denied that his plan aimed at 'giving everybody something for nothing'. Freedom from want could not be 'forced on or given to a democracy'; it had to be desired by the people. Beveridge stressed that a good society depended not on the state but on the individual. He spoke of the retention of 'personal responsibilities'. Individuals would be encouraged to save as private citizens. These ideas were very much in the Liberal tradition, as was his belief that his proposals would not involve an increase in government expenditure.

'Beveridge's five giants'. What was the cartoonist's view of the problems facing Beveridge?

As a good Liberal, Beveridge at every point assumed the continuation of **capitalism**. The political movement called socialism can be defined in various ways, but one attitude common to all its forms is a conviction that the capitalist system is exploitative and unjust and, therefore ultimately indefensible. Throughout the Beveridge Report there is an essential understanding that post-war welfare reform will take place within the framework of continuing capitalism. It is for that reason that historically the Report has to be seen as belonging to the mainstream of liberal rather than socialist thinking and planning.

William Beveridge stood as a Liberal candidate in the 1945 election, hoping to retain the seat he had won a year earlier. But his defeat meant that he was unable to oversee the progress of his plan through Parliament. Nevertheless the introduction of the welfare state by Attlee's government between 1945 and 1951 (see page 11) was both a fulfilment of the Beveridge plan and a fitting tribute to its creator.

Labour's welfare programme

When Beveridge's Report first appeared it met an eager response from the Labour Party. But the fact was all the parties accepted the Report's basic objectives. There was broad agreement that social reconstruction would be a post-war necessity in Britain. This showed how much ground had been made in Britain by the principle of **collectivism**. This in turn was evidence of the influence of the moderate socialism that the Labour Party espoused. Yet Churchill did not regard the Report as socialist; his reluctance to put the Report into practice was on the grounds of cost rather than principle. It is noteworthy that the Labour members of his War Cabinet supported him in 1942 and 1943 in defeating Commons motions demanding legislation to implement the Report.

However, in office after 1945 with a massive majority, Labour turned its attention to applying the main proposals in the Beveridge Report. Labour's election campaign had promoted the notion that after six years of monumental effort the people were entitled to a just reward. It would also be a fitting recompense for the sufferings of the nation during the depression of the inter-war years. The Beveridge plan had provided the new government with its blueprint for social reconstruction.

The Labour government's strategy for an integrated social-welfare system took the form of four major measures, which came into effect in the summer of 1948. In a Prime Ministerial broadcast on the 4 July 1948, the eve of the introduction of the measures, Attlee explained in plain terms the intention behind them:

> The four Acts which come into force tomorrow – National Insurance, Industrial Injuries, National Assistance and the National Health Service – represent the main body of the army of social security. They are comprehensive and available to every citizen. They give security to all members of the family.

Key question
What were the main features of the welfare state as introduced under Attlee?

Key terms

Capitalism
The predominant economic system in the Western world by which individuals and companies trade and invest for private profit.

Collectivism
The people and the state acting together with a common sense of purpose, which necessarily meant a restriction on individual rights.

The main features of the measures to which Attlee referred were:

- The National Insurance Act created a system of universal and compulsory government–employer–employee contributions to a central fund from which would come payments when needed for unemployment, sickness, maternity expenses, widowhood and retirement.
- The Industrial Injuries Act provided cover for accidents occurring in the workplace.
- The National Health Service Act brought the whole population, regardless of status or income, into a scheme of free medical and hospital treatment. Drug prescriptions, dental and optical care were included. Under the Act the existing voluntary and local authority hospitals were co-ordinated into a single, national system, to be operated at local level by appointed health boards.
- The National Assistance Act complemented National Insurance by establishing National Assistance Boards to deal directly and financially with cases of hardship and poverty.

Key dates

Family Allowances Act: 1945

National Insurance Act and Industrial Injuries Act: 1946

National Assistance Act: 1948

Two other measures need to be added to the four listed by Attlee: the Education Act of 1944 and the Family Allowances Act of 1945. These were introduced before Labour came into office but were implemented by Attlee's government:

- The Education Act 1944 (the Butler Act) was introduced by R.A. Butler, a Conservative, and may be regarded as the first organised attack on one of Beveridge's five giants: ignorance. It provided compulsory free education within a tripartite secondary education system. At the age of 11 years pupils were to take an examination (the '11 plus') to determine whether they were to attend a secondary-grammar (for the academically inclined), a secondary-technical (for the vocationally gifted) or a secondary-modern (for those not suited to either of the former two categories). Selection for the appropriate type of education would be determined by the '11 plus'.
- The Family Allowances Act 1945 provided a weekly payment of five shillings (25p) for every child after the first. The money was paid directly to the mother and did not require a means test.

Key question
How far was the Attlee government's introduction of the welfare state the implementation of socialist principles?

The debate over the principles of the welfare state

The Labour government's implementation of the welfare state has been described as a social revolution. It was certainly an event of major significance, but it is important to see it in context. It was a not a revolution forced on an unwilling people and it was not a revolution that pushed down existing structures. Quite the opposite: it built upon what was already there. Beveridge had, indeed, described his plan as a revolution but he had been keen to stress that it was a British revolution, by which he meant it was not destructive but constructive, and built upon precedent. He said it was 'a natural development from the past'; the nation was ready for such a revolution.

Interestingly, Attlee's government, when introducing the welfare measures, was also careful to point out that, far from representing revolutionary socialism, the welfare state was a responsible act of **social reconstruction**. Ernest Bevin expressed the government's basic view in a speech in the Commons in June 1949:

> From the point of view of what is called the welfare state and social services, I beg the House not to drag this business into a kind of partisan warfare. This so-called welfare state has developed everywhere. The United States is as much a welfare state as we are, only in a different form.

In saying this, Bevin was responding to the criticism of the Conservative opposition who voted against nearly all the major clauses of the various welfare measures. He was hoping to take the question out of the political arena, arguing that the welfare state was not peculiar to Britain. This now looks somewhat naïve; it had become a political issue and the American system at the time bore little relation to the one that Britain was adopting.

The welfare state: fulfilment of socialism or liberalism?

Bevin's claim is instructive since it shows that the Labour government was not hell-bent on pursuing revolutionary socialist policies. In the light of such views, it is perhaps best to see Labour's impressive achievement in the field of social services not as an entirely new departure but as the implementation of welfare policies that represented progressive thinking in all parties. Although Churchill and the Conservatives opposed the measures at every turn, subsequent events were to show that this was purely tactical and expedient. All the Conservative governments that were to follow between 1951 and 1997 committed themselves to the preservation and, indeed, the extension of the welfare state in all its main aspects. It is true that the main parties would continually row about how it was funded and how efficiently it was managed, but there was no serious difference between them over the need to keep the welfare state in existence.

It can now be seen that, rather than being the advent of reconstructive socialism, Labour's moves towards a welfare state marked the high point of reforming liberalism. It was very much in the tradition begun by the Liberal governments between 1906 and 1914. Although the Liberal Party by 1945 had ceased to be a major political force, it could be argued that the coming of the welfare state marked the final great triumph of liberalism as a set of ideas. It had set the agenda for the foreseeable future.

Resistance to the introduction of the NHS

Yet when due note has been taken of liberal influence and of the ultimate **consensus** between the parties over welfare, the clear historical fact remains that it was the Labour Party under Attlee that between 1945 and 1951 found the commitment and

Social reconstruction Shaping society so as to provide protection and opportunity for all its citizens.

Consensus Common agreement between the parties on major issues.

consistency of purpose to turn good intentions into workable and permanent structures. This was often, moreover, achieved in the face of determined opposition. One of the most controversial examples of this was the resistance of the British Medical Association (BMA) to the introduction of the National Health Service (NHS). The Act setting up the NHS was passed in 1946 and was intended to come into effect in 1947. However, the resistance of the medical profession meant its introduction was delayed until 1948.

Professions are notoriously reluctant to put the public first. George Bernard Shaw once memorably described them as 'conspiracies against the people', suggesting that all professions invariably place their members' interests above the needs of the public they supposedly exist to serve. It was certainly the case that the majority of the consultants and **GPs**, fearing a loss of their privileges and a reduction in their income, initially refused to co-operate with Aneurin Bevan, who as Minister of Health had the task of planning and implementing the NHS. A poll of doctors in March 1948 revealed that, of the 80 per cent of the profession who voted, only 4735 supported the NHS scheme while 40,814 were against it. The doctors' basic objections were:

- They did not wish to become mere 'salaried civil servants' of the government.
- They feared government interference in doctor–patient relations.
- They were concerned that the regional management boards which would run the NHS would take away their independence as practitioners.
- They saw the proposed NHS as a form of nationalisation (see page 16) which treated the medical profession as if it were an industry.

Although not formally stated, one of the doctors' grievances was Bevan himself. The BMA felt that Attlee had made a mistake in appointing as Minister of Health a man renowned for his aggressive left-wing views, who would make negotiations very difficult. The doctors complained that Bevan looked upon the NHS as a political crusade rather than a practical plan for improving health care. They were able to quote such statements of his as, 'a free health service is pure Socialism and as such it is opposed to the hedonism of capitalist society'. In fairness, however, it should be said that, despite his reputation as a bullying fanatic, Bevan could be utterly charming when he chose. Many of those who opposed his views remarked that in his personal dealings with them he was courteous and understanding.

In the end, Bevan had to buy off the BMA. It was only in return for a guarantee that they would not lose financially and would be allowed to keep their private practices that the doctors eventually agreed to enter the NHS. Bevan remarked bitterly that in order to establish the NHS with its ideal of medical care provided free to all at the point of treatment he had won the doctors over only

Key date

NHS began: 1948

Key term

GPs
General practitioners, family doctors.

by 'stuffing their mouths with gold'. As it finally came into effect in 1948 the NHS had these main features:

- Primary care would be provided by GPs, who would work as independent contractors and be paid for each patient on their books.
- Dentists and opticians, while providing NHS treatment, would continue to operate as private practitioners.
- Hospitals would be run by 14 regional boards, which would appoint local management committees to oversee matters at local level.
- Community services such as maternity care, vaccination and the ambulance service were to be provided by local authorities.
- Medical prescriptions would be provided free of charge.

'It still tastes awful.' 'Matron' Bevan forcing doctors to take the 'nasty' medicine of the NHS. How accurately does the cartoon depict the relationship between the BMA and Aneurin Bevan?

Further particular concessions that Bevan had to make to the BMA's demands included:

- Private practices and hospitals, in which doctors charged their patients fees, were to be allowed to continue, thus enabling GPs to be both NHS and private doctors.
- 'Pay beds' for private fee-paying patients were to be reserved in NHS hospitals.
- Teaching hospitals were to be run by independent governors outside government control.

Regardless of his long and often bitter struggle with the medical profession, Bevan still believed that the NHS would not only solve the nation's major social problems, but also pay for itself. A healthy society would mean far fewer workers being absent. Efficiency and wages would rise. Higher wages would produce higher tax yields. From that increased revenue the state would be able to finance its welfare provision.

Such thinking now seems sadly unrealistic. Bevan declined to listen when he was told that the demand for treatment would outstrip supply and that government revenue would be insufficient to meet the cost of drugs, medical appliances and machinery. This had already begun to happen by the mid-1950s. But he was less culpable in regard to another development that undermined the NHS. He could not know that there would be a major population shift in the second half of the century caused by people living longer and in old age making demands on a service that could be financed only by a dwindling proportion of people of working age who were paying tax. Nor was Bevan aware that his scheme would fall foul of two particular developments: bureaucracy and the 'dandruff syndrome'.

Bureaucracy

From its inception to the present day, the NHS has continued to grow as a supplier of jobs. By the 1980s it had become the largest single employer in Europe. Many of the posts created were managerial and administrative positions which provided handsome incomes for the holders, but were not directly related to treatment for patients. For decades a controversy has continued to rumble on over how the NHS can be reformed so that it can best fulfil its primary task of providing patient care. However, the strong vested interests among its millions of employees have so far thwarted attempts at genuine reform.

The 'dandruff syndrome'

The second problem which Bevan could not foresee was the tendency that affects all systems that are provided to the consumer without charge. Since all medical treatment was free, there was no limit to the number of people entitled to call on the services of doctors and nurses. This led to time and resources being wasted on trivial complaints, e.g. dandruff. The gap between Bevan's estimation of cost and the reality is clear from these comparative figures:

Year	Health and Social Security budget
1949	£597 million (equivalent to 4.7% of **GDP**)
1990	£91 billion (equivalent to 14% of GDP)

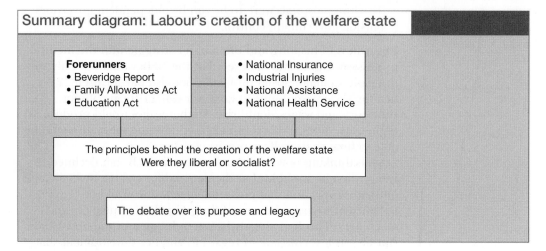

Summary diagram: Labour's creation of the welfare state

Forerunners
- Beveridge Report
- Family Allowances Act
- Education Act

- National Insurance
- Industrial Injuries
- National Assistance
- National Health Service

The principles behind the creation of the welfare state
Were they liberal or socialist?

The debate over its purpose and legacy

GDP
Gross domestic product: the annual total value of goods produced and services provided in Britain.

3 | The Economy Under Labour 1945–51

Nationalisation

From its earliest days, the Labour Party had advanced the principle that government had the right to direct the key aspects of the economy in order to create efficiency and social justice. When it came into office with an overwhelming majority in 1945, the times were ripe for it to fulfil its aims. In its election manifesto, *Let us Face the Future*, the party promised to implement an ambitious programme for the **nationalisation** of Britain's major industries. These were specified as:

- fuel and power industries
- iron and steel
- inland transport, which included rail, road and air services.

The nationalisation programme

Labour's public ownership programme makes impressive reading:

- 1946: coal, civil aviation, Cable and Wireless (a company providing long-distance communications) and the Bank of England
- 1947: road transport and electricity
- 1948: gas
- 1949: iron and steel.

Coal, Britain's most vital industry, yet one which for decades had been subject to disruption and underproduction, was the first earmarked for public ownership. The government considered

Key question
How extensive was the Labour government's restructuring of the economy?

Nationalisation
Clause IV of the Labour Party's constitution committed it to achieving 'the common ownership of the means of production, distribution and exchange'. In practice, common ownership or public control meant government control.

Key dates

Nationalisation of coal, civil aviation, Cable and Wireless, Bank of England: 1946

Nationalisation of road transport and electricity services: 1947

Nationalisation of iron and steel: 1949

that the modernisation that this would bring could also be achieved in the gas and electricity undertakings. Nationalisation would bring greater safety, productivity and efficiency, with the result that all the other industries associated with fuel and power production would benefit. It was also reckoned that the ending of private ownership in transport, which would be the prelude to the co-ordination of the road, rail and canal system, would similarly improve the quality of the nation's essential services.

Iron and steel

The odd-man-out in the list of enterprises scheduled for nationalisation was the iron and steel industry. It had in fact been included only because of a Labour conference decision of 1944 that had imposed it on the unwilling Labour leaders. Since steel was the only profit-making industry, it had stout defenders willing to fight against nationalisation. This made the legislation relating to its takeover by the state a fierce battleground.

The key factor here was that nationalisation involved compensating the former owners of the concerns that were taken into public ownership. In a declining industry, coal for example, nationalisation might well be a blessed relief to the owners since it bought them out at a price that cut their losses. However, in a concern that was still profit-making, compensation was a much more difficult issue to resolve. It raised the question of what was a fair settlement, but, more significantly still, it opened up the larger issue of whether the state had the right to overrule the declared objections of the owners and shareholders. It became an argument over justice in a free society.

Opponents of the nationalisation of the steel industry protested on four main grounds:

- it was not a public utility, but a privately owned manufacturing concern
- it was successfully run and making profits
- large investments had recently been made into it
- it had an excellent record of employer–employee relations.

Conservative resistance

The row over iron and steel proved a godsend to the Conservatives. They had been badly damaged by their heavy defeat in 1945, and their morale and reputation were low. Now in 1948 the proposal to nationalise steel created a rallying ground for them. Up to that point, the Conservative opposition had offered only token resistance to nationalisation. There was a sense in which the war seemed to have won the argument for state direction. The principle of public ownership itself was rarely discussed; most of the debates were taken up with the dry detail of the methods for making the change and with the levels of compensation. The iron and steel bill changed all that. The Conservatives now had a cause to defend. In the Commons and in the constituencies, they began to launch a series of spirited onslaughts on the nationalisation programme as an abuse of government power.

Government victory over iron and steel

However, in the end the government was able to push through the nationalisation of iron and steel in 1950. The path to success was greatly eased by the passing of the **Parliamentary Reform Act of 1949**, a measure which effectively prevented the Conservatives from using their majority in the House of Lords to block the steel bill. This allowed nationalisation to become law before the scheduled end of the Labour term in office in 1950.

Keynesianism

Every so often a particular financial or economic theory arrives to dominate its time. For most of the period between the late 1940s and the late 1970s, Keynesianism provided the basic frame of reference. John Maynard Keynes (1883–1946), a Cambridge academic and one of the wartime government's chief economic advisers, believed that economic depressions, such as the one that had afflicted the economy in the 1930s, were avoidable if particular steps were taken. His starting point was demand. He calculated that it was a fall in demand for manufactured products that caused industrial economies to slip into recession. If demand could be sustained, decline could be prevented and jobs preserved.

Keynes maintained that the only agency with sufficient power and influence to keep demand at a high enough level was the government itself. He urged, therefore, that:

- The government should use its budgets and revenue powers to raise capital, which it could then reinvest in the economy to keep it at a high level of activity.
- This artificial boost to the economy would lead to genuine recovery and growth. Companies and firms would have full order books and the workers would have jobs and earnings.
- Those earnings would be spent on goods and services with the result that the forces of supply and demand would be stimulated.
- The government should be prepared to abandon the practice of always trying to balance the budget between income and expenditure. It should be willing to run **deficit budgets** in the short term even if this meant borrowing to do so. The government would eventually be able to repay its debts by taxing the companies and workers whose profits and wages would rise considerably in a flourishing economy.

The six years of government-directed war effort, during which Keynes was an influential figure at the Treasury, helped to give strength to his arguments. What is interesting is that although Keynes thought in terms of limited government action, it was the notion of government being an *essential* part of economic planning that become widely accepted. This new conviction had the effect of giving added legitimacy and justification to the economic reform programme followed by Clement Attlee's Labour governments after 1945.

Key question
According to Keynes, what role should government play in the economy?

Key terms

Parliamentary Reform Act of 1949
First introduced in 1947, this measure, which became law in 1949, reduced the delaying power of the House of Lords over a Commons' bill to two sessions and one year.

Deficit budgets
Occur when a government spends more than it raises in revenue.

Key question
How did Labour attempt to deal with the financial problems it inherited?

Key terms

Balance of payments
The equilibrium between the cost of imports and the profits from exports. When the cost of imports outweighs the income from exports, financial crisis follows.

Invisible exports
The sale of financial and insurance services to foreign buyers, traditionally one of Britain's major sources of income from abroad.

The government's financial problems

Attlee's government inherited crushing financial difficulties in 1945. By the end of the war Britain carried the following burdens:

- debts of £4198 million
- a **balance of payments** crisis: in the financial year 1945–6, Britain spent £750 million more abroad than it received
- exports of manufactures had dropped by 60 per cent in wartime
- **invisible exports** had shrunk from £248 million in 1938 to £120 million in 1946
- costs of maintaining overseas military commitments had quintupled between 1938 and 1946.

To meet this crisis Hugh Dalton, Chancellor of the Exchequer (1945–7), negotiated a loan of $6000 million from the USA and Canada. The government's hope was that, in accordance with Keynesian theory, the loan would provide the basis of an

'Economic blizzard.' Freezing cold, accompanied by heavy snowfalls, persisted in Britain between January and March 1947, leading to fuel shortages and regular cuts in domestic and industrial electricity supplies. Some four million workers were laid off as a direct result of the weather conditions. Why was the country so poorly prepared for dealing with the situation?

industrial recovery. But such recovery as did occur was never enough to meet expectations.

Part of the problem was that the US dollar was so strong at the end of the war that it dominated international commerce. The consequence was that Britain began to suffer from what was known as the '**dollar gap**'. This drained Britain of a substantial part of the loan it had negotiated while at the same time making it harder to meet the repayments.

What made the situation still worse was that Britain had agreed with the USA, its Cold War ally, to increase its spending on defence from £2.3 billion to £4.7 billion. Despite demobilisation in 1945, Britain, as one of the occupying forces in Europe and as a member of the United Nations Security Council, continued to maintain a large peacetime army. In 1950 this stood at nearly a million men. In addition to the expense this entailed, there was the financial burden Britain had shouldered when Attlee's government in 1948 committed Britain to the development of its own **independent nuclear deterrent**. Ernest Bevin, the Foreign Secretary, declared: 'We've got to have it and it's got to have a bloody Union Jack on it.'

By the late 1940s Britain was spending 14 per cent of its **GNP** on defence. Faced with these burdens, the Labour government's only recourse under Dalton and his successor, Stafford Cripps, was to adopt a policy of austerity. The basic aim was to use rationing and tight economic controls to prevent **inflation**. Such measures, it was hoped, would keep employment high and allow the government to continue with its welfare programme. Controls on imports were imposed to keep dollar spending to a minimum. But this led to further shortages and rationing. In 1949, in an effort to relieve the situation and make British goods easier to sell abroad, the pound sterling was devalued from $4.03 to $2.80.

The government's deflationary policies did not please the trade unions, particularly when they were asked to show restraint in these difficult times and operate a **wage freeze**. There were thinly veiled threats from the government that if the unions did not do this voluntarily, wage restrictions would have to be legally imposed. Despite being the government's natural supporters and the chief provider of Labour Party funds, the unions were not prepared to be docile. As they saw it, a Labour government was in power to provide for the needs of the workers, not involve itself in financial deals which kept the USA happy but left British workers vulnerable. Arthur Deakin, General Secretary of the large and influential **TGWU**, had warned the government in its first year of office that the unions would resist any moves to weaken their members' interests:

> We shall go forward building up our wage claims in conformity with our understanding of the people we are representing. … Any attempt to interfere with that position would have disastrous consequences.

Key dates

Government committed to develop independent nuclear deterrent: 1947

Government forced to devalue the pound: 1949

Key terms

Dollar gap
Since the pound was weaker than the dollar, the goods that Britain desperately needed from North America had to be paid for in dollars.

Independent nuclear deterrent
In 1947, to the anger of its left wing, the Labour government initiated a research programme that led to the detonation of a British atom bomb in 1952 and a hydrogen bomb in 1957.

GNP
Gross national product. The annual total value of goods produced and services provided by Britain at home and in trade with other countries.

Inflation
A decline in the purchasing power of money, which meant Britain had to spend more dollars to buy its imports.

Key terms

Wage freeze
An undertaking not to press for higher wages until Britain's economy had improved.

TGWU
Transport and General Workers Union.

Key figure

George Marshall 1880–1959
One of America's most distinguished soldier-statesmen of the twentieth century.

Key date

Britain began to receive Marshall Plan aid: 1948

The hard times were made harder by the coinciding of this period of austerity with Labour's creation of the welfare state, which placed further heavy financial burdens on an already strained economy. Yet Britain's financial problems would have been even greater had it not been for the relief provided by the Marshall Plan, which began to operate from 1948.

Britain and the Marshall Plan

After 1945, the world's trading nations all experienced severe balance of payments difficulties. Worried that this would destroy international commerce, the USA, the only economy with sufficient resources, adopted a programme in 1947 to provide dollars to any country willing to receive them in return for granting trade concessions to the United States. Whatever America's self-interest may have been, it is difficult to see how Europe could have recovered without a massive inflow of American capital. Under the plan, which bore the name of the US Secretary of State, **George Marshall**, Europe received $15 billion, Britain's share being 10 per cent of that.

The Marshall Plan ranks as one of the major achievements of Ernest Bevin as foreign secretary. It was he who did so much to convince the USA of the necessity of such a plan both for shoring up Europe against the threat of the USSR and for sustaining an international economy, without which the USA would not be able to maintain its strength as the world's greatest industrial power.

Desperate though Britain was for Marshall aid, the left-wing of the Labour Party was frustrated and angered by the government's acceptance of it. For many Labour MPs, the financial arrangement tied Britain to the USA in the relationship of beggar and master and so denied the government any chance of acting independently in the Cold War world.

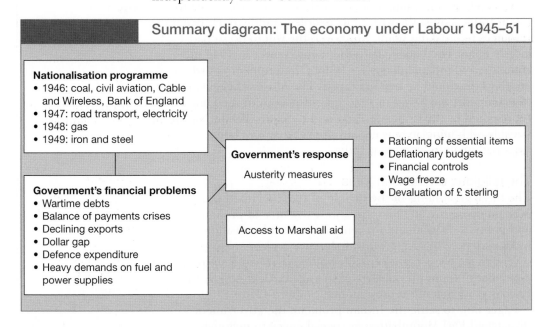

Summary diagram: The economy under Labour 1945–51

Nationalisation programme
- 1946: coal, civil aviation, Cable and Wireless, Bank of England
- 1947: road transport, electricity
- 1948: gas
- 1949: iron and steel

Government's financial problems
- Wartime debts
- Balance of payments crises
- Declining exports
- Dollar gap
- Defence expenditure
- Heavy demands on fuel and power supplies

Government's response

Austerity measures

Access to Marshall aid

- Rationing of essential items
- Deflationary budgets
- Financial controls
- Wage freeze
- Devaluation of £ sterling

4 | Assessing the Labour Government's Achievements

Indian Independence 1947

Harold Wilson, a later Labour Prime Minister (see page 81), believed that the granting of independence to India in 1947 was his party's greatest achievement. It was during the Second World War that Britain had begun to accept that its possession and retention of colonies involved unbearable burdens. The early defeats suffered by British forces at the hands of the Japanese revealed Britain's weakness east of Suez. Seizing the moment, the Indian nationalists had intensified their efforts to force Britain out of India. In 1942, Mohandas Gandhi inaugurated the 'Quit India' movement. Violence and reprisals followed, with the misery made worse by a famine in Bengal. The local police and army remained largely loyal and British control was unbroken, but at the cost of many lives and more political repression.

Mohandas Gandhi 1869–1948

Gandhi was arguably the most influential revolutionary of the twentieth century; his philosophy of non-violent protest became the model for civil rights movements everywhere. He was certainly the single most important influence in the growth of Indian nationalism. As a young lawyer in South Africa he had organised passive resistance to the race laws there. On returning to India he set about employing the same techniques as a means of undermining the British hold on India. A devout Hindu, Gandhi nonetheless sought mutual respect and tolerance between all religions and castes. His simple, even saintly, lifestyle endeared him to the great mass of the Indian peasantry to whom he was the *Mahatma* (great soul).

At the close of the Japanese war in 1945, it was clear that to retain India against the wish of its peoples would stretch Britain's resources to breaking point. Moreover, the will to do so had largely gone. The Labour Party came into power in 1945 fully committed to independence for India. The problem was when and how this could be best arranged. The Muslim League, led by Mohammed Jinnah, was increasingly suspicious of the Hindus, represented by the Congress Party and its leader Pandit Nehru. A sizeable Sikh minority was equally apprehensive of being swamped in an independent India.

The religious divisions in India

The three great faiths of the people of India – Hinduism, Mohammedanism and Sikhism – were a source of profound social and political division and prevented a peaceful transition to independence. To such groups, federation within a single sovereign state was not acceptable, although it had been proposed a number of times previously and was again suggested by the Labour government's representative, Stafford Cripps.

Eager now to settle the Indian problem, the government dispatched Earl Mountbatten as special envoy to negotiate

Key question
What did Labour achieve during its six years of office from 1945 to 1951?

Key date

Independence of India: 1947

Key term

Mahatma
Great soul.

Britain's final withdrawal. Given the reluctance of the parties concerned to consider federation, partition seemed the only solution. After much haggling, the Hindu Congress and the Muslim League agreed to the Mountbatten proposals: India, the subcontinent, was to be divided into two distinct states: India, overwhelmingly Hindu; Pakistan and East Pakistan, predominantly Muslim. The Indian princes would give up their rule in return for the freedom to retain their wealth. The date for the formal end of British rule was brought forward from 1948 to 1947.

Post-independence problems

Given the scale of the problem, this compromise was doubtless the best solution that could be arrived at, but how far it was from being a lasting one was soon revealed by the tragedy that ensued. Jinnah and the League resented having had to settle for a 'moth-eaten' Pakistan; Congress was dismayed at seeing India broken up, while the Sikhs, not being in a majority in any single region, were resolved to resist subjection in whichever of the new states they found themselves. In the same week in which the transfer of power from Britain became law, civil war broke out. Muslim–Hindu–Sikh passions spilled over into desperate acts of mutual violence.

The independence of India had thus come at a terrible price. The creation of the separate states of India and Pakistan led to a massive cross-migration of refugees: Muslims from India into Pakistan, Hindus and Sikhs from Pakistan into India. The communal riots and massacres that accompanied all this resulted in the killing of over three million men, women and children; one million alone dying in the Punjab.

Key question
How radical were the policies of Attlee's governments?

Main achievements of the Attlee governments 1945–51

The record of Attlee's governments showed that despite working throughout under the shadow of serious economic and financial difficulties they achieved a high degree of activity and success. This was a tribute to the enthusiasm and to the administrative and political skills of their leading ministers. They:

Key term

NATO
The North Atlantic Treaty Organisation. A defensive alliance formed in 1949 by 10 Western European countries as a safeguard against Soviet expansion. The USA eagerly accepted the invitation to join.

- implemented a large-scale nationalisation programme
- created the welfare state
- helped convince the USA of the need for the Marshall Plan
- granted Indian independence
- initiated a major housing programme, resulting in a million new homes being built
- played a key role in the formation of **NATO**
- started the programme that turned Britain into a nuclear power.

So large was Labour's majority in the 1945 election that its opponents feared it would enable the new government to usher sweeping socialist changes into Britain. It is true that during the next six years many significant and lasting reforms were introduced, but the Labour governments made no attempt either to disrupt the capitalist system in Britain or to destroy the social structure.

That indeed was the complaint voiced against Attlee's government by the **Labour left**, who argued that Labour, with its unassailable majority, was in a position to bring about a genuine transformation of British society. But instead, they asserted, it threw away the opportunity by settling for half measures. Its nationalisation programme was not really an attempt to take central control of the economy. With the exception of steel, it was restricted to non-profit-making concerns and made no effort to take over the private banks or insurance companies.

Another accusation from left-wing critics was that, by borrowing heavily from the USA in order to meet its financial difficulties, Attlee's government lost its freedom of action in foreign policy. Dependent on America, Britain found itself locked into a lasting Cold War hostility towards the Soviet Union.

A powerful argument from an opposite political viewpoint was that the Labour government had indeed thrown away a historic opportunity to reform Britain – not, however, by doing too little but by doing too much. Writers, such as Corelli Barnett, have claimed that what Britain needed after the war was the reconstruction of its industrial base. Priority should have been given to financial recovery and investment in the nation's **infrastructure**. This would have provided the means for Britain to re-establish itself as a major manufacturing economy, able to respond to the post-war international demand for commodity goods.

Instead, runs Barnett's argument, Britain made a priority not of industrial recovery but of social welfare. However, welfare was costly and Britain, being practically bankrupt at the end of the war, had to borrow heavily to fund it. Saddled with large debts, Britain was able to achieve only low economic growth. To strengthen his case, Barnett quoted the example of West Germany, which, by delaying its welfare state until it had achieved industrial recovery, put itself on the path to an economic miracle.

There have also been suggestions that Labour failed to make an impact in areas where it should have been at its most influential. In 1951, despite six years of government by a supposedly radical party which for five of those years had enjoyed an unassailable majority:

- Britain's class structure remained largely unaltered.
- Social reform had not greatly raised the conditions and status of women.

Criticism of the NHS

An even more telling criticism is that the NHS, Labour's proudest creation and the one which best defined its character as a party of the working class, failed to fulfil the expectations invested in it. The charge is that it was not the poor and disadvantaged sections of the population who benefited most

Key terms

Labour left
A significant number of Labour MPs, some of whom were Marxists, were strongly sympathetic towards the Soviet Union. At this stage, the full horrors of Stalin's regime had yet to be revealed, so it was still possible to believe that the USSR was a model socialist state.

Infrastructure
The interlocking systems and installations which enable a nation's industrial economy to operate, e.g. transport, power supply, sewerage and communications.

from the introduction of the NHS, but the already privileged middle classes. It was they who no longer had to pay for medical treatment, but who could now call on the services of the best qualified GPs whose practices tended to be in the more prosperous areas where the middle classes lived. In contrast, it was the underprivileged who still lacked access to the best treatment and who were worst hit when the Labour government, backtracking on its promise to maintain free health care, introduced prescription charges.

It was this issue that produced the most serious challenge that Attlee had yet faced from within the Labour Party. In 1951, forced by its financial difficulties to make savings in public expenditure, his government imposed charges on dental treatment and the provision of spectacles, as well as on prescriptions. Aneurin Bevan, the man who had constructed the NHS, led a number of ministers in resigning from the Cabinet. Those who followed him in this became known as Bevanites; they protested that the charges contravened the founding principle that the NHS should be free to all at the point of treatment.

Key dates

Bevanite rebellion over prescription charges: 1951

Election reduced Labour overall majority to five seats: 1950

Key question
Why did Labour lose office in 1951?

The end of the Attlee government

The Bevanite rebellion helped to sound the death knell of Attlee's government. Reduced by the 1950 election to an overall majority of only five (a majority that was so tight that, when there was a close vote in the Commons, sick Labour MPs had to be brought from their hospital beds and helped through the division lobby), the government now had to contend with mounting dissatisfaction within its own ranks. The open challenge to prescription charges encouraged those Labour MPs and members of the party who had previously swallowed their grievances to voice their doubts over the direction the government had taken over economic, welfare and foreign policy.

Such divisions stimulated the Conservatives and sharpened their attacks. In such an atmosphere, another election could not be long delayed. The 1951 election was a close-run thing with the Conservatives gaining a narrow victory. It was doubtless with some relief that a weary and beleaguered Labour government left office.

Key term

King's Speech
The formal address delivered by the monarch at the beginning of each parliamentary year setting out the government's policies.

Table 1.2: Election results 1950

Political party	No. of votes	No. of seats	Percentage of vote
Labour	13,266,592	315	46.1
Conservative	12,502,567	298	43.5
Liberal	2,621,548	9	9.1
Others	381,964	3	1.3

Key question
Why was foreign policy a divisive issue within the Labour Party?

Labour's internal dispute over foreign policy

Early in his government Attlee faced a challenge in Parliament over his foreign policy. Interestingly, it came not from the opposition but from within his own party. In 1946, in an amendment to the **King's Speech**, a group of some 60 backbench

Labour MPs representing the left of the party criticised the government for its pro-American stance.

> We hope that the Government will so review its conduct of International Affairs as to afford the utmost encouragement to, and collaboration with, all Nations striving to secure full Socialist planning and control of the world's resources. We get the impression that not only is there a complete and exclusive Anglo-American tie-up, but a tie-up between the two front benches.
> (Richard Crossman, House of Commons, 18 November 1946)

Moved by **Richard Crossman**, the Amendment called on Attlee's government to co-operate less with the USA and more with the Soviet Union. Crossman's complaint was that pro-Americanism was not simply current government policy but represented the attitude of the whole British political establishment.

Attlee replied by pointing out that the government was not anti-Soviet and pro-American through prejudice, but simply because the USSR under Stalin was continuing the aggressive, anti-Western approach that had characterised Russian policy since the days of the tsars. This made co-operation with the Soviet Union impossible.

Behind this disagreement between Attlee and the left-wing of his party lay a fundamental and lasting difference of opinion as to the real character and purpose of the Labour Party. The Marxist fringe believed that Labour's essential role was to work for the replacement of the capitalist system by a socialist one; but the mainstream Labour Party saw itself as a radical but constitutional force, prepared to work within the existing political system to achieve its aim of social reform. It was as British statesmen rather than international socialists that Attlee and Ernest Bevin, his Foreign Secretary, approached the problem of Britain's policies in the post-war world. Their intention was to protect British interests, which in the nature of things after 1945 also meant Western interests, in the face of Soviet expansionism. Bevin often said that his natural desire was not to be anti-Soviet, but the hostile attitude of the Kremlin obliged him to be so in practice.

The left of the Labour Party took this bitterly. They had anticipated that with a Labour Party in power, Anglo-Soviet relations would vastly improve: 'left would understand left'. However, the rapid development of the Cold War after 1945 shattered this hope. Britain found herself siding with the United States against the Soviet Union. The argument of the Labour left was that this was not inevitable; their accusation was that, in leaning so heavily on the USA for financial aid, the government was destroying the chance of genuine British independence in international affairs.

Bevin's angry reaction to these insults was to accuse the left of a total lack of political realism. In the world as it was, and not how the left would like it to be, the Soviet Union was a threat and without American dollars from the Marshall aid programme and military support, Britain and Europe could not be sustained.

Richard Crossman 1907–74
An MP from 1945 to 1974; educated at Winchester and Oxford; owned a country house with 200 acres of land; a leading Marxist intellectual in the Labour Party and a strong supporter of Aneurin Bevan; co-authored 'Keep Left', a 1947 pamphlet that urged the government to follow truly socialist principles.

Key figure

What is especially notable is that, interesting though the ideas of the Bevanite left wing were, in the event they had little impact on the shaping of Labour policy. The importance of Bevin's being Foreign Secretary at this critical period was that he established the tradition of post-war British foreign policy: pro-American and anti-Soviet. This was an approach that was to be followed by all the British governments, Labour and Conservative, throughout the duration of the Cold War between 1945 and the early 1990s. Bevin's policies were a triumph for the centre and right of the Labour Party.

The same might be said of the policies of the Labour governments from 1945 to 1951 overall. Whatever changes may have been introduced under Attlee, at no time was there a serious attempt to work outside the capitalist system. As with economics so with foreign policy; in the things that mattered, Attlee and Bevin were traditionalists at heart. Given this, a dispute with the left of the party was bound to follow. The **broad church** of the Labour Party meant that internal conflict characterised it throughout the second half of the twentieth century and into the twenty-first.

Reasons for Labour's 1951 defeat
Labour handicaps

- Attlee's government was worn down by heavy economic and financial difficulties.
- Collectively and individually, the government was exhausted after six troubled years in office.
- A number of its ministers, e.g. Attlee himself, Herbert Morrison and Ernest Bevin, had been working continuously since 1940.
- Serious divisions had developed between the right and left of the party over economic, welfare and foreign policies.
- There was resentment among some trade unions at Labour's slowness in responding to workers' demands.
- The shrinking in the 1950 election of its large majority made governing difficult and damaged party morale.
- Labour found it difficult to shake off its image as a party of rationing and high taxation.
- In their call for the austerity that they claimed the times demanded, leading ministers such as the ascetic Stafford Cripps as Chancellor of the Exchequer and the aggressive Manny Shinwell, Minister of Fuel and Power, did not present an attractive picture to the electorate.
- Britain's entry into the **Korean War** in 1950 angered Labour's left wing; they argued that, although technically British forces fought as part of a United Nations force, in reality the Labour government was sheepishly following the USA in a Cold War engagement.

There were, of course, more positive aspects to the victory of the Conservatives. Their heavy and unexpected defeat in 1945 had left them shell-shocked. However, by the late 1940s their fortunes

Key terms

Broad church
Containing many conflicting viewpoints.

Korean War
US-dominated UN armies resisted the takeover of South Korea by the Chinese-backed Communists of North Korea from 1950 to 1953. Britain suffered the loss of 1788 servicemen, with another 2498 being wounded.

had begun to improve. Much of this was due to the reorganisation of the party undertaken by Lord Woolton, the Conservative Party Chairman. It was also at this time that the younger Tory MPs, such as **R.A. Butler**, began to bring new ideas and confidence to the party. The nationalisation issue gave them a cause round which they could rally and on which they could attack the government.

Conservative advantages

- The Conservatives had begun to recover from the shock of their defeat in 1945.
- The 1950 election saw an influx of bright young Conservative MPs eager for battle against a tiring government.
- Under the direction of the dynamic **Lord Woolton**, 'a cheerful cove', as a colleague put it, the Conservative Party had reformed its finances and constituency organisation and was much better positioned to fight for seats and votes than in 1945.
- The attack on the government's nationalisation of iron and steel provided a strong platform for opposition attacks.

Table 1.3: Election results 1951

Political party	No. of votes	No. of seats	Percentage of vote
Conservative	13,717,538	321	48.0
Labour	13,948,605	295	48.8
Liberal	730,556	6	2.5
Others	198,969	3	0.7

The explanation of Attlee's losing office in 1951 is not so much Labour decline as Conservative recovery. While Labour had gained an added two million votes between 1945 and 1951, the Conservatives had added nearly four million. Yet they only just squeezed into power. What benefited them was the Liberal Party's decision to put up only 109 candidates, a drop of 366 compared with 1950. The nearly two million ex-Liberal votes that became available went largely to the Conservatives.

The election figures for 1951 reveal one of the oddest aspects of British electoral politics. It is possible for a party to poll more votes than its opponents yet still be defeated. After six years of government, Labour had in fact more than held its share of the vote. Remarkably, the 1951 election saw Labour gain the highest aggregate vote ever achieved by any party up to that point. It outnumbered the Conservatives by a quarter of a million and had nearly one per cent more of the vote. The ratio of votes to seats was:

- Labour   47,283 : 1
- Conservatives   42,733 : 1
- Liberals   121,759 : 1

It was clearly not the case that Labour had been dumped out of office by a disillusioned electorate. It was more a matter on this occasion of Labour's being the victim not the beneficiary of the unfairness of the British electoral system (see page 2).

(see page 2).

Key figures

R.A. Butler
1902–82
MP, 1929–65;
Minister of Education, 1941–5;
Chancellor of the Exchequer, 1951–5;
Home Secretary, 1957–62; Foreign Secretary, 1962–4.

Lord Woolton
1883–1964
Managing director of a chain of department stores; Minister of Food in Churchill's wartime government; Minister of Reconstruction, 1943–5; Conservative Party Chairman, 1946–55.

Key dates

Start of Korean War: 1950

Election success for Conservatives, but Labour gained highest popular vote yet: 1951

Key question
How important were Attlee's governments in the long term?

The legacy of the Attlee governments 1945–51

While there may be legitimate criticisms of the Labour government regarding particular policy failures, there is a broader significance to the years 1945–51. In governing during that period the Labour Party laid down the policies that were to be followed in all essentials by successive Labour and Conservative governments during the next 35 years. Until Margaret Thatcher came into power in 1979 and deliberately challenged this consensus (see page 117), there was a broad level of agreement on what were the major domestic and foreign issues and how they were to be handled.

Conservative and Labour strategies were based on:

- economic policies based on Keynesian principles of public expenditure and state direction
- welfare policies based on the implementation of the Beveridge Report
- education policies based on the notion of creating equal opportunity for all
- foreign policies based on a pro-American, anti-Soviet stance
- imperial policies based on the principle of independence for Britain's former colonies.

This common area of agreement did not prevent serious political rivalry and constant accusations by each party that its opponents were failing to pursue the correct policies. However, when in government, the Labour and Conservative parties followed fundamentally similar policies.

Whatever the later questions concerning the Labour governments' performance there was little doubt among contemporaries that something momentous had occurred between 1945 and 1951. They were conscious that Labour had created the welfare state, that it had carried into peacetime the notion of state-directed planning, which had always been one of its main objectives, and that in doing so it had established Keynesianism as the basic British approach to economic planning (see page 18). R.A. Butler, a leading Conservative, put the Labour reforms into historical perspective by describing them as 'the greatest social revolution in our history'. What gives particular significance to Butler's words is that the Conservative Party came, in all major respects, to accept that revolution.

The distinctive characteristic of the policies followed by Conservative governments from 1951 was how closely they coincided with those introduced by the Attlee governments. In the words of a modern historian, Dilwyn Porter, 'Attlee's patriotic socialists gave way to Churchill's social patriots'. Just as Labour had moved to the right by accepting capitalism and the mixed economy, so the Conservatives moved to the left by accepting Keynesianism and the managed economy.

In opposition, the Conservatives had opposed every nationalisation measure and many of the welfare proposals. Yet, in government themselves after 1951, they fully denationalised only one industry – steel – and built on the welfare programme which they had inherited. Labour could justly claim that it had converted the Conservative Party to welfarism. This was perhaps one of Attlee's most enduring legacies.

Some key books in the debate

Stuart Ball, *The Conservative Party and British Politics 1902–51* (Longman, 1995).
Corelli Barnett, *The Audit of War* (Macmillan, 1986).
Peter Clarke, *Hope and Glory: Britain 1900–1990* (Penguin, 1996).
Dennis Kavanagh and Peter Morris, *Consensus Politics From Attlee to Major* (Blackwell, 1994).
David Kynaston, *Austerity Britain 1945–51* (Bloomsbury, 2007).
Andrew Marr, *A History of Modern Britain* (Macmillan, 2007).
Kenneth Morgan, *The People's Peace, British History 1945–90* (OUP, 1990).
Nick Tiratsoo (ed.), *From Blitz to Blair: A New History of Britain Since 1939* (Phoenix, 1997).

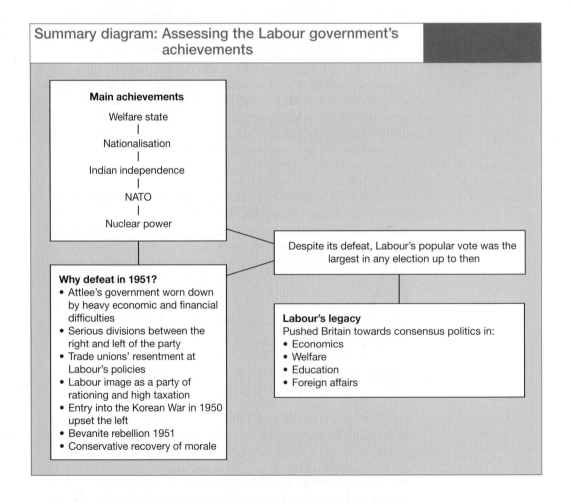

Summary diagram: Assessing the Labour government's achievements

Main achievements

Welfare state
|
Nationalisation
|
Indian independence
|
NATO
|
Nuclear power

Despite its defeat, Labour's popular vote was the largest in any election up to then

Why defeat in 1951?
- Attlee's government worn down by heavy economic and financial difficulties
- Serious divisions between the right and left of the party
- Trade unions' resentment at Labour's policies
- Labour image as a party of rationing and high taxation
- Entry into the Korean War in 1950 upset the left
- Bevanite rebellion 1951
- Conservative recovery of morale

Labour's legacy
Pushed Britain towards consensus politics in:
- Economics
- Welfare
- Education
- Foreign affairs

Study Guide: AS Questions

In the style of Edexcel

Source 1

'It still tastes awful.' A cartoon published in Punch *on 21 January 1948.*

Source 2

From: a letter written by Archibald McIndoe to a friend early in 1948. McIndoe was a leading surgeon.

Bevan has accused us of deliberately misleading our colleagues and encouraging them to flout the will of the people. There will be a 90 per cent vote amongst doctors against the National Health Act, and tempers are rising on all sides. Unfortunately, the economic sanctions which Bevan can draw against us are grim and I think there will be a considerable degree of ratting* when the appointed day comes along.
[*Ratting: giving up the fight]

Source 3

Comments made by Aneurin Bevan about the way in which he eventually gained the co-operation of doctors.

I won them over only by stuffing their mouths with gold.

Study Sources 1, 2 and 3.
How far do Sources 2 and 3 support the impression given in Source 1 of the way Bevan dealt with the medical profession in 1948? Explain your answer, using the evidence of Sources 1, 2 and 3. (20 marks)

Exam tips

The cross-references are intended to take you straight to the material that will help you to answer the question.

This is an example of your first question that is compulsory. It is a short-answer question, and you should not write more than three or four paragraphs. Note that you are only required to reach a judgement on the evidence of these sources. The question does not ask you to write what you know about Bevan and the implementation of the NHS. However, you will apply your own knowledge to the sources when you use them. For example, you should know about Bevan's role as Minister of Health and also about the resistance of the medical profession to his proposals.

In the case of this question, you will first of all have to analyse the impression given in Source 1, then you can begin to consider how the evidence of Sources 2 and 3 relates to it. The text on pages 12–16 and 24–5 will also provide valuable information.

When analysing a cartoon, keep in mind that every element of it has been deliberately created for impression. Note the size of 'Matron Bevan' compared with the doctors – suggesting that Bevan was in a powerful position.

You could identify three elements to the impression in Source 1:

- The strength of Bevan's position indicated by his size relative to each of the doctors.
- The opposition of the doctors to the NHS, indicated by their resistance and unhappiness as they stand in line to get their 'medicine' from the pot labelled NHS.
- The doctors' unwilling acceptance of the NHS, indicated by their swallowing of the 'medicine' but the nasty taste it leaves in their mouths.

What evidence can you find in Sources 2 and 3 which relates to these points: either to confirm or to challenge this impression? Source 2 clearly confirms the opposition of the doctors to the NHS in 1948, and the strength of Bevan's position. It also suggests that the doctors are likely to give up the fight. Make these points and select a few key words from the source to support them. Note that Source 3, from Bevan himself, also supports the impression of the doctors' resistance (how does it do this?), but suggests that Bevan himself was under pressure to give way. How else does it challenge the impression given in Source 1? And what evidence is there in Source 2 that suggests Bevan faced considerable opposition?

When you deal with (a)-type questions you are weighing up the evidence. Bear in mind that the evidence of the sources you are given will point in different directions. So in this case, you will know immediately that there is some evidence supporting elements of the impression in Source 1 and some evidence challenging or modifying elements. You will be placing evidence on both sides. Where is there more weight? It will never be a good idea to deal with the sources one by one. Develop a short plan alongside the three bullet points above with 'Support' in one column 'Challenge' in the other, enter the evidence from Sources 2 and 3, and then come to a conclusion.

In the style of OCR B

Answer **both** parts of your chosen question.

(a) How is the defeat of the Conservatives in 1945 best explained?
[Explaining attitudes, motives and circumstances]   (25 marks)

(b) What was it about foreign policy during the years 1945–51
that made it so controversial within the Labour Party?
[Explaining ideas, attitudes and beliefs]   (25 marks)

Exam tips

The cross-references are intended to take you straight to the material that will help you to answer the question.

General Introduction

Each part question will be different so each needs full and separate treatment. Spend equal time on each part.

This exam requires answers that explain and make sense of the past. Your task is to construct that historical explanation. The information in the square brackets below each question identifies the kind of explanation you need to start working with. For a good answer, work through four stages: (i) identify various factors that explain the question set. There will always be more than one and they will be a mixture of ideas, actions and events. Try to think of each as a circle of explanation; (ii) work out the role that each factor played; (iii) decide which was/were more important than the others, explaining and justifying why. You now have a series of circles of explanation that relate to each other; (iv) establish why and how some factors influenced others (again, with supporting justification). Your circles now link, and overlap.

Working through each step in rough gives you your essay plan. Writing up each step gives you your essay: well structured, focused on the question. If you complete only step (i), your answer will be just a basic list of ideas, actions and events, so it will not score well. If you complete steps (ii) and (iii), your answer will have arranged those ideas, actions and events according to their relative importance. Such an answer will score in Level 4 (16–20 marks) if you really have explained things carefully. To reach the top (21–25 marks), you have to go one stage further and simultaneously explain the interaction of component ideas, actions and events: not just putting them in rank order of importance but establishing cause and effect from one to another. Do all of that and you show you do not merely know what happened (various separate circles) but understand why (a chain of interconnected circles of explanation).

(a) Refer to pages 2–4 of the text as they will help you to answer this question. Given the command phrase ('How ... best explained?'), your essay needs to develop a hierarchy of explanations, establishing relative importance between causal actions, ideas and attitudes. The information in the square brackets prompts you to start with a focus on causal explanation, and then to turn to the other two. There are two sides to this so you need to consider negatives that explain Tory defeat and positives that show why Labour won, but always link explanations to Conservative failure. One circle should consider Churchill himself, but the question is not just about him. Build one circle of explanation around the link in people's minds between the Conservatives and the failures in the 1930s: 'uncaring' policies during the depression and military weakness in the face of Hitler. Another circle could focus on the high hopes for the future and the widespread feeling that the Conservatives were not really committed to social and economic reconstruction (unlike Labour). Another circle should look at the election itself: Churchill's '*Gestapo*' gaff, poor Conservative planning, and the supposed influence on troops of the education corps.

Do not forget to show interactions between these circles. Churchill may have 'won the war', but his party was discredited by the past and judged unable to meet the needs of the future. Labour may have had a poor pre-war record, but seemed in tune with the people in 1945. Was Conservative defeat inevitable? Was a landslide defeat inevitable?

(b) Pages 24–9 of the text will help you to answer this question. The prompt in square brackets reminds you to focus on the empathetic mode. You need to map opposition within the party to government policies and the international situation, examining internal divisions within Labour and the reasons for them. You might start your first circle of explanation with the Labour left and its 1946 attempted amendment to the King's Speech. That will allow you to examine not just attitudes within Labour to the USA and the USSR, but attitudes inside the party to capitalism, socialism and communism. Labour divisions were deep and complex. Your next circle could examine how the emerging Cold War got in the way of political ideals. Was Bevin right that Soviet aggression made Anglo-Soviet relations increasingly difficult and that foreign policy must be realistic? Was Attlee right that Britain's interests had to come before everything? Or were Crossman and Bevan right that socialist governments needed to co-operate and the East/West division was neither inevitable nor desirable? Do not forget to place this conflict within the wider struggle being fought for the soul of Labour. Battles over foreign policy were caused by the same ideological splits that caused rows over economic policy and NHS funding.

2

The Conservatives in Office 1951–64

POINTS TO CONSIDER

Having gained a marginal victory over Labour in 1951, the Conservatives went on to govern for the next 13 years. During that time they continued in all major respects the policies begun by the previous government. This was because the social and economic policies of the 1945–51 Labour government had set a pattern that was largely followed by all succeeding governments up to 1979. This chapter considers how the Conservative administrations dealt with the issues and policies they inherited from Labour. The major themes covered are:

- The Churchill and Eden governments 1951–7
- Harold Macmillan's government 1957–63
- Britain's relations with Europe 1945–63
- The Labour Party 1951–64
- The Conservatives' last years 1963–4

Key dates

1951	Conservative election victory
1952	UK's first atomic bomb tested
1953	End of the Korean War
1955	Conservative election victory
1956	The Suez affair
1957	UK's first hydrogen bomb tested
	Homicide Act
	Rent Act
1958	Life peerages introduced
1959	Conservatives won general election
	UK a founding member of EFTA
1960	Macmillan's 'wind of change' speech
	Labour conference adopted unilateralism
1962	Commonwealth Immigration Act
	Cuban missile crisis
1963	UK's application to join the EEC vetoed
	Profumo affair
	Macmillan retired as Prime Minister
1963–4	Alec Douglas-Home led Conservative government

Table 2.1: Conservative Prime Ministers 1951–64

Years	Prime Minister
1951–5	Winston Churchill
1955–7	Anthony Eden
1957–63	Harold Macmillan
1963–4	Alec Douglas-Home

1 | The Churchill and Eden Governments 1951–7

Winston Churchill's government 1951–5

Churchill was 77 years old when he became Prime Minister for the second time. He regarded his return to office in 1951 as a belated thank you from the British people for his wartime leadership. He was now too old and frail to be much more than a figurehead. He did not need to do much; what sustained him was his past reputation as a statesman. For some months in 1953 he was out of action altogether following a stroke. Nobody seemed to notice. Yet his period in government between 1951 and 1955 witnessed a number of important developments.

Key events and developments 1951–5
- Rationing was ended.
- The steel industry was denationalised.
- The Conservative Party committed itself to building 300,000 houses a year.
- The government continued with Keynesian policies.
- The accession of Queen Elizabeth II in 1952 ushered in a new 'Elizabethan age'.
- Britain detonated its first atomic bomb in 1952.
- The Korean War ended in 1953 (see page 27).

'Butskellism'
With hindsight, it can be seen that the key figure in Churchill's government of 1951–5 was not the Prime Minister but R.A. Butler, his Chancellor of the Exchequer. Although Butler never became Conservative leader or Prime Minister, being passed over on three occasions in 1955, 1957 and 1963, he held all the other major offices of state (Chancellor of the Exchequer, 1951–5; Home Secretary, 1957–62; Foreign Secretary, 1962–4), and was a formative influence in the development of modern Conservatism. He was a force in pushing the party in a progressive direction. As Minister of Education in Churchill's wartime Coalition, Butler had been responsible for the Education Act of 1944 (see page 11). Arguably this was to remain his greatest achievement; it indicated his concern for social issues, something that the Conservatives were to adopt as one of the planks in their political platform.

After his party's heavy defeat in 1945, Butler went on to play a central role in restoring Conservative morale during the Attlee years. He was a leading light among a group of Conservatives who had began to study ways in which they could modernise their

Key question
Why was R.A. Butler such an influential figure in this period?

Key dates

Conservative election victory: 1951

UK's first atomic bomb tested: 1952

End of Korean War: 1953

party's attitude and policies so as to prevent Labour claiming a monopoly of modern thinking. An interesting product of this was the presentation in 1947 of a document known as the 'industrial charter' in which Butler and his colleagues accepted that Britain should operate a mixed economy, containing both private industry and state-directed concerns, and in which the trade unions would have a legitimate and respected role to play.

It was Butler who set the pattern of economic policy that was followed throughout the period of Conservative government to 1964. His policies between 1951 and 1955 showed that he had accepted the new form of Keynesian economics adopted by the preceding Labour government (see page 18). In essentials, he continued Labour's main aims of:

- trying to maintain full employment while at the same time achieving economic growth
- expanding the welfare state
- keeping to Britain's heavily committed military defence programme (which included the costly Korean War, 1950–3)
- developing a nuclear weapons programme.

Butler acknowledged that the deflationary policies of the Labour government before 1951 had had beneficial effects in the short term (see page 19). The cost of British goods had dropped and exports had picked up. There was also a major uplift in the international economy in the early 1950s, largely a result of the Marshall Plan (see page 26), which led to increased demand for British products. Yet Butler was faced, as Labour had been, with the hard fact that Britain was heavily in debt, a result of its wartime borrowing and continuing heavy defence commitments. All this had produced a severe and continuous balance of payments deficit. A strong criticism made at the time and voiced by later observers was that after 1945 British governments, both Labour and Conservative, had over-reached themselves. They had tried to rebuild a modern competitive industrial economy, but had crippled themselves by taking on the huge costs involved in running a welfare state and maintaining an extensive defence programme.

Butler's ideas were seen to be so close to those of the Labour Party that his name was used to coin a particular term – 'Butskellism'. The word, first used in 1954 by a journal, *The Economist*, joined together the names of Butler, seen as representing the Conservative left, and **Hugh Gaitskell**, regarded as a key figure on Labour right. It suggested that the left and right wings of the two parties met in the middle to form a consensus on such matters as finance, the economy and the welfare state.

From time to time, it has been argued that there was insufficient common ground between Butler and Gaitskell and their two parties for the word to be more than a clever piece of terminology. However, while it is true that there were differences between Butler and Gaitskell over detail, particularly in financial matters where Gaitskell favoured high direct taxation and greater government direction while Butler believed in economic control

Key figure

Hugh Gaitskell 1906–63
MP, 1945–63; Minister of Fuel, 1947–50; Chancellor of the Exchequer, 1950–1; Leader of the Labour Party, 1955–63.

through use of **interest rates**, the two men did share a noticeably similar approach in a number of key areas. Kenneth Morgan, a leading authority on modern British political history, suggests that 'Butskellism' existed as 'a state of mind':

> It implied a coherent attempt to maintain a social consensus and to try to 'set the people free' through greater liberalisation, lower [indirect] taxation and decontrol, without dismantling the popular welfare and industrial fabric of the Attlee years.

What is clear is that all the succeeding administrations, Labour and Conservative, tried to govern from the centre, believing that that was the position the bulk of the electorate would support.

Anthony Eden's government 1955–7

Table 2.2: Election results 1955

Political party	No. of votes	No. of seats	Percentage of vote
Conservative	13,286,569	344	49.7
Labour	12,404,970	277	46.4
Liberal	722,405	6	2.7
Others	346,554	3	1.2

A handsome man who set the hearts of Tory ladies aflutter, **Anthony Eden** had long been regarded as the heir apparent to Churchill as Conservative leader. However, he had had to wait far longer than he had expected since Churchill did not finally retire until 1955. The election that Eden called soon after becoming Prime Minister in 1955 produced an increased Conservative majority. This was to prove the only real success of his short administration.

It was Eden's fate to live the greater part of his political life in the shadow of Winston Churchill, the man he admired and whom he was destined to succeed, but not until 1955 when he himself was ageing and past his best. It is true that Eden had held the prestigious office of Foreign Secretary for 10 years under Churchill. However, given that throughout that time Churchill had made foreign affairs his particular area of interest, Eden's role as Foreign Secretary was reduced to that of the ever-present loyal confidant and background figure.

Having had to wait so long, Eden by the time he reached the highest office in 1955 was a man in a hurry. Irritated by criticism in the Tory press that his uninspiring domestic policies 'lacked the **smack of firm government**', he was determined to silence criticism by achieving success in foreign affairs, in which he felt he had a special expertise. This drew him into the ill-fated Suez affair, the event which overshadowed his years as Prime Minister and destroyed his reputation as a statesman.

The Suez affair 1956

Colonel Nasser, who had become President of the new Egyptian republic in 1952, had at first been on good terms with the West. He had been promised US and British loans for the construction

Aswan Dam
A dam on the Nile river that was intended to modernise Egypt by providing a huge supply of hydroelectric power.

Soviet bloc
The countries of Eastern Europe which were dominated by the Soviet Union.

of the **Aswan Dam** on the upper Nile, a project on which he had staked his own and his country's future. However, when the USA learned that Nasser had also approached the **Soviet bloc** countries for aid, it withdrew its original offer. In July 1956, Nasser, in desperation, announced the nationalisation of the Suez Canal as a means of raising the necessary finance. Foreign ships would have to pay to pass through what was now an Egyptian waterway.

Eden declared that such a man as Nasser could not be allowed 'to leave his thumb on Britain's windpipe', a reference to the threat to the essential oil supplies that came to Britain from the Middle East through the canal. He began to plan ways to bring Nasser down. The French, long resentful of Egypt's support of

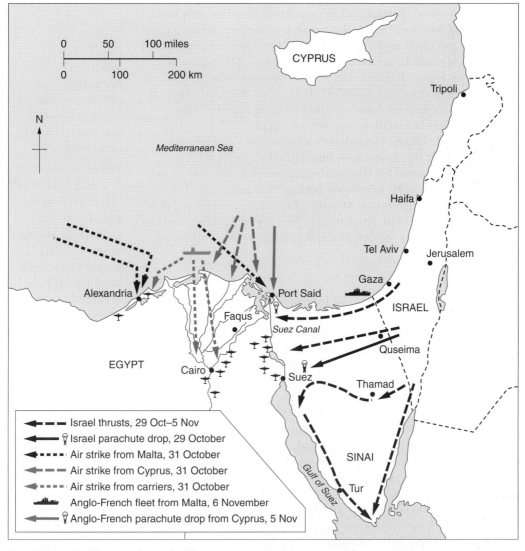

Figure 2.1: The Suez invasion 1956.

Arab nationalists in **French Algeria**, were very willing to join the British in anti-Nasser moves. Eden also hoped that the Americans would favour such a policy; he had been led to believe that the USA would give at least moral backing to Anglo-French attempts to free the canal. The Americans did, indeed, join Britain and France in seeking to apply pressure to Egypt by the creation of a Canal Users' Association.

Nasser, however, despite the international line-up against him, refused to budge. Britain and France then referred the issue to the **UN Security Council**. This proved fruitless, since the Soviet Union used its **veto** to block proposals in the council to have Egypt condemned internationally.

All this confirmed Eden in his belief that only force could shift Nasser. He began secret discussions with France and **Israel**, which was eager to launch a major strike against Egypt. Plans were prepared for a combined military invasion of Egypt. The strategy, finalised in mid-October 1956, was that the Israelis would attack Egypt across Sinai. Britain and France, after allowing sufficient time for the Israelis to reach the canal, would then mount a joint assault on the canal region from the north, under the pretence of forcing Egypt and Israel to observe a ceasefire. The plan was accepted by Eden's Cabinet. On 29 October, the Israelis duly attacked across the Gaza Strip; on 30 October the Anglo-French ultimatum was delivered and on the following day the two European allies began their invasion of Egypt.

The United Nations immediately entered into an emergency debate in which the Americans, infuriated by Eden's having totally ignored them, led the condemnation of Israel and its two allies. Over the special telephone hotline that linked the US President and British Prime Minister, Eisenhower swore at Eden in four-letter expletives. Britain, deprived of US backing, used its veto for the first time to defeat a UN resolution demanding an immediate ceasefire.

Soviet involvement

Besides resentment at not being informed of Britain's plans, what angered the Americans was that in the Cold War atmosphere of the day, Eden's actions threatened to allow the Soviet Union to seize the initiative. As it happened, the USSR had been initially distracted by its own problems arising from the Hungarian crisis that coincided with the Egyptian issue. After Stalin's death in 1953, the Soviet Union appeared to allow greater freedom to its **satellites**. However, when, in October 1956, Hungary pushed too hard for independence Khrushchev, the new Soviet leader, sent in tanks to occupy the Hungarian capital, Budapest. Desperate appeals for Western assistance were made by the Hungarians. But while the West expressed outrage at Soviet actions, intervention was not seriously considered. The military, diplomatic and geographical difficulties were simply too great. Moreover, the Anglo-French-Israeli attack on Egypt made it difficult for the West to adopt the moral high ground over matters of invasion.

Key terms

French Algeria
Algeria, part of the French empire, had a large Arab population most of whom supported the Algerian independence movement.

UN Security Council
The body set up to resolve international disputes; its permanent members were the USSR, the USA, Britain, France and China.

Veto
Each individual member of the UN Security Council had the right to cancel out the collective or majority decision of the others.

Israel
In 1948, in the face of the undying hatred of its Arab neighbours, Israel became a sovereign Jewish state, taking most of the territory known as Palestine.

Satellites
The countries of the Soviet bloc under the control of the USSR.

By the first week of November, the Hungarian rising had been crushed and the USA's refusal to accept the legitimacy of the allied invasion had become clear beyond doubt. This encouraged the Soviet Union to make its biggest move yet over Egypt. On 5 November, it issued a formal Note to Britain. Condemning the Anglo-French invasion of Egypt as the bullying of the weaker by the stronger, the Note warned that the USSR was prepared to use rockets against the Western invaders:

> We are fully determined to crush the aggressors and restore peace in the Middle East through the use of force. We hope at this critical moment you will display due prudence and draw the corresponding conclusions from this.

Key question
Why did Eden call off the Suez campaign?

The British withdrawal from Suez

It is unlikely that the USSR would have dared carry out its threat to attack Britain and its forces directly; it was Britain's temporary international isolation that allowed the Soviet Union to take a righteous stance and engage in a bluff that it calculated would not be called. Nevertheless, it was the case that the day after the receipt of the Note, Eden gave way and Britain accepted the UN demand for disengagement. But while the possibility of Soviet intervention undoubtedly helped to concentrate Eden's mind, the still more pressing reasons for his ordering a withdrawal from Suez were:

- the strength of opposition among the British people; Gaitskell and Bevan made withering attacks on what they described as Eden's mad venture
- the fury of President Eisenhower and the Americans at not being consulted
- Britain's failure to gain international backing
- condemnation of Britain at the UN
- the reluctance of all but a few of the Commonwealth countries to support Britain
- the international **run on sterling**, which threatened Britain with economic collapse with no prospect of the USA's being willing to bale Britain out.

Key terms

Run on sterling
A catastrophic fall in Britain's currency reserves caused by large withdrawals of deposits by international investors.

European dictators
As Foreign Secretary between 1935 and 1938, Eden had developed a deep distrust of Germany's Adolf Hitler and Italy's Benito Mussolini.

Eden's personal role

Historians, reflecting on the Suez crisis, have made much of the role played personally by Anthony Eden. It has been suggested that the crisis took the form it did largely because of his perception of the problem and how it might be solved. Eden's deep distaste for Nasser, whom he saw in the mould of the **European dictators** of the 1930s, led him always to put the worst construction on the Egyptian leader's actions. In view of the delicate international balance in the Middle East, this was of considerable significance. Anxious for the maintenance of essential oil supplies, Eden suspected that beneath Nasser's campaign to modernise Egypt lay an essentially anti-British motive. He concluded that in the end it might be that Nasser would have to be stopped by military force. Mistaking the initial collective British and Western disapproval of the Egyptian seizure of the canal as implying support for any moves he might initiate, Eden had colluded with France and Israel for a pretext to invade Egypt and topple Nasser.

Already on dangerous ground, Eden did not help his cause by the manner and style in which he acted. Tetchy and short-tempered, he did not try to hide his distaste for those who disagreed with him. This mattered most in his dealings with the USA, the ally that the British government most needed at this critical juncture. Eden's undisguised annoyance with Eisenhower was hardly likely to win the Americans over to his point of view. A particular blindness of Eden's was his failure to appreciate that with a presidential election imminent in the USA, the American government was simply not prepared to become embroiled in a costly, military venture that recalled old-style imperialism.

It has also to be said Eden's chronic poor health, which deteriorated further during the crisis, weakened his judgement. The strain of Suez wore him out. J.P. Mallalieu, a Labour MP, gave a striking description of the physical and mental state to which the Eden had been reduced by the pressure of events:

> The Prime Minister sprawled on the front bench, head thrown back and mouth agape. His eyes, inflamed with sleeplessness, stared into vacancies beyond the roof except when they switched with meaningless intensity to the face of the clock, probed it for a few seconds, then rose again in vacancy. His hands twitched at his horn-rimmed spectacles or mopped themselves in a handkerchief, but were never still. The face was grey except where black-ringed caverns surrounded the dying embers of his eyes.

Eden's wife recorded that during the weeks of the crisis it felt as if the Suez Canal was flowing furiously through her drawing room. Within weeks of the crisis Eden stepped down as Prime Minister. The official reason was ill-health and it was certainly true that he was seriously unwell, but the Suez disaster had shattered his standing at home and abroad. He could not have carried on as head of government even had he been fully fit.

The significance of the Suez affair for Britain

It is important to note that Britain was not defeated militarily in Egypt. Indeed, British forces were withdrawn from Suez when they were on the verge of successfully completing their mission. That was why the Israelis were so bitter with the British for leaving the job half done. The truth was that Britain's withdrawal was a failure not of military resolve, but of political will. Fearing the consequences of being internationally isolated, Eden's nerve broke and he accepted that Britain could no longer continue with a policy that the world condemned. It was an admission that in the post-war world Britain could not act alone. Such thinking led a number of people in both political parties to consider

Key question
What were the consequences for Britain of the Suez venture?

whether Britain should consider closer union with Europe (see page 63).

The Suez crisis was a landmark in Britain's foreign policy. In attacking Egypt, Britain had attempted to act independently of NATO and the USA, without consulting the Commonwealth, and in disregard of the UN. The international and domestic protests that the Suez venture aroused meant that it was the last occasion Britain would attempt such independent action. British imperialism had made its last throw. It is true that there would be occasions in the future when Britain would use armed force unilaterally, but this would only be, as for example over the Falklands (see page 123), when it considered its own sovereign territory had been occupied by a hostile power.

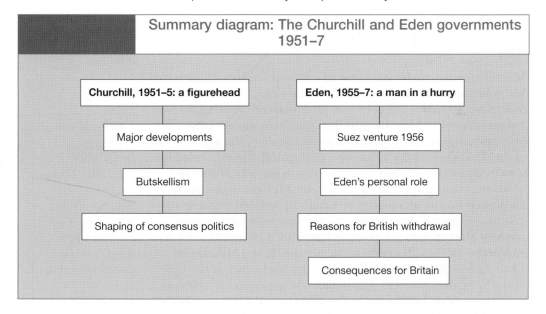

Summary diagram: The Churchill and Eden governments 1951–7

Churchill, 1951–5: a figurehead
- Major developments
- Butskellism
- Shaping of consensus politics

Eden, 1955–7: a man in a hurry
- Suez venture 1956
- Eden's personal role
- Reasons for British withdrawal
- Consequences for Britain

2 | Harold Macmillan's Government 1957–63

Key question
In what sense did Macmillan follow 'a middle way'?

Eden was followed as Prime Minister not by R.A. Butler, who, until Suez had been generally regarded as the likely successor, but by Harold Macmillan. Although an outstanding figure in the Conservative Party, Butler had a diffident and detached manner that made him reluctant to engage in the infighting that party politics requires. Nor had he impressed when he had stood in for Eden during the Suez crisis.

Macmillan, in contrast, had a much sharper political sense. Although he had firmly supported Eden over Suez, he came out of the escapade relatively unscathed. As Chancellor of the Exchequer, he made a rallying call to the Cabinet on 3 January 1957. Admitting that the military operation had swollen Britain's debts by £564 million, he told his colleagues that they must learn lessons from Suez, but not be overwhelmed by it: 'The Suez operation has been a tactical defeat. It is our task to ensure that, like the retreat from **Mons and Dunkirk**, it should prove the prelude to strategic victory.'

Key term

Mons and Dunkirk
Celebrated occasions in the First and Second World Wars when British forces recovered from initial defeats to win the final military struggle.

Profile: Harold Macmillan 1894–1986

1894	– Born into the Macmillan publishing family
1917	– Badly wounded in action
1924	– Elected as Conservative MP
1930s	– Opposed appeasement policy
1938	– Published *The Middle Way*
1940–2	– Minister of Supply
1942–5	– Minister with special responsibility for the war in North Africa
1951–4	– Minister for Housing and Local Government
1954–5	– Minister of Defence
1955	– Foreign Secretary
1955–7	– Chancellor of the Exchequer
1957–63	– Prime Minister and leader of the Conservative Party
1984	– Became the Earl of Stockton
1986	– Died

Macmillan's appearance was that of a typical English gentleman. Yet by birth he was half Scottish, half American. He had a gallant service record in the 1914–18 war, an experience which gave him a particular respect for the working class. This was deepened by his witnessing, as MP for a Durham constituency, the grim effects of the depression in the north-east of England. He expressed his unorthodox Conservatism in 1938 in his book, *The Middle Way*, which may be regarded as an early appeal for consensus politics. He argued for the acceptance of Keynesianism and pressed the case for extending the direction by the state of a broad range of services. Having held key posts in Churchill's 1940–5 Coalition and in the 1951–5 government, he became Prime Minister in 1957. Although he was Chancellor of the Exchequer at the time of the Suez affair in 1956, Macmillan was generally regarded as not being deeply implicated in the government's failure. This left him well placed to heal the wounds in the party. He was the first Prime Minister to commit Britain to entering Europe and was an outspoken supporter of independence for the African colonies. He proved himself a keen Cold Warrior by supporting the USA in its conflicts with the Soviet Union, notably in 1962 when he stood by President Kennedy during the **Cuban missile crisis**.

Despite his seemingly relaxed style, Macmillan worked extremely hard and could be ruthless on occasion: in 1962 in the 'Night of the Long Knives' he dismissed half his Cabinet. Despite considerable unhappiness in his private life he maintained an 'unflappable' air in public. He had a dry sense of humour and took particular delight in the satirists' portrayal of him as 'Supermac', originally intended as an ironic reference to his government's uncertain economic performance. His own comment on this was famously that under Conservatism Britain had 'never had it so good'.

Cuban missile crisis
In October 1962, the USA, having discovered that Soviet nuclear missiles were being installed on the island of Cuba, ordered their removal. After days of acute tension, the Soviet Union gave way and ordered their dismantling and withdrawal.

Key term

Cuban missile crisis: 1962

Key date

Macmillan's rousing speech undoubtedly helped his bid for leadership. A week later he became Prime Minister. These were still the days when the Conservative Party did not elect its leader; he was appointed by an inner circle who took soundings from MPs and party workers. It was not a democratic system, but both Macmillan and his successor in 1963, Sir Alec Douglas-Home (see page 71), 'emerged' as Prime Minister as a result of this informal and secretive process.

In forming his first Cabinet in 1957 Macmillan made Butler Home Secretary. This proved an important move. At the Home Office Butler took a basically liberal approach towards legal and social issues, placing the emphasis in penal matters on reform rather than punishment. A significant example was the introduction of the Homicide Act in 1957 which effectively ended the death penalty except for certain rare categories of murder.

Butler's liberal stance as Home Secretary hinted strongly that the Conservative Party under Macmillan was prepared to modify its traditional social attitudes. Its opponents would find it harder to dismiss it simply as a party of reactionaries. Butler's liberal attitude was one on which subsequent home secretaries, such as Labour's Roy Jenkins, would build (see page 90), providing another example of the consensus that applied to so many areas of British politics and government in the second half of the twentieth century.

Key date

Homicide Act: 1957

'Introducing Supermac' published in the *Evening Standard* newspaper, 6 November 1958. Macmillan as Superman, the popular comic-book hero for whom nothing was impossible. Macmillan became the butt of the political and social satirists who flourished in the late 1950s and 1960s in the press and the theatre, and in particular in the BBC programme, *That Was The Week That Was*. Why, despite its mocking intention, did the cartoon become one of Macmillan's favourites?

INTRODUCING: **SUPERMAC**

HOW TO TRY TO CONTINUE TO STAY TOP WITHOUT ACTUALLY HAVING BEEN THERE

NOTE: MAC'S TORSO IS, OF COURSE, PADDED

Conservative economic policy 1957–64

Although Britain had picked up economically in the Churchill
and Eden years, the ending of rationing being an example of
this, its recovery was not as pronounced as had been hoped.
Compared with what was happening in Europe and the USA, the
British economy appeared sluggish. Nevertheless Macmillan's
chancellors of the exchequer after 1957 made no serious attempt
to change Britain's economic and financial strategies. They
continued Butler's main lines of policy:

* to operate a mixed economy
* to follow a loose form of Keynesianism.

The aim of these policies was to avoid the extremes of inflation
and deflation by a series of adjustments to meet particular
problems as they came along. If inflation (seen in Britain in the
second half of the twentieth century as the major threat to
economic stability) rose too quickly, measures to slow it down were
introduced. These invariably involved raising interest rates to
discourage borrowing and increasing import controls to limit
purchases from abroad, with the aim of reducing the trade gap.
The annual budgets were an important part of the mechanism. As
a check on overspending or too rapid a rise in wages, taxes might
be increased. Treasury officials spoke of such moves as preventing
the economy from 'overheating'.

Alternatively, if there was a fall in demand for goods, which
meant difficulties for manufacturers and retailers, the Chancellor
of the Exchequer of the day might introduce 'a give away' budget
in which taxes and interest rates were lowered. It was hoped this
Keynesian approach would encourage more spending and thus
result in a demand-led recovery.

Budget politics

A common criticism voiced by both parties when in opposition
was that budgets were too often used as short-term measures to
buy votes in general elections. Interesting illustrations of vote-
catching were the Conservative budgets of the late 1950s and
early 1960s. In his 1959 budget, Heathcoat Amory made an effort
to boost support for the government in the forthcoming election,
by introducing a range of tax cuts. This was at a time when the
prevailing high inflation suggested that financial restraint would
have been more appropriate. The result was increased consumer
spending, which led to still higher inflation and a wider trade
gap. Faced with this, Heathcoat Amory changed tack and adopted
deflationary measures which included tax and interest rate rises,
cuts in public spending, and an attempt to put a limit on wage
increases.

Successive Conservative chancellors continued with these
restrictive measures until the 1964 election loomed. To regain lost
popularity, Macmillan's government in 1963 returned to an
expansionist budgetary policy; taxes and interests rates were
again lowered. The consequence was another boom in consumer
spending. Since the sudden demand for goods could not be met

Key question
What economic
policies did the
Conservative
government follow
under Macmillan?

**Macmillan's
Chancellors of the
Exchequer**
Peter Thorneycroft
  1957–8
Derick Heathcote
  Amory 1958–60
Selwyn Lloyd
  1960–2
Reginald Maudling
  1962–4

from British stocks there was a sharp increase in the import of foreign manufactures. The net result was that by the end of 1964 Britain had a balance of payments deficit of over £800 million.

Stop–go and stagflation

What such a train of events suggested to some observers was that Britain lacked a genuine economic strategy. The series of adjustments made by governments did not really add up to an integrated plan. Policy lagged behind events; it did not direct them. This is what led to the coining of the terms **stop–go** and **stagflation** to denote the failure of governments to develop policies that encouraged a consistently performing economy. All this pointed to the difficulty of managing a modern economy, which is always vulnerable to the play of unforeseeable circumstances. When Harold Macmillan was asked by a reporter what he regarded as the most difficult feature of government planning, he replied 'events, dear boy, events'.

Britain's industrial growth rate

Britain's economic record cannot be taken in isolation. A major worry was that Britain was performing poorly in comparison with its chief international competitors. Its GDP growth rate was the lowest in western Europe.

Table 2.3: GDP growth rate 1951–64

Country	Percentage growth
Italy	5.6
Germany	5.1
France	4.3
UK	2.3

The figures in Table 2.3 should not be interpreted to mean that Britain was simply less productive or less efficient than those other countries in the list. A major reason for Britain's relatively weak performance was its heavy defence expenditure. It still maintained costly military and naval bases around the world and it was running an expensive nuclear-arms development programme. None of the other countries listed in the table carried the burdens that Britain did. By 1964, the last year of the Conservative government, Britain was spending £1.7 billion on defence, which amounted to 10 per cent of its GDP. Compared with its major industrial competitors, Britain was committing an extraordinary proportion of its **R&D** investment on defence. Only the USA spent more (see Table 2.4).

Table 2.4: Percentage of R&D spent on defence 1963–4

Country	Percentage
Japan	0.9
Netherlands	1.9
Italy	2.6
West Germany	10.8
France	26.2
UK	34.5
USA	40.6

Key terms

Stop–go
When consumption and prices rose too quickly, the government put on the 'brake' by increasing taxes and raising interest rates, thus making it more difficult to borrow money. When production and exports declined, the government pressed the 'accelerator' by cutting taxes and lowering interest rates, thus making it easier to borrow money.

Stagflation
A compound word of stagnation and inflation. It referred to the situation in which industry declined but inflation still persisted, with the result that the economy suffered the worst of both worlds.

R&D
Research and development. Economic research and development provide the means of industrial growth.

Living standards under the Conservatives

In July 1957 Harold Macmillan made a statement that, although challenged by his opponents, came to be regarded as a representative description of the character of his administration from 1957 to 1963 and perhaps of that of the whole period of Conservative government:

Let's be frank about it: most of our people have never had it so good. Go around the country, go to the industrial towns, go to the farms, and you will see a state of prosperity, such as we have never seen in my lifetime – nor indeed in the history of this country.

Wages

Despite periods of serious hardship for some of the population in Britain under the Conservatives, the broad picture was one of a continuous rise in living standards. The various financial problems that confronted the nation did not prevent the great majority of the population from gaining in material prosperity. This is an area where figures speak loudest. Wages rose ahead of prices. One example of the overall improvement in working people's income is that the average weekly wage of the adult male worker increased from £8 6s (£8.30) in 1951 to £18 7s (£18.35) in 1964. It was not simply that wages increased in overall amount. The key fact was a growth in **real wages**; income kept ahead of prices. People were able to buy more with their money. This meant that although inflation continued to climb throughout the period it never overtook the increase in real wages.

Table 2.5: Growth in real wages 1951–64 (calculated as an average hourly rate percentage increase for each individual worker)

Financial year	Percentage increase
1951–5	2.2
1955–60	2.9
1960–4	4.0

Credit

Another vital factor in the raising of living standards was the greater availability of credit, a facility provided by finance companies that enabled people to borrow much larger sums of money than they could obtain by saving. With loan repayment spread out over a number of years on 'easy terms', usually a relatively small amount each month, people were able to buy items they previously could not have afforded.

Access to credit (also known as hire purchase) enabled consumers to buy an unprecedented range of manufactured goods. A consumer boom began. In the period 1950–65 the sales of private cars nearly quadrupled from 1.5 million to 5.5 million. In addition, foreign holidays, clothing and **mod cons** came within the reach of ordinary people in ways that would have been impossible without the existence of credit.

Key question
How justified was Macmillan's claim that under the Conservatives the British people had 'never had it so good'?

Key terms

Real wages
The purchasing power of earnings when set against prices. When prices are high money will buy less; when prices are low the same amount of money will buy more.

Mod cons
Short for modern conveniences, e.g. central heating, and household accessories such as vacuum cleaners, refrigerators, radios and TVs.

Housing

Perhaps the most impressive feature of the consumer boom was the growth in house buying. Housing had been a proud claim of Attlee's government, which had built over 600,000 homes by 1951. The Conservatives tried to better the Labour record. To great acclaim at the 1950 Conservative conference, the party leaders had responded to emotional pleas from the floor by committing themselves to build 300,000 houses annually. Macmillan was instrumental in the fulfilling of that pledge. As Housing Minister between 1951 and 1954, he achieved the target of 300,000 new homes each year. Although the pace slowed considerably after that, when the Conservatives went out of office in 1964 they could claim to have built 1.7 million homes, 60 per cent of those being private dwellings.

Rent Act 1957

Key date

Rent Act: 1957

It was during his own administration in 1957 that Macmillan presided over the introduction of the Rent Act which, by abolishing rent control, put six million properties on the market. The downside of this was that rents rose considerably, making it difficult for tenants at the lower end of the scale to afford leases. But that was the trade-off Macmillan felt had to be made in order to stimulate the rented property market.

'A property-owning democracy'

What made this housing explosion possible was the relative ease with which money could be borrowed and repaid over long periods of time. Encouraged by the government, banks and building societies advanced the necessary capital in the form of mortgages that allowed increasing numbers to own their own homes, thus creating the conditions for what the Conservatives called a '**property-owning democracy**'. It was such developments that Harold Macmillan had in mind when he declared in 1957 that the British people had 'never had it so good'.

Key term

Property-owning democracy
A society in which as many people as possible are encouraged to become homeowners, an extension of the principle that the ownership of property is an essential component of democracy.

There is no doubt that Macmillan was being politically astute in calling attention to the undoubted material improvement in people's lives and implying that it was largely the result of Conservative policies. Yet although Macmillan was always an optimist on the surface, remarking on one occasion that if you weren't optimistic you might as well be dead, he did harbour fears. In the same 'never had it so good' speech of 1957 he went on to warn that the new prosperity could be threatened by inflation. It was also a concern that the affluent times might not last that drew him towards the idea that Britain had to join the forerunner of the European Union, the Common Market (see page 61).

Unemployment

As Macmillan was well aware, despite the evident improvement in the material well-being of so many in the population, problems remained. Although the Conservatives willingly inherited the Labour Party's commitment to full employment as a basic economic aim, achieving this proved much more difficult. Table 2.6 shows that the lowest annual figure for joblessness was well over a quarter of a million in the mid-1950s, rose rapidly in the late 1950s, and, after falling in the early 1960s, reached an embarrassingly high figure in Macmillan's final year in government. The persistence of high unemployment cast doubt on just how realistic it was to claim that the people had 'never had it so good'.

Table 2.6: Number of workers unemployed in Britain 1951–64

Year	Number	Year	Number
1951	367,000	1958	536,000
1952	468,000	1959	621,000
1953	452,000	1960	461,000
1954	387,000	1961	419,000
1955	298,000	1962	566,000
1956	297,000	1963	878,000
1957	383,000	1964	501,000

Education

Controversy between the major parties over state schooling rumbled on throughout the second half of the twentieth century. The central disagreement was between those who wished to end separate three-tier schooling (see page 11) altogether and replace it with a system of comprehensive schools, and those who defended the grammar schools since they were proving successful in providing education for working-class children.

Main arguments for the comprehensive system:

- Selective education meant the undervaluing of the majority of children who did not meet the artificial standard of selection imposed.
- The selection process, such as the 11 plus exam, was psychologically dubious and unreliable.
- Selection was socially divisive, since it operated a system which separated groups of children from each other.
- Under selection, the greater share of public funds went to the top layer of schools leaving the lower layers impoverished.
- The inferior education children received in the lower layers marked them as failures.
- The record showed that bright pupils performed as well academically in comprehensive schools as in grammars.

Main arguments against the comprehensive system:

- In practice, comprehensive schools had denied able children from disadvantaged backgrounds the chance to benefit from a specialist school education fitted to their needs.
- Since the quality of schools depended on the area in which they were situated, there was no alternative in a deprived catchment area to a poor comprehensive now that grammar schools were being abolished.

- Wealthy parents had the choice of moving to a better area so that their children could go to a better comprehensive school. Poorer parents had no such choice. The result was not, therefore, greater educational fairness and opportunity but less. Selection by ability had been replaced by selection according to parental income.
- Most comprehensive schools streamed their pupils or put them into 'sets' according to academic attainment, thus, in practice, preserving the differentiation of children into distinct types.

Yet, while it is true many Conservatives, particularly at local level where the fate of particular schools was being decided, strongly opposed the spread of comprehensives, the Conservative Party in its official policy came to accept that this form of schooling best fitted British needs. Edward Boyle, Minister of Education from 1962 to 1964, was one of the younger Conservatives under Macmillan who pushed for the abolition of the 11 plus (see page 11) and the provision of better education for all children.

The fact is that, judged by what it did or what it allowed while in government, the Conservative Party chose not to resist the movement for non-selective education. The following list shows that the Conservatives, far from being a barrier to the spread of comprehensive schools, were in office when the first purpose-built schools appeared:

- Ysgol Gyfun Llangefni in Anglesey, north Wales, 1954
- Kidbrooke School in south London, 1954
- Sandfields School in Wales, 1958
- Risinghill School in Islington, north London, 1960.

The Conservatives' conversion, though grudging, was another sign of how a consensus had developed among the British political parties. A single statistic illustrated this: in the second half of the twentieth century more comprehensive schools were built under Conservatives than under Labour. One of the key developments in Boyle's time was the publication of the Robbins Report in 1963, which is best seen as an attempt to extend the comprehensive principle into higher education.

The main recommendations of the Robbins Report were as follows:

- expansion of the existing universities
- emphasis to be given to scientific education
- the 12 existing colleges of advanced technology (CATs) to be upgraded to university status
- larger grants to be provided so that no potential students would be deterred by lack of income.

Key question
Why was there increased social mobility in the Macmillan years?

Class

One of the charges made by those who fought to defend the grammar schools was that those who wished to impose a comprehensive system were not really concerned about education but were using the schools issue to fight a class war, trying to impose equality by social engineering. However, while it was still customary to regard Britain as a class-conscious if not a class-ridden society, things were changing. Class was ceasing to matter as much as it did; three key reasons suggest themselves:

- The war had weakened class divisions. The national war effort and the common experience of dangers like the blitz, and hardships like rationing, had made many people realise how artificial class divisions were. Churchill had recognised that important social shifts were occurring. He described the working-class trade unions as having become 'an estate of the realm'.
- The creation of the welfare state under Attlee and its acceptance by the Conservatives after 1951 were an acknowledgement that the well-being of the whole population was a matter of national concern.
- The growing affluence of Britain in the 1950s and 1960s, the spread of wealth across a much broader section of the population, and the consequent rise in living standards had the effect of blurring class distinctions.

Here it is important to stress that the term class does not have a fixed meaning. As Arthur Marwick, one of Britain's most esteemed social historians, points out, classes do not belong in 'the same category as the facts of geography, demography and economics.' The term class should not be given the rigid meaning that **Karl Marx** gave it: 'Classes', Marwick says, 'evolve and change as circumstances change'. This does not prevent our using the word in a descriptive sense; class can be helpfully applied to broad groups which experience common social and economic change. Most people in mid-twentieth-century Britain would have accepted that there were three major social groups or classes:

- upper classes, drawn from the traditional landed aristocracy
- middle classes who worked in trade or the professions
- working classes who worked for wages in manual labour.

These were not exact definitions, of course; there were grades within each class, particularly the middle class. It was also increasingly possible to move from one class to another. It was this mobility that became evident in the Macmillan years.

Karl Marx 1818–83 A highly influential German revolutionary who taught that conflict between strictly opposed classes was the driving force of history.

Key figure

Social mobility

One of R.A. Butler's claims was that modern Conservatism, far from perpetuating class differences in Britain, was actually ending them:

> We have developed instead an *affluent*, open and democratic *society*, in which the class escalators are continually moving and in which people are divided not so much between 'haves' and 'have-nots' as between 'haves' and 'have-mores'.

The speech in 1960 in which he used those words clearly complemented Macmillan's 'never had it so good' speech three years earlier. Between them, the two speakers had defined the aim of the Conservative government as being the development of a socially mobile society which left its individual members free through their own efforts to enjoy the fruits of the nation's increasing wealth.

The key to the social shift and the blurring of class divisions was the availability of financial credit (see page 48). In a pre-credit age, only the rich had been able afford to buy ostentatiously. But now that borrowing and purchasing on credit were possible for nearly everybody, having possessions was no longer a clear guide to social status.

Since people on a regular wage could buy things on hire purchase, there was an increase in the number of consumers and in production to meet that demand. This was the great equaliser in class terms. Indeed, a process developed in which working-class incomes often exceeded lower middle-class ones. Yet it was still possible for lower middle-class people living in genteel poverty to regard themselves as in some way socially superior and more respectable than car workers or plumbers who were earning much more than they were. This suggests that in Britain class was as much an attitude of mind as of possessions and wealth.

Responses to Conservative social and economic policies

Supporters of Macmillan's policies argued that while it was true that the gap between rich and poor widened in Britain between 1951 and 1964, it had to be understood that wealth and poverty were relative terms. The truth was that the material quality of life was improving for everybody. Sympathetic observers compared the process to a cruise ship going through a set of locks. The first-class passengers keep their superior position in the higher decks, but the less well-off in the lower decks also rise as the vessel goes up. The reality was that the great majority of those designated poor in Britain, for example, had access to resources that their forebears could not even have imagined.

Critics challenged these claims by faulting the Conservatives on the following points:

- They had not developed coherent economic policies but had simply employed 'stop–go' tactics to prevent the economy swinging too wildly between deflation and inflation.
- Apart from a wish to keep the value of the pound sterling, they had no structured financial strategy. They had used budgets and tax adjustments not in a responsible way but as a technique for buying votes at election time.
- A major error was the government's failure to invest in industrial research and development. It had shown equal misjudgement in not making efforts to improve Britain's poor employer–worker relations. The result of all these shortcomings was 'stagflation'; by the mid-1960s Britain had one of the poorest growth rates among the advanced industrial nations.

There were also moralists who argued that Macmillan's pursuit of a property-owning democracy was a vain endeavour since it was based not on genuine national prosperity, but on heavy borrowing by government and consumers. The scale of debt which this created was economically dangerous and socially harmful since it encouraged materialism, consumerism and irresponsibility.

Social tensions

Key question
In what ways did immigration increase social tension?

One of the most notable features of Britain in the second half of the twentieth century was its development as a multiracial society. A key stage in this occurred in 1948 with the sailing of a converted troopship, the *Empire Windrush*, from Kingston, Jamaica, to Britain. The ship carried hundreds of West Indian workers; the majority were young males, but there were also a number of older men and families. They were coming to find work. The official welcome they received was a warm one. Cinema newsreels enthusiastically recorded the event and assured the newcomers that they would soon find homes and jobs.

Under existing law, the newcomers had full rights of British citizenship. This stimulated further emigration from the West Indies. The government encouraged this with organised appeals for Caribbean workers to fill the vacancies, principally in the hospital and transport services that Britain's acute post-war labour shortage had left. By the mid-1950s employers in Britain has extended their recruitment to the Indian subcontinent. Textile firms in London and the north of England eagerly took on workers from India and Pakistan.

However, by the late 1950s, disturbing reactions had begun to occur among some of the white host population. 'No coloured' notices appeared in boarding house windows and on factory gates. Mutterings were heard to the effect that the newcomers were attracted to Britain as much by the generous welfare benefits as by the prospect of work. The actual number of white residents who believed such slanders may have been small, but troublemakers were able to exploit the housing shortage, which was a major problem in the poorer areas, by suggesting that it was all the fault of the immigrants.

Race relations problems have never been simply about numbers. Those who spoke of Britain being 'swamped by waves of immigrants' were grossly exaggerating. The proportion of people of non-European origins has never been more than six per cent of the overall population of Britain. Moreover, as Table 2.7 shows, in every decade of the century up to the 1970s net emigration exceeded net immigration.

The main difficulties arose over accommodation. When immigrants first arrived in Britain they tended to live in the poorer areas of cities and urban areas where the cheaper properties for buying or renting were to be found. This was understandable and unavoidable given their limited resources. But since Britain's inner cities suffered from a severe shortage of affordable housing there was bound to be competition between residents on low incomes and newcomers. The same problems arose in the job market. Where work was scarce, those who could

Table 2.7: Emigration from, and immigration into, the UK (to nearest 100,000)

Decade	Outflow	Inflow
1900–9	4,404,000	2,287,000
1910–19	3,526,000	2,224,000
1920–9	3,960,000	2,590,000
1930–9	2,273,000	2,361,000
1940–9	590,000	240,000
1950–9	1,327,000	676,000
1960–9	1,916,000	1,243,000

not get a job tended to blame immigrants for squeezing them out of employment by taking work at lower pay rates than whites were prepared to accept.

Riots 1958–9

Tension turned to violence in 1958 when a series of riots broke out in a number of urban areas in Britain, most notably in Nottingham, Bristol and some of the poorer London districts. There was a pattern to the trouble everywhere it happened; gangs of white youths went round insulting black residents whose young men frequently retaliated. The most disturbing incident occurred in August in London's Notting Hill where a crowd of over 600 white males tried to batter their way into black-owned properties. Television newsreels showed disturbing scenes of police battling to keep white and black mobs apart, while the fire services struggled to quench the fires started by the throwing of petrol bombs.

To quell the trouble, at least in the short term, severe prison sentences were imposed on the white ringleaders who were found guilty of inciting the disturbances. Macmillan's government also set up an official inquiry under Lord Salmon to examine the underlying reasons for the outrages. The Salmon Report suggested that the chief factors were:

- sexual jealousy of young white males who resented white women going out with black males
- the anger of whites at the willingness of blacks to work for low wages
- bitterness at the rise in rents which, whites believed, were a result of the readiness of blacks to live in cramped conditions and, therefore, pay higher collective rents than individual whites could afford
- white 'teddy boys' who used violence against immigrants becoming 'local heroes' to whites fearful of the growing number of black residents.

The Report approached the riots very much as a law and order issue. It put the problem down to white reaction to increased immigration and made no overt reference to racism or discrimination suffered by immigrants. The government then acted in the same spirit as the Report. Interpreting the disorder as a sign that immigrant numbers had to be controlled, it

Key term

Teddy boys
Young men of the 1950s with a strong tendency to violence when gathered in numbers; they took their name from their style of dress which recalled the fashions of King Edward (Teddy) VII.

introduced a **Commonwealth Immigrants Act** in 1962. This proved a highly controversial measure and was condemned in many quarters as being racist since it placed restrictions on would-be entrants according to their ethnic origin.

In opposition, the Labour Party stoutly opposed the bill, but, when in office itself, it introduced a second Commonwealth Immigrants Act in 1968. Both major parties had concluded that limitations on entry into Britain were necessary in the interests of good race relations. To make that point, the Labour governments introduced Race Relations Acts in 1965 and 1968 (see page 88). One consequence of the news that an Immigration Act was being prepared was a rush of immigrants into Britain in the period before its terms came into force. Between 1960 and 1962, over 230,000 **New Commonwealth** citizens arrived. This in fact marked an immigration peak, but it was such numbers that fuelled the anxieties of those who called for a complete block on entry.

Key date

Commonwealth Immigration Act: 1962

Key terms

Commonwealth Immigrants Act
Attempted to limit immigration by creating a voucher scheme which restricted the right of entry to those who actually had jobs to go to.

New Commonwealth
Largely West Indians, Indians, Pakistanis and Bangladeshis.

Old Commonwealth
Largely Australians, New Zealanders, Canadians and South Africans.

Table 2.8: Commonwealth immigrants living in the UK

Year	Old Commonwealth	New Commonwealth	Total
1961	307,697	289,058	596,755
1971	528,810	765,095	1,293,905

'They just ain't civilised – like we are … !' In May 1959, in the west London borough of Notting Hill, Kelso Cochrane, a West Indian man, was stabbed to death in the street by a group of six whites. Despite witness statements being collected, no charges were brought, a situation that led many immigrants to fear that the law would not really protect them. The youths depicted wear the hairstyle, long jackets, drain-pipe trousers and crêpe-soled shoes of the typical 'teddy boy' uniform of the day. What bitterly ironic point is being made by the cartoonist?

A 'youth subculture'

Social disorder did not always involve race. Britain by the 1960s had seen the development of what has been termed a 'youth subculture'. This referred to the unwillingness of some young people to accept the standards and values of their elders. This could easily descend into antisocial behaviour and hooliganism, as evident in the affrays that began in 1964 between '**mods and rockers**'.

Some explanations for the anti-social behaviour of the young:

Key term

Mods and rockers
Mods drove motor scooters and were rather more smartly dressed than rockers, who rode proper motorbikes; their pre-arranged fights usually took place in seaside resorts on bank holidays.

- The growing affluence of society enabled some young people on good wages to feel independent and ready to ignore traditional ways.
- Conversely, there were pockets of poverty which left those who did not share in the general prosperity embittered and alienated.
- The teenagers and 20 year olds of the 1960s were the first generation not to have lived through the grim times of the depression and the Second World War. Deliberately targeted by advertisers, eager to sell them the clothes and pop records, young people were encouraged to regard themselves as special and different.
- The psychological theories of the day encouraged people, especially the young, to throw off traditional restraints and act out their feelings and desires.
- The scandals associated with some of those in the upper echelons of society hardly set a good example of responsible behaviour (see page 69).
- The 1960s were a boom time for satire; the regular mocking on television and in the papers meant that the nation's political leaders played a part in undermining traditional notions of respect and deference.

Macmillan and the end of Empire

Key question
What policy did Macmillan's government follow towards Britain's remaining colonies?

It is one of the most striking examples of consensus politics in Britain that it should have been the Conservatives, traditionally regarded as the party of imperialism, who took a predominant role in the dismantling of the British Empire. Fully accepting the implications of Attlee's government decision to grant independence to India in 1947 (see page 22), the Conservative government under Harold Macmillan continued the process of abandoning the empire. Despite the protests of the right wing of the party, represented by such bodies as the League of Empire Loyalists, the Conservatives had come to recognise that there was in post-war Britain, and, indeed, in the world at large, a broad agreement that the age of imperialism had passed. Two world wars fought for the right of peoples to be free had made it no longer acceptable for any nation to impose itself upon another or control the people against their will. The failure of the Suez venture in 1956 had re-emphasised that point.

Colonialism, therefore, was dead or dying. Macmillan put this memorably in 1960 when he spoke of the need to recognise 'the

Key date
Macmillan's 'wind of change' speech: 1960

wind of change' blowing through Africa. He meant that, in the light of the growing national consciousness of the African peoples, the only politically realistic and morally acceptable policy was to grant independence to those peoples who wanted it. What gave particular significance to his message was that it was delivered in a speech he gave to the South African Parliament while on a tour of African countries. White-dominated South Africa was at this stage the home of **apartheid**, a system that enshrined the notion that certain people and races were not yet capable of governing themselves.

Macmillan backed his words by presiding over an extraordinary transition. Between 1957 and 1968 Britain gave independence to all its remaining colonies in Africa and the majority of those elsewhere. Despite the protest of white settlers, this proved, for the most part, a remarkably smooth and bloodless process. Where there were problems in the British retreat, as in **Kenya**, they arose not over whether independence was to be granted but when.

Southern Rhodesia (Zimbabwe)

The major exception to the story of peaceful transition was Southern Rhodesia. There the white settler community which held the political power refused to accept the principles of 'majority rule' and 'one person, one vote'. They claimed that to introduce majority rule into Rhodesia would give authority to the backward black Africans, who were incapable of exercising it responsibly. Having failed to reach agreement with successive British governments, Ian Smith, the Prime Minister and leader of the white Rhodesian Front party, declared **UDI** in 1965. For the next 15 years Rhodesia defied international condemnation, which sometimes took the form of economic sanctions, a particular case being an embargo on tobacco, one of the colony's most profitable exports.

Eventually the sanctions and a dispiriting civil war between black African guerrilla fighters and the white settlers in Rhodesia forced Smith to the conference table. Talks with Margaret Thatcher's Conservative government, which had opposed sanctions, produced a new settlement involving the acceptance of majority rule. Free elections in 1980 saw a victory for Robert Mugabe, who had been a 'freedom fighter' against UDI during the civil war. The new nation adopted the name Zimbabwe.

The main problem that remained after independence was how long the majority of black Zimbabweans would continue to tolerate the possession of the nation's best land by the minority white farmers. With the approval of Zimbabwe's neighbouring African governments, President Mugabe introduced a policy of dispossessing the white farmers and redistributing the land among his followers. Sadly, this was accompanied by growing violence. Violence, indeed, became a feature of Mugabe's rule,

Key terms

Apartheid
In theory, the notion of separate and equal development for different racial groups in South Africa; in practice, the subjection of other races to white rule.

Kenya
Between 1952 and 1960 clashes between British forces and Kenyan nationalists resulted in the death of 13,000 native Kenyans and 100 Europeans.

UDI
Unilateral Declaration of Independence.

which adopted increasingly dictatorial methods. His efforts to reconstruct Zimbabwe along Marxist economic lines led to the spoliation of his country. By the early years of the new century, rampant inflation had destroyed Zimbabwe's currency and, according to UN estimates, reduced two-thirds of the population to starvation level. When criticised by Western observers, such as Britain, the USA and the European Union, Mugabe's response was invariably to say that he would not take lectures from former colonialist exploiters. He was on strong

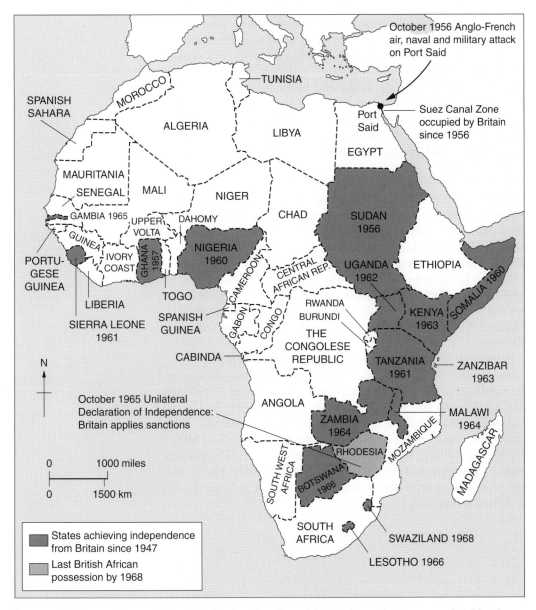

Figure 2.2: Map of Africa 1947–68 indicating the dates when independence was gained by the British colonies.

grounds; although the West condemned his methods, its
imperial guilt inhibited it from direct interference in Zimbabwe.
His reaction also usually won the applause of many African
states that shared his objection to the West's attempt to take a
moral stance.

The effect on Britain of its loss of Empire

A once commonly held view was that when Britain gave up its
Empire during the second half of the twentieth century it suffered
a serious economic loss. However, the imperial balance sheet
reveals that Britain as a nation had paid out more in grants and
aid than it got back in profits. Despite the often-repeated charge
that Britain continually drained its colonies of their resources,
figures indicate that in the period from 1870 to independence in
1947 Britain on a yearly average took less than one per cent of
India's net GDP.

Even more significantly, at the end of the war in 1945, Britain,
having agreed in 1940 to pay all India's war costs, found itself
owing the subcontinent a sum of £1200 million. It was now the
debtor nation. It was the same story with the colonies overall.
Britain was in debt to them at the end of the war to the tune of
£454 million.

Whatever profits individuals and companies might have
made, Britain, overall, was a net loser financially. In the end,
Empire was abandoned not because it was making too little
but because it was costing too much. Macmillan was doubtless
sincere when he publicly supported the principle of colonial
independence; nevertheless, the basic reason why Britain
ceased to be an imperial power was because it could no longer
afford to remain one. Bankrupt after the war and heavily reliant
on the USA for financial aid, Britain could not realistically
continue funding the defence and economic needs of the
colonies.

A more difficult question is whether the loss of empire
damaged Britain's morale and left its people feeling diminished.
It is difficult to see that Britain's decision to give up its colonies
was regarded by the bulk of the population as other than a
logical and mature thing to do. Certainly people seemed
untroubled by it. The historian Bernard Porter, recalling his
feelings as a young man in the 1960s, has written: 'The process of
losing an empire had little effect on British politics. Life in the
metropolis went on much as before. The rest of us lived through
it all hardly noticing it.'

Imperial guilt
The feeling among
the ex-colonial
powers that their
previous possession
of colonies
disqualified them
from taking direct
action in African
affairs.

Summary diagram: Harold Macmillan's government 1957–63

Macmillan's characteristics as leader: Supermac image

Conservative economic policy

Methods	Target	Results	Persistent problems
• Maintaining the mixed economy • Operating mild Keynesian policies	• Attack on inflation	• Stop–go • Stagflation • Budgetary politics • Spreading affluence	• Slow growth of GNP • High defence costs • Limited R&D

Living standards	Social tensions	Macmillan and Empire
• 'Never had it so good' years • Consumer boom • Housing boom • Property-owning democracy • Unemployment • Education • Class shifts	• Immigration • Riots 1958–9 • Youth subculture	• Acceptance of 'wind of change' • Decolonisation 1957–68

Key question
Why was Britain slow to join the movement for European union after 1945?

Key terms

'The six'
France, Germany, Italy, Belgium, the Netherlands and Luxembourg.

Common market
A trading system between equal states with the minimum of regulation.

Protectionist
Making non-common market goods uncompetitive by denying them entry or placing tariffs on them.

3 | Britain's Relations with Europe 1945–63

European developments 1945–57

After 1945 there was a significant movement among the Western European nations towards mutual co-operation. This culminated in 1957 with the signing of the Treaty of Rome by **'the six'**, which created the European Economic Community (EEC). The Treaty's key terms were:

- the establishment of a **common market** and a customs union to monitor all aspects of trade between the member states
- the adoption of a Common Agricultural Policy (CAP)
- member states were required to operate a **protectionist** policy against all non-member nations.

The Common Agricultural Policy

CAP rested on the notion of ending rural poverty by a system in which 'poor areas' in the Community were to be subsidised by a transfer of money from the 'rich areas'. The subsidy system, which provided the farmers with guaranteed prices for their produce regardless of actual demand or cost, meant high prices for the consumer. This deliberate and sustained dear food policy became one of the most controversial aspects of the operation of the EEC.

The political character of the EEC

The EEC defined itself formally as an economic organisation but it was driven as much by political considerations. This was because from the first the EEC was dominated by Germany and

France. Germany's desire was to re-establish itself as a respectable and acceptable nation that had wholly thrown off its Nazi past. For its part, France was motivated primarily by a fear of a resurgent Germany. Far better, therefore, to control Germany within a formal organisation to which they both belonged than try to compete separately against it.

As for the other four members, the Benelux countries and Italy, they judged that the post-war years offered them an opportunity to extract as many economic concessions as possible from Germany, their more powerful, but guilt-ridden, neighbour. This, they judged, could best be achieved within a European union organised as a **federation**.

Britain's attitude towards European union

Significantly, Britain, not having experienced occupation by a hostile power in wartime, was not convinced in the way that 'the six' were of the need for a formal European union as a means of preserving peace. British governments showed little interest in Europe. When pressed to join the **Schuman Plan** in 1950, Clement Attlee had rejected it unequivocally. He told the House of Commons: 'We are not prepared to accept the principle that the most vital economic forces of this country should be handed over to an authority that is utterly undemocratic and is responsible to nobody.'

Interestingly, the Conservatives at this time shared exactly the same view towards Europe as the Labour government. Harold Macmillan directly echoed Attlee when he declared, also in 1950, that Britain was not prepared to take risks with the British economy by subjecting it to the control of a foreign organisation. 'We will allow no supra-national authority to put large masses of our people out of work in Durham, in the Midlands, in South Wales and in Scotland.'

Over a decade later such sentiments still prevailed in the Labour Party. At the party conference in October 1962, Gaitskell firmly rejected the idea of Britain's joining the EEC. Were the nation to take such a step, he warned, it would have fatally undermined its standing 'as an independent European state. I make no apology for repeating it. It means the end of a thousand years of history.' Yet, already, by the time Gaitskell made his dramatic statement, the Conservative government had begun to have second thoughts about Europe and was seriously considering committing Britain to the EEC.

Britain moves towards European membership 1956–63

In the decade after the Second World War, British governments had remained convinced that Britain's economic future lay not in Europe but in its continued relationship with the United States and the Commonwealth. However, in the 1950s and 1960s the poor performance of the British economy compared to that of the EEC countries (see page 47) cast serious doubt on whether Britain could continue to remain detached. Equally disturbing for

Key terms

Federation
The essence of a federation is that the member states forgo a significant degree of individual sovereignty in order for the union of states to have effective executive power.

Schuman Plan
A scheme by which the European nations pooled their most productive resources – coal and steel – in a European Coal and Steel Community (ECSC).

Key question
What led Britain eventually to consider joining the EEC?

Key dates

UK a founding
member of EFTA:
1959

UK's first hydrogen
bomb tested: 1957

Key terms

EFTA
The European Free
Trade Association
formed by Britain,
Norway, Sweden,
Austria, Portugal,
Switzerland and
Denmark.

**Special
relationship**
The term coined by
Churchill in 1946 to
describe the
common values and
perceptions that, he
believed, made the
USA and Britain
natural allies.

City-orientated
Relating to the
money markets in
London's
international
financial centre,
known as 'the City'.

Britain was the failure of **EFTA** to match the economic success of
the EEC. Set up in 1959 as a genuinely free-trade counterbalance to the protectionist EEC, EFTA was never able to match
the influence of the EEC and by 1972 most of its members had
joined that organisation.

There had also been important shifts on the wider
international front. The Suez affair of 1956 (see page 38) had put
a question mark against Britain's status as an independent world
power and raised doubts about the Anglo-American **special
relationship**. Added to this, was Britain's difficulty in remaining a
truly independent nuclear force. Although Britain had joined the
nuclear club, detonating its first atom bomb in 1952 and its first
hydrogen bomb in 1957, the advance of weapon technology
meant that by the late 1950s its method of delivering the
weapons by bomber was outmoded. To maintain its strike power
Britain had to begin buying US Polaris submarines from which
nuclear warheads could be launched (see page 64).

Such developments obliged British politicians to adjust their
thinking. Equally significant was the decline within the
Conservative Party of the traditionally influential agricultural
lobby and its replacement by the younger, **City-orientated**,
managerial element, who were becoming increasingly pro-
European in their sympathies. They were not moved by the
notion of European unity as an ideal. Their approach was hard-
headed and practical; they feared being left behind economically
by their European competitors. Their view was essentially: 'if you
can't beat 'em, join 'em'.

It was against this background that Prime Minister Macmillan
appointed Edward Heath as minister with special responsibility
for negotiations with 'the six'. In 1961 Macmillan declared that
the government was now considering applying to join the EEC.
In announcing this remarkable new departure, he promised that
Britain would join only on condition that the existing privileges
and interests of EFTA and the Commonwealth would be
preserved. He later explained his attitude in these terms:

> The possible damage that might be inflicted on British agriculture
> and Commonwealth trade was a question of vital importance.
> Much would therefore depend upon the issue of any negotiations.
> We must persuade 'the six' of the value of the Commonwealth to
> the Free World, and the meeting of Commonwealth leaders
> concurred in the belief that neither the Commonwealth countries
> nor British public opinion would accept that Commonwealth
> interests should only be safeguarded during the transitional period.

Britain's application to join the EEC in 1963 vetoed by France

Key question
Why did France block
Britain's entry into the
EEC in 1963?

Macmillan's concern for the rights of the Commonwealth and
EFTA made Britain's readiness to negotiate appear grudging. It
suggested that Britain wanted to have its cake and eat it. It was
for this reason that President De Gaulle used the French veto to

block Britain's first formal application to join the EEC, made in 1963. He explained it thus:

UK's first application to join the EEC vetoed: 1963

Key date

> How far is it possible for Great Britain at the present time to accept a truly common tariff, as the continent does, for this would involve giving up all Commonwealth preferences, renouncing all claims for privileges for her agriculture, and treating as null and void obligations entered into with countries forming part of the Free Trade Area?

There was a powerful logic to De Gaulle's doubts concerning British sincerity. His rhetorical question in reaction to Macmillan's claim that 'we must persuade "the six" of the value of the Commonwealth to the Free World' made sound sense. How, indeed, could Britain assert such sentiments and then genuinely undertake the removal of all the preferential claims and privileges currently enjoyed by EFTA and the Commonwealth? Strong grounds for De Gaulle's scepticism had been provided in 1962 when the independent Commonwealth countries of Africa, fearing a compromising of their newly won freedom, had rejected a specially negotiated offer to become associate members of the EEC.

De Gaulle's reservations did not end with economics. More important for him were the political implications of British entry. These were spelled out by the French Agricultural Minister:

> It is very simple. At present, in 'the six' there are five hens and one cockerel. If you join, with other countries, there will be perhaps seven or eight hens. But there will be two cockerels. I am afraid that is not acceptable to us.

De Gaulle's opposition to British entry has to be seen in historical perspective. As a committed patriot, De Gaulle had been appalled at the **humiliation of France** in 1940. Conscious that its liberation in 1944 had depended not on French arms but on those of the USA and Britain, De Gaulle believed passionately that France should atone for its failings by reasserting itself in the post-war world. It should make itself pre-eminent in a Europe that was independent of Britain and America, whose cultural values he regarded as decadent and whose political influence he found distasteful. When he returned to lead his country in the late 1950s, he saw in the EEC a way of achieving this objective, an objective that would be threatened if Britain was permitted to join.

A personal meeting between De Gaulle and Macmillan in December 1962 had done nothing to ease these fears. Indeed, the failure to reach an Anglo-French understanding on joint nuclear-arms development, followed only days later by the Anglo-American agreement in which the USA agreed to supply Britain with Polaris missiles (see page 63), served to confirm De Gaulle's suspicions that Britain was the thin edge of a large US wedge about to be thrust into Europe. De Gaulle saw the EEC as a

Key term

Humiliation of France
In a six-week period in May and June 1940, France had been totally overwhelmed by German forces and forced to surrender and accept occupation.

counterbalance to American power and did not want British membership undermining this.

Having been rejected by France, largely at the personal insistence of De Gaulle, Britain's only recourse was to wait until he was no longer president and then apply again. Britain had assumed the role of beggar, pleading, cap in hand, to be allowed to join the feast. It was a humiliating position and can be seen as damaging Britain's relations with Europe from that point on. When Britain was eventually accepted into Europe it was on terms not of British making. Britain had applied to the EEC out of fear, had been rejected out of French pride, and had revealed to itself and to the world how economically weak and diplomatically isolated it was.

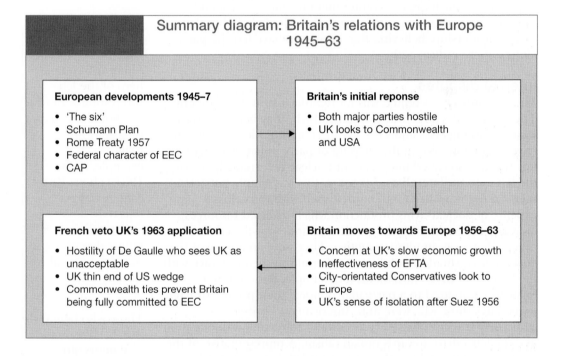

Summary diagram: Britain's relations with Europe 1945–63

European developments 1945–7
- 'The six'
- Schumann Plan
- Rome Treaty 1957
- Federal character of EEC
- CAP

Britain's initial reponse
- Both major parties hostile
- UK looks to Commonwealth and USA

French veto UK's 1963 application
- Hostility of De Gaulle who sees UK as unacceptable
- UK thin end of US wedge
- Commonwealth ties prevent Britain being fully committed to EEC

Britain moves towards Europe 1956–63
- Concern at UK's slow economic growth
- Ineffectiveness of EFTA
- City-orientated Conservatives look to Europe
- UK's sense of isolation after Suez 1956

4 | The Labour Party 1951–64

Key question
What problems did the Labour Party experience in opposition?

In British politics, rows within parties are often more lively and more intense than disputes between parties. One explanation for the Conservatives' remaining in office for so long after 1951 was the condition of the Labour Party, which for much of that period remained disunited. This was despite having in Hugh Gaitskell, who succeeded Attlee in 1955, a leader who was undoubtedly one of the most gifted politicians of the day. Possessed of a sharp analytical mind, he was also blessed with a perfect voice for public speaking and he used its tone, timbre and cadences to great effect to express anger, sorrow or humour. Arguably the most impressive example of his oratory and his greatest parliamentary performance was in 1956 when with controlled fury he forensically shredded and destroyed Eden's attempt to justify the British occupation of the Suez Canal zone.

However, the fates conspired against Gaitskell. His untimely death in January 1963 at the young age of 57 meant that he never became Prime Minister, a role for which his abilities and experience made him especially fitted. His greatest political misfortune was that he became leader of the Labour Party when it was going through one of its most disruptive periods. The truth was that the Labour Party, despite its creative years in office between 1945 and 1951, had yet to decide exactly what type of party it was and what aims it should pursue. The identity problem was to trouble it throughout its existence right down to 2007. Despite its remarkable achievement in introducing the welfare state, many of the party regarded this as simply the first step in the march towards a truly socialist Britain. The left of the party argued for a much greater commitment to state control and direction of the economy and society. They had chafed under Attlee's leadership, believing that he should have led the party along a more radical path.

Internal disputes

The **Bevanites** represented this more radical strand of thought. They wanted the large trade unions, which, they believed, spoke for the working class and were led by committed left wingers, to have the major voice in the shaping of party policy. A key issue was Britain's so-called independent nuclear deterrent. Many of the left were **unilateralists**. For some, this was simply patriotism: they did not want Britain to burden itself with the colossal expense of nuclear-arms production which diverted resources away from providing for the needy and underprivileged. For others, there was an ulterior motive. They were anxious that the Soviet Union should not fall too far behind in the arms race with the West. The **CND** movement, for example, although not formally committed to a particular political standpoint, attracted to its ranks those who were anti-American and pro-Soviet.

As party leader, Gaitskell resisted both trade union domination and the left's drive towards unilateralism. A representative of the moderate centre-right of the party, Gaitskell believed that his victory over Bevan in the 1955 leadership contest had given him the authority to steer the party away from policies that would alienate it from the electorate. He became even more convinced of this by the outcome of the 1959 election.

The 1959 election

Before the election, it had been widely held that Labour had a strong chance of winning. The election was the first to be held since the Suez affair, providing the electorate with a chance to punish the Conservative government for its involvement. There was also a feeling that the budgetary policies followed by the government might count against it. However, opinion polls and the election itself showed that these factors had been exaggerated.

In fact, the election came at a bad time for Labour. It was another of Gaitskell's misfortunes that his time as Labour Party

Bevanites
Followers of Aneurin Bevan, a hero of the left. Interestingly, Bevan was not always as radical as his followers. For example, at the 1957 Labour Party conference, he rejected unilateralism as a policy, describing it as an 'emotional spasm'.

Unilateralists
Those who believed that Britain should give up its atomic weapons without waiting for a multilateral agreement between the nuclear powers to do so.

CND
Campaign for Nuclear Disarmament. Founded in 1958 to agitate for unilateral nuclear disarmament, it was dominated from the first by left wingers.

leader coincided with a period of economic recovery which, while it was not entirely due to the policies of Macmillan's government, was skilfully presented in Conservative propaganda as if it were. Harold Macmillan's famous reference in 1957 to the British people's 'never having had it so good' was a clever piece of populism (see page 48) and was equally effectively used by the government in the run-up to the 1959 election in the form of the slogan 'Life is better with the Conservatives. Don't let Labour ruin it.'

In an attempt to counter the impact of that slogan, Labour's campaign team tried to woo the voters with a scheme that promised a substantial increase in state pensions without an accompanying rise in taxation. However, the scheme was too hurriedly drafted and raised questions about how it would be paid for that embarrassed rather than helped the Labour candidates in their campaigning.

To the opposition's list of electoral handicaps should be added its attitude towards the European issue. In 1962 Gaitskell had followed Attlee in publicly declaring that the Labour Party was against Britain's joining the EEC (see page 62). Although it would later change its position on this, the Labour Party at this stage hardly appeared progressive and forward looking. This point was made by a significant number of Gaitskell's party who suggested that he had adopted the wrong stance. The party's internal doubts were certainly not a vote winner.

Table 2.9: Election results 1959

Political party	No. of votes	No. of seats	Percentage of vote
Conservative	13,749,830	365	49.4
Labour	12,215,538	258	43.8
Liberal	1,638,571	6	5.9
Others	255,302	1	0.9

Key date

Conservatives won general election: 1959

The election results in Table 2.9 show that the Conservatives had gained 21 seats, while Labour had lost 19, the net effect being that the government had increased its overall Commons majority from 58 to 100. Labour had clearly failed to impress the electorate.

Reasons for Labour's defeat in 1959

The party was damaged by:

- disagreements over the true character of the party
- divisions over how far the party should push for socialist policies, such as nationalisation
- splits over the issue of unilateralism
- uncertainty over whether Britain should join the EEC.

In the election campaign itself Labour was:

- outmanoeuvred by the Conservatives who claimed to be leading Britain towards prosperity

- handicapped by the public perception that Labour's plans would result in the raising of taxes.

Labour's reaction to its defeat

Anger over a third consecutive election defeat produced recriminations within the Labour Party. Gaitskell accused the left of weakening the movement by their demands for unilateralism. The left replied by attacking him over his betrayal of party principle by dropping nationalisation as a primary goal. Some on the right of the party rallied to Gaitskell's defence by forming the **CDS**. This group argued vigorously that it was undemocratic and improper for the left to use their influence with the leaders of the large trade unions, such as the Transport and General Workers, to foist their extremist minority views on the Labour Party, the majority of whose members were moderates.

Attempts by the left to undermine Gaitskell and impose unilateralism on Labour came to a dramatic climax at the 1960 party conference. Able to rely on the **block vote** of the major unions, the unilateralists forced their policy on the party. Gaitskell in his speech as leader appealed to the delegates, some of whom tried to shout him down, not to give in to the demands of the **'fellow travellers'** in the party. With great emotion he declared that for the Labour Party to ignore the views of the electorate by adopting a unilateralist policy that would alienate the majority of voters was political suicide. Gaitskell promised: 'We will fight, and fight, and fight again to save the party that we love.'

Although he lost the vote in 1960, Gaitskell may be said to have won the argument, since a year later the conference agreed to drop unilateralism as party policy. It is notable that Gaitskell's argument in 1960 was essentially the one repeated 25 years later by Neil Kinnock when he turned on the 'loony left' and berated it for its lack of common sense and realism (see page 140).

Key terms

CDS
Campaign for Democratic Socialism. A number of CDS members went on to break from Labour in 1981 and form a new political party, the Social Democratic Party.

Block vote
Labour Party procedures allowed individual trade union leaders to cast their conference votes on behalf of all the members of their union, which could number millions.

'Fellow travellers'
Crypto-Communists and Soviet sympathisers.

Key date

Labour conference adopted unilateralism: 1960

'And may I say to Hon. members opposite me … .'
A cartoon from the *Evening Standard*, 5 March 1960 (showing Macmillan sitting on the left and Gaitskell standing on the right). Explain the irony behind the cartoonist's caption and his depiction of Gaitskell's physical position.

Summary diagram: The Labour Party 1951–64

Problem of party unity

- Gaitskell succeeded Attlee after defeating Bevan for leadership
- Gaitskell led the party from a centre-right position

Opposed internally

- Bevanite left
- Unilateralists and CND

Why Labour lost 1959 election

- Weakened by internal divisions
- Disadvantaged by rising UK's prosperity
- Mounted a poor election campaign

Election defeat intensified internal wrangles

- 1960 Conference saw victory of left
- Trade union block vote forced unilateralism as official policy
- Gaitskell's 'fight and fight and fight again' speech rallied party
- 1961 Conference rejected unilateralism

Key question
What factors weakened the Conservative governments in their last years?

5 | The Conservatives' Last Years in Government 1963–4

Macmillan was unlucky in that the final years of his premiership were marred by scandals which, while seldom the direct fault of the government, reflected badly on it:

- The Vassall affair 1963. The government was obliged to appoint an official investigation into the case of John Vassall, a civil servant in the Admiralty who in 1962 had been caught spying for the Soviet Union. There were suggestions that senior Admiralty figures had tried to protect Vassall. The inquiry found no clear evidence of this, but the talk of cover-ups suggested the government was not in control of its departments.
- In January 1963, it was revealed that Kim Philby, a senior official in the Foreign Office, had for decades been passing information to the USSR as well as recruiting agents and running a spy network. To avoid arrest, Philby fled to Moscow where he remained until his death in 1988. Somewhat unfairly, Macmillan's government took the brunt of the blame for the security services having failed for so long to spot a deadly traitor in the heart of the establishment.
- The Argyll divorce case. In 1963, a lurid court case, in which the Duke of Argyll sued his wife, Margaret, for divorce on the grounds of adultery, provided the public with a host of salacious details including a list of 88 men with whom, at various times in various numbers, the duchess had had group sex. The list was said to include two (unidentified) government ministers, one of whom appeared in a pornographic photo that was shown in court. In granting the divorce, the judge said it was beyond doubt the Duchess had engaged in 'disgusting sexual practices'. A popular comedian of the day, Tommy Trinder, remarked on radio that the Duchess should have married not the Duke of Argyll, but Plymouth Argyll.

The Profumo affair 1963

All these incidents troubled Macmillan and his government, but the scandal that gave them the most concern was the Profumo affair. In March 1963 the behaviour of Macmillan's Minister for War, John Profumo, became headline news. It was revealed that Profumo had had a sexual liaison with Christine Keeler, a prostitute who numbered members of the Soviet embassy among her clients. The risk to national security was obvious and was eagerly seized on by the media. In March 1963 Profumo solemnly declared in the House of Commons that there was no truth in the rumours that he had had improper relations with Miss Keeler, only to have to admit three months later that he had lied to Parliament. He resigned his position, but his disgrace spread far beyond him, implicating the government and Conservative Party.

Distasteful details emerged that Profumo had first met Keeler at Cliveden, a famous country house in Buckinghamshire used as a high-class brothel by Dr Stephen Ward, a fashionable osteopath who used his contacts to procure girls for upper-class men. Since Ward as a popular doctor had many Conservatives on his books, the party was damaged by association, even though most of those he treated were genuine patients. Ward was subsequently put on trial, charged with living off immoral earnings. Fearing that the court case was going heavily against him, he committed suicide rather than face the consequences. At another trial not connected with Ward's, Christine Keeler was found guilty of perjury and sentenced to nine months' imprisonment.

The impact of the Profumo affair

The scandal did not in itself bring down the government, but the fact that Macmillan believed Profumo's original denial of impropriety suggested that the Prime Minister was losing his political grip. Macmillan said ruefully that it was a sorry state of affairs that he should be criticised for believing the word of a friend and colleague who had personally assured him that there was no truth in the rumours.

It was not merely the tabloids that kept the issue before their readers. *The Times* weighed in with a portentous leader headed 'It *is* a moral issue' in which it argued that the scandal was about more than a Minister lying in Parliament, serious though that was. The affair had invaded the public sphere and could not be dismissed simply as a reprehensible individual indiscretion. It reflected on the character of British public institutions and government. *The Times* caught the prevailing response of most people; while neither the Prime Minister nor the government was directly to blame for the failings of one minister, the Profumo affair seemed somehow to emphasise that after 12 years in office the Conservative Party had weakened its claim to lead the nation. There was a feeling that Macmillan and the government he led had become faintly ridiculous and outmoded.

Profumo affair: 1963 | Key date

Key figures

Lord Hailsham 1907–2001
MP, 1938–50 and 1963–70; Leader of the House of Lords, 1960–3; Minister for Sport, 1962–4; Minister of Education, 1964.

Lord Home 1903–95
MP, 1931–45, 1950–1 and 1963–74; Secretary for Commonwealth Relations, 1955–60; Leader of the House of Lords, 1957–60; Foreign Secretary, 1960–3 and 1970–4; Prime Minister, 1963–4.

Key term

Night of the Long Knives
A deliberate over-dramatisation used by the press to compare Macmillan's reshuffle with Hitler's massacre of his leading supporters in Germany in 1934.

Key dates

Life peerages introduced: 1958

Macmillan retired as Prime Minister: 1963

Alec Douglas-Home leads Conservative government: 1963–4

The struggle to succeed Macmillan 1963

When Macmillan, in 1963, unwell and weary after six years in office and damaged by the Profumo affair, announced his intention of resigning, he asked for the party to follow the 'customary processes' in choosing a new leader. This meant sounding out the Cabinet and the MPs to find out whom the majority would accept. At the time, most of the press thought it was a straight fight between Butler and **Lord Hailsham**, a contender with the right aristocratic connections to appeal to old-fashioned members of the party but who was a somewhat abrasive character.

Butler seemed to be well placed to become Prime Minister. His work as Home Secretary and then Foreign Secretary under Macmillan appeared to have been highly successful. In 1962 he had been one of the few leading Cabinet members to survive the '**Night of the Long Knives**', Macmillan's Cabinet reshuffle, in which he elevated a number of younger Conservatives and demoted some of the established ones. Macmillan then raised him to the position of Deputy Prime Minister. However, in 1963 Butler once again did little to push his leadership claims at the critical moment despite his appearing to be in a strong position. There was also the fact that although Macmillan admired Butler's abilities, he disliked him as a person and did not wish to see him become Prime Minister.

Douglas-Home succeeds Macmillan

Then, to everybody's surprise outside the party and many within it, an outsider and late runner entered the race – **Lord Home**, Macmillan's Foreign Secretary. To make himself eligible, since convention now required that the Prime Minister be a commoner, he renounced his peerage. Hailsham did the same for the same reason. That they were able to do this had a certain irony, since the right to give up their titles existed only because of the work of the Labour radical Tony Benn (see page 105), who had successfully campaigned for an Act which became law in 1963 that allowed him to renounce his hereditary peerage and drop his title of Lord Stansgate and so remain in the House of Commons.

Macmillan deliberately kept the party waiting before announcing the date of his resignation, thereby giving Home time to press his candidacy. Eventually from his hospital bed where he was being treated for prostate problems, Macmillan sent his letter of resignation to the Queen, in which he included a recommendation that Sir Alec Douglas-Home be invited to be the next Prime Minister. The Queen acted on the advice and on 16 October 1963 Douglas-Home became Prime Minister. He was to hold the office for one day short of a calendar year.

There is little doubt that it was Macmillan's support as retiring Prime Minister that won the day for Douglas-Home. It made the consultations Macmillan had asked the party to engage in little more than a charade. It had always been Macmillan's intention to block Butler; the only question was whom did he support. He had initially backed Hailsham but then switched to Home, judging that on balance he was a safer choice. There was considerable resentment among some party members that Butler had been ignored for a third time. Enoch Powell (see page 88) and **Iain Macleod** declared that they would not serve under Home, whose leadership, they believed, would give the electorate the wrong image of Conservatism.

The manner in which Macmillan and the party grandees were able to nominate Sir Alec Douglas-Home as his successor indicated that class and the old-boy network were still a force. Nine of those most closely involved in the manoeuvrings that saw Home emerge as leader were old Etonians. However, what was significant was that this proved to be the last time the party would employ such a dated process. Following its defeat in the 1964 general election, the party would adopt an open, democratic system involving the balloting of Conservative MPs. The following year, Edward Heath became the first Conservative leader to be elected under the new arrangements.

Iain Macleod 1913–70
MP, 1950–70; Minister of Health, 1952–5; Minister of Labour, 1955–9; Colonial Secretary, 1959–61; Chancellor of the Exchequer, 1970. One of the best parliamentary speakers of his day, he was disliked by the Conservative right for his progressive views on social issues and decolonisation.

Summary diagram: The Conservatives' last years in government 1963–4

Weakening factors	Power struggle over succession
• Macmillan and the government rocked by scandals 1963 • Government embarrassed by French rejection of UK's EEC application • Prime Minister and government mocked by satirists	• Ailing Macmillan announced his intention to retire 1963 • Hailsham, Butler, Douglas-Home rival candidates to the premiership • Antiquated system of selecting leader saw Douglas-Home 'emerge' as new Prime Minister • Result largely a matter of Macmillan's backing Douglas-Home • Whole matter seen as ridiculous by many in the population • Last time such a system would be used

Study Guide: AS Questions

In the style of Edexcel

Source 1

From: a speech by Harold Macmillan in July 1957 to a Conservative Party rally in Bedford.

Most of our people have never had it so good. Go around the country, go to the industrial towns, go to the farms, and you will see a state of prosperity such as we have never seen in my lifetime – nor indeed in the history of this country.

Source 2

From: Michael Lynch, Britain 1945–2007, *published 2008.*

Despite periods of serious hardship for some of the population in Britain under the Conservatives, the broad picture was one of a continuous rise in living standards. The various financial problems that confronted the nation did not prevent the great majority of the population from gaining in material prosperity. This is an area where figures speak loudest. Wages rose ahead of prices. It was not simply that wages increased in overall amount. The key fact was a growth in real wages. Income kept ahead of prices.

Source 3

From: Derrick Murphy, Britain 1914–2000, *published in 2000.*

The years 1957–9 tend to be remembered as the high point of the decade's affluence, while in fact it was only in the particular circumstances of the first half of the decade that the party was able to deliver lower taxes and higher public spending without serious consequences. When Macmillan delivered his well known speech in July 1957 declaring that 'most of our people have never had it so good' he was not welcoming an age of affluence but trying to warn the country that high public spending, rising standards of living, full employment and low inflation were not simultaneously possible. The economic difficulties which had begun in the second half of 1955 had made the Cabinet acutely aware of the underlying problems in the economy.

Use Sources 1, 2 and 3 and your own knowledge.
Do you agree with the view that the 1950s can be seen as a period of great prosperity for the people of Britain? Explain your answer, using Sources 1, 2 and 3 and your own knowledge.

(40 marks)

Exam tips

The cross-references are intended to take you straight to the material that will help you to answer the question.

This is an example of a (b)-type question, worth two-thirds of the marks for the unit. You should expect to write a substantial answer to this question – leaving yourself about 35–40 minutes to write your answer after you have analysed the sources and planned a response.

Examiners will award you a maximum of 16 marks for making use of the provided sources and 24 marks for deploying your own knowledge. You must identify points raised by the sources, and then you can use your own knowledge to develop those further and to introduce new and relevant points that the sources do not contain. But you should start your plan with the sources. That makes sure that you do not get so carried away with planning and writing a standard essay answer that you forget to use the sources properly. For the highest marks, you should develop techniques which enable you to use your own knowledge in combination with material from the sources: integrating the two.

Try working with a set of columns which allows you:

- to sort your material into that which agrees with the claim in the question and that which counters it
- to plan in an integrated way where your own knowledge can extend a point found in the sources.

Some examples are given below.

AGREE (evidence from sources)	AGREE (evidence from own knowledge)	DISAGREE (evidence from sources)	DISAGREE (evidence from own knowledge)
Source 1 states that most people 'had never had it so good' and refers to greater prosperity than ever before and implies that it exists all over the country, while Source 2 provides direct evidence of the 'great majority … gaining in material prosperity' and a 'growth in real wages'.	The greater availability of credit (pages 48 and 53) fuelled a consumer boom and gave ordinary people access to goods such as cars and foreign holidays that they would never have been able to afford without credit.	Source 1 needs to be treated with caution: it is a rally speech, designed to please party supporters.	
		Source 2 refers to periods of 'serious hardship' for some of the population of Britain. Source 1 also refers to 'most' people, not all, suggesting limitations to this prosperity.	

AGREE (evidence from sources)	AGREE (evidence from own knowledge)	DISAGREE (evidence from sources)	DISAGREE (evidence from own knowledge)
		Source 3 refers to 'economic difficulties', beginning in 1955 and suggests that by 1957 there were 'underlying problems in the economy'.	

Additional points are given below. Try slotting these remaining points into a plan. You will need to decide into which column they should go and how they should be grouped. Do some of them add to points in the plan above, or are they new points? Can evidence to support them be found in the sources, from the sources with additional material from your own knowledge or do they come entirely from your additional knowledge gained from Chapter 2?

- The period saw a huge growth in house buying.
- The Rent Act of 1957 stimulated the rented property market.
- Rents rose, making it difficult for lower earners to afford leases.
- Britain's GDP was the lowest in Europe.
- Inflation was high by the end of the 1950s.

And now what is your overall conclusion?

In the style of OCR A

'Social tensions were the **most** important domestic problem facing the Conservatives during the years 1957–64.' How far do you agree?   (50 marks)

Exam tips

The cross-references are intended to take you straight to the material that will help you to answer the question.

The question gives you a specific factor to consider (pages 43–60 and 69–72 contain the relevant information). Whether you think it was very significant or not, you must spend serious time assessing its importance before you move on to examine other alternative possibilities. Whatever conclusion you come to, you must also explain clearly why you think that it was/was not the most important problem facing the Conservatives – and justify your claim with evidence. The question also gives you one factor as a potential '... **most** important problem ...'. Do not ignore it, or dismiss it rapidly. Weigh its importance against the other important problems so you must decide between the various problems faced and arrange them in a ladder of relative importance, one against the others. Under social problems, look at specific issues such as housing (including the Rent Act), unemployment and education, but also consider social mobility and class, immigration and youth culture.

The major alternative problem to consider in order to examine the assertion in the question would be the performance of the economy – poor economic performance (low GDP), slow economic growth further undermined by constant interference by governments (e.g. tax cuts) to create short-term benefits to win elections – which in turn encouraged inflation, unsustainable consumer booms and significant growth in imports. Do not sit on the fence. Whatever option you choose, justify your argument with firm evidence.

In the style of OCR B

Answer **both** parts of your chosen question.

(a) How is the failure of policy over Suez in 1956 best explained?
[Explaining intentions and actions]   (25 marks)

(b) Why did the British government change its policy on EEC
membership during 1961–3?
[Explaining motives and circumstances]   (25 marks)

Exam tips

The cross-references are intended to take you straight to the material that will help you to answer the questions.

Revise the General Introduction at the start of the Exam tips in Chapter 1 (page 33).

(a) Given the command phrase ('How … best explained?'), your essay needs to develop a hierarchy of explanations, establishing relative importance between intentional and causal explanations. One approach might be to focus on the interaction between three individuals: Nasser, Eden and Eisenhower. Alternatively, your circles of explanation could look at international relationships: between the USA and a declining Britain, and between the USA and the USSR. Whichever way you approach this question, your one key circle will have to focus on Eden. Was his plot too devious? Did he misread American attitudes? Certainly he miscalculated badly, bringing disaster on himself. Equally, another circle must examine and explain Washington's behaviour (and did it change during the crisis wrong-footing Eden?). As you consider the relative significance of the possible explanations, you might decide to write off Labour and Commonwealth opposition as having carried little weight, but you will have to weigh factors like Eden's loss of nerve and international condemnation against US refusal to prevent a run on sterling and the impact of the coming US presidential election. If the best explanation lies in politics, was it politics in London or Washington, or the political relationship between the USA and the USSR (pages 38–43)?

(b) The prompt suggests you start by considering motives and then switch to examining actions, or the other way round. Either way, your circles of explanation need to consider reasons for a major change. One circle of explanation will need to consider the impact of imperial decline, of Britain's weak economic position and the connections between them. With decolonisation happening fast from 1957, did Macmillan see that Britain needed to find a new role to play in a new international grouping? Another circle needs to examine what had changed between 1959 when Britain had set up EFTA as a rival to the EEC (do not get side-tracked into explaining why Britain did not sign the Schuman Plan or the Treaty of Rome). Was Macmillan's decision economic (the poor performance of EFTA and of the British economy) or political (did Suez and Polaris missiles show Britain as too dependent on the USA; did Britain overvalue the Commonwealth)? One circle could look at changes within the Conservative Party during the 1950s that reduced the influence of the farming lobby and increased the influence of the business lobby. The new view may have been realistic in business terms, but it made many MPs see opportunities where their predecessors had seen none. You could make a link here to Edward Heath. He was not the cause of the policy change, but he symbolised the new view and fought for it with great skill. (Refer to pages 61–5.)

Study Guide: A2 Question

In the style of AQA

To what extent was Labour's defeat in the 1959 general election the result of internal divisions in the party?   (45 marks)

Exam tips

The cross-references are intended to take you straight to the material that will help you to answer the question.

To answer this question, you need to draw up a plan, listing the points you will make in support of the proposition – that internal divisions brought defeat – and those that can be used to balance the argument by suggesting there were other factors involved. Before you begin to write, decide what your argument will be and try to ensure that your answer follows a single line, arguing logically and coherently towards a well-supported conclusion.

You will need to mention:

- the problems inherent in Labour Party ideology and the meaning of socialism and its commitment to nationalisation
- the position of the trade unions
- divisions over unilateral disarmament.

Try to balance these against:

- Labour's association with high taxation
- Labour's attitude to the EEC
- the state of the economy and Tory promises
- the Conservative record.

Pages 46–8 and 65–8 of the text will help you to answer this question.

3 The Years of Consensus 1964–79

POINTS TO CONSIDER

The period 1964–79 was notable for its consensus politics. Successive Labour and Conservative governments tended to follow very similar policies. This was principally because they were beset by economic problems for which they could find few clear answers. Edward Heath's government tried briefly to diverge from the consensus, but circumstances soon ended the experiment. This chapter covers the following topics:

- Wilson's government 1964–70
- Heath's government 1970–4
- Labour in office 1974–9

Key dates

1964	Labour's election victory under Wilson
	National Plan introduced
	IMF loaned the UK £1 billion
1965	Race Relations Act
1966	Election gave Labour an increased majority
	Prices and incomes freeze introduced
	Three-month seamen's strike
1967	Appointment of Ombudsman
	Dockers' strike
	UK's second EEC membership application rejected
	Pound devalued
	Abortion Act
	Sexual Offences Act
1968	Immigration Act
	Race Relations Act
1969	Open University established
	'In Place of Strife' introduced for discussion
	Death penalty abolished
1970	Heath became Prime Minister following Conservatives' election victory
1971	Industrial Relations Act
1972	Local Government Act
	Miners' strikes
	Government pay freeze reintroduced

1973	UK formally joined the EEC
	A 'state of emergency' led to three-day working week
	Beginning of oil price crisis
1974	Miners went on strike again
	Heath government defeated in election
	Wilson became Prime Minister
1975	Referendum on EEC membership
1976	Callaghan succeeded Wilson as Prime Minister
	IMF crisis
1977	Lib–Lab pact
1978–9	Winter of discontent
1979	Labour lost election

Key question
What problems underlay Wilson's government?

1 | Harold Wilson's Governments 1964–70

Sir Alec Douglas-Home's single year as Prime Minister from 1963 to 1964 was, even as Conservative supporters admitted, an undistinguished time. The odd manner in which he had emerged as party leader and Prime Minister threw a shadow over his government and, although he was a man of considerable personal charm and old-world courtesy, he did not compare well as a parliamentarian with Harold Wilson, Labour's leader. Douglas-Home invariably came off worse in the Commons' debates and **Prime Minister's Questions**. It was no great surprise, therefore, that Wilson pulled away from Douglas-Home in the opinion polls, a development confirmed by Labour's victory in the 1964 general election.

Table 3.1: Governments and Prime Ministers 1964–79

Period	Party	Prime Minister
1964–70	Labour	Harold Wilson
1970–4	Conservative	Edward Heath
1974–6	Labour	Harold Wilson
1976–9	Labour	James Callaghan

The 1964 election

The Labour Party's success, after 13 years in opposition, suggested that the tide had turned in its favour. It presented a more youthful image, not simply because Wilson was a younger man than Home or Macmillan, but because Labour seemed more in tune with young people and their idea of a progressive Britain. The notion of the '**swinging sixties**' may have been largely a creation of the media but astute Labour politicians acknowledged its power as an image and were anxious not to appear unfashionable. Wilson also cleverly played on the contrast between himself as the plain straight-speaking Yorkshireman and Home as the huntin'-shootin'-fishin' aristocrat who was out of touch with real people and their wants. Wilson tapped into the mood of the day by speaking of Britain's need to respond to the

Key terms

Prime Minister's Questions
A weekly session when selected members of the House of Commons put direct questions to the Prime Minister.

Swinging sixties
The 1960s saw the relaxing of many of the old taboos in regard to lifestyle and social behaviour; the music of the Beatles and the Rolling Stones, and the fashions of London's Carnaby Street typified the youthful character of the age.

'white heat of the technological revolution'. The situation was similar in many ways to 1945 when Labour had successfully presented itself as the force of progress standing against the effete political establishment.

Table 3.2: Election results 1964

Political party	No. of votes	No. of seats	Percentage of vote
Labour	12,205,814	317	44.1
Conservative	12,001,396	304	43.6
Liberal	3,092,878	9	1.2
Others	348,914	0	1.3

Yet the voters did not turn overwhelmingly to the Labour Party in 1964, any more than they had to the Conservatives in 1951. It was a close finish. There were even suggestions among some Conservatives that they might have won the 1964 election had Butler rather than Douglas-Home been leader, an unproveable but arresting suggestion given how narrow the Labour victory turned out to be.

The telling statistic was not the recovery of Labour, but the falling away of support for the Conservatives. The figures show that while Labour, compared with 1959, had slightly increased its share of the vote from 43.8 per cent to 44.1 per cent, the Conservatives had slipped six points from 49.4 per cent to 43.6 per cent. This was just enough to give Labour an overall majority of four seats. The Conservative decline indicated that, after 13 years of the same party in power, a significant number of electors wanted a change. The Conservatives' decision to move closer to the principle of the planned economy had opened them to the charge that they were losing their traditional moorings and were ceasing to offer a distinct alternative to the Labour Party.

Reasons for Labour's victory in 1964 include the following:

- Weariness and lack of spirit undermined the Conservative government after 13 unbroken years in office.
- The scandals tainting the Conservative Party in 1963–4 weakened its claim to integrity and competence.
- The antiquated system which had produced Douglas-Home as leader and Prime Minister damaged the Conservative attempt to project a modern image.
- Unemployment reached over 800,000 in 1963, denting Macmillan's earlier claim that Britain had 'never had it so good'.
- The government's humiliating failure in having its 1963 application to join the EEC rejected exposed how weak Britain had become internationally.
- The Labour Party presented a younger, 'with-it', image that was in tune with the changing times.
- In the comparison between the two party leaders, Harold Wilson was more impressive in the public eye than Alec Douglas-Home.

Key date

Labour's election victory under Wilson: 1964

- The Conservative government was the main target of satire which began to flourish in the early 1960s in the theatre and on radio and television.
- Wilson's skilful election campaign, in which he presented himself and his party as better fitted to lead the nation in the technological age that Britain had entered, edged him to victory.

Labour's difficulties in government

A factor that should be stressed at the outset is that Wilson's government was beset, as were all the Labour and Conservative administrations that followed, by constant economic difficulties. These arose from the fact that Britain in the second half of the twentieth century was undergoing a major shift in its economic and social structure. It was changing from an industrial economy to a post-industrial one.

- manufacturing industries were shrinking
- service and finance industries were expanding.

The transition was not smooth or consistent and so caused considerable social disruption. This, indeed, was the root cause of Britain's post-war difficulties. For all the talk of Keynesian planning (see page 18), the truth was that central and local government had only a marginal influence in shaping this transition. It was a case of responding to developments rather than directing them.

Such were Britain's difficulties in this period that some commentators used such terms as 'Britain in decline' or 'Britain, the sick man of Europe'. They meant that Britain had failed to match the growth rates achieved by the industrial economies of Western Europe, Japan and the USA. This was something that had become evident during the Macmillan years (see page 47) and was to continue to worry Wilson's and later governments. One explanation for Britain's relatively poor performance is that it spent too much on defence and too little on investment in industry. The figures in Table 3.3, which show the proportions spent on research and development (R&D), support this argument.

Table 3.3: Percentage of R&D budget spent on defence

Country	1963–5	1966–70	1971–5	1976–9
Japan	0.9	0.9	0.7	0.6
Netherlands	1.9	2.3	2.0	1.6
Italy	2.6	2.4	2.1	1.9
West Germany	10.8	10.3	6.9	6.2
France	26.2	22.5	18.4	19.6
USA	40.6	31.9	27.7	25.4
UK	34.5	25.6	28.9	29.3

The National Plan 1964

Wilson's government began well enough. The creation of a new Department of Economic Affairs under George Brown, which drew up a 'National Plan', and created a new Ministry of Technology, suggested that the government was intent on modernising. The National Plan was a programme aimed at stimulating industrial production and exports by encouraging co-operation between government, employers and trade unions. Despite setting itself grand expansion targets, few of these were met and by 1967 the National Plan had been quietly abandoned. But in the interim the electorate were sufficiently impressed by the government's modernising programme to give Labour a majority of 110 seats over the Conservatives in the 1966 election, which was called by Wilson after only 18 months in office.

National Plan introduced: 1964

Election gave Labour an increased majority: 1966

Key dates

Profile: George Brown 1914–85

1914	– Born into a working-class family in Lambeth, London
1945–70	– Elected MP for Belper, near Derby
1951	– Minister of Works
1964–6	– Minister for Economic Affairs
1966–70	– Foreign Secretary
1985	– Died

Brown was a prominent and outspoken figure on the right of the Labour Party. He was deputy leader between 1960 and 1970 but his relations with Harold Wilson, who defeated him in the leadership contest in 1963, were never entirely happy. He tried to make a success of the new Department of Economic Affairs, which he led from 1964 to 1966, but he too often clashed with the Treasury over financial questions.

Brown's lack of tact proved a handicap when he became Foreign Secretary (1966–70). The British media were quick to seize on his indiscretions. Fond of a drink or two, Brown was often described by the newspapers as being 'tired and emotional', a euphemism for being drunk. He became a peer in 1970. A study of Brown's career during the Wilson years helps to show the internal dissensions and rivalries that afflicted the Labour Party in this period.

Table 3.4: Election results 1966

Political party	No. of votes	No. of seats	Percentage of vote
Labour	13,064,951	363	47.9
Conservative	11,418,433	253	41.9
Liberal	2,327,533	12	8.5
Others	452,689	2	1.7

Tensions with the unions

Matters did not go well from the election onwards. Wilson was committed to the idea that inflation and Britain's balance of payments deficit were the major threat to Britain's economic progress and that, consequently, wage and salary increases must be kept in check. As early as 1963, he had warned the Labour Party, the trade unions and the employers that they had to become more realistic in their approach to wage demands and settlements:

> We are redefining our socialism in terms of the scientific revolution. The Britain that is going to be forged in the white heat of this revolution will be no place for restrictive practices or outdated methods on either side of industry.

Key dates

Prices and incomes freeze introduced: 1966

Three-month seamen's strike: 1966

Dockers' strike: 1967

Pound devalued: 1967

IMF loaned the UK £1 billion: 1964

Confirmed in government by his 1966 election success, Wilson pressed forward with his ideas for cuts in government spending and a wage 'freeze'. A Prices and Incomes Board was set up with the power to regulate pay settlements. Wilson's attitude disappointed the left of the party and angered the trade unions, which had hoped a Labour government would bring them benefits not lectures on their need to be responsible and shore up the capitalist system. The leader of Britain's largest union, the TGWU, Frank Cousins, whom Wilson had made his Minister of Technology in 1964, resigned over the creation of the Prices and Incomes Board.

How serious the gap between government and unions was became evident in a series of strikes over pay in 1966 and 1967, the most disturbing being lengthy stoppages by the seamen's and the dockers' unions. Wilson interpreted these as more than industrial disputes; he characterised them as a deliberate attack by a group of Marxist extremists on Britain's industrial well-being. In 1966, he spoke in the Commons of: 'a tightly knit group of politically-motivated men who are now determined to exercise back-stage pressures endangering the security of the industry and the economic welfare of the nation'.

Key terms

IMF
The International Monetary Fund. A scheme intended to prevent countries going bankrupt. It began operating in 1947 and by 1990 had been joined by over 150 countries. Each of the member states deposited into a central fund from which it could then draw in time of need.

Devaluation
Reducing the value of the pound against the dollar with the principal aim of making it easier to sell British goods abroad since they would be cheaper in real terms.

Devaluation 1967

Wilson believed that the industrial troubles were a key factor in the increase in Britain's trade deficit. He judged that this deficit had grown so considerably that in 1967 he felt he had to approach the **IMF** for another large loan, having already borrowed from it in 1964. Again, he blamed the trade union troublemakers, claiming that the government had begun to surmount the financial problems only to be 'blown off course by the seven weeks' seamen's strike'. The IMF loan was only a stopgap, which, in Wilson's eyes, was a worrying sign that the government was losing control over its own finances.

So concerned did Wilson become that late in 1967 he took the step he had been determined to avoid since coming to power three years earlier – the **devaluation** of the pound. This involved reducing the exchange of sterling from $2.80 to $2.40. After the Chancellor of the Exchequer, James Callaghan, had announced the measure in the Commons, Wilson made a prime ministerial broadcast on television. In solemn tones, he informed the nation of what the government had been reluctantly forced to do. In a rather pathetic attempt to save face, for which he was mocked ever after, Wilson assured viewers that devaluation did not mean that the pound in their pockets was worth any less.

Perhaps, if devaluation had been introduced earlier and in a less theatrical way it could have been passed off as a mere financial adjustment. But Wilson, remembering that Attlee had had to devalue sterling in 1949, wanted to avoid the tag that Labour was the party of devaluation. However, by delaying the measure and then turning it into a drama Wilson unwittingly made devaluation appear as a great political and economic failure by the government. That was how it was perceived by many inside as well as outside the Labour Party. A depressed Callaghan stood down as Chancellor of the Exchequer over it. The trade unions were angered by Wilson's attempt to lay most of the blame for the government's financial plight on the strikers.

It is now recognised that Wilson had overestimated the seriousness of the balance of payments crisis. In fact, in the private sector of the economy there was no deficit but a substantial profit, as Table 3.5 shows.

Table 3.5: UK balance of payments 1963–9

Year	Balance in the private sector (in £ millions)	Balance in the public (government) sector (in £ millions)	Overall balance (in £ millions)
1963	+548	−619	−71
1964	−78	−666	−744
1965	+425	−677	−252
1966	+706	−754	−48
1967	+332	−793	−461
1968	+387	−785	−398
1969	+1326	−924	+402

Table 3.5 is drawn from the work of W.A.P. Manser, a modern economic historian, whose book, *Britain in Balance: The Myth of Failure* (1971), contained the following thought-provoking conclusion:

> The plain testimony of the figures is unequivocal. Britain does not run up a commercial deficit. For the cause of her payments imbalance we need look no further than official activity. If there were no government spending, there would be no deficit and no balance of payments problem.

Nevertheless, whatever academic economists might have concluded, Wilson was convinced at the time that Britain's sluggish industrial performance was caused in large part by poor industrial relations. The strike figures appeared to support this belief (see Table 3.6). The Conservative governments (1951–64) had certainly been troubled by industrial action, but the number of stoppages grew in Wilson's time, giving the lie to the idea that with Labour in power the unions would be appeased.

Britain's second application to join the EEC 1967

It was economic fears at home that prompted Harold Wilson's Labour government to make Britain's second attempt to join the EEC four years after the French veto of the first application (see

Key question
Why did Britain make another application to join the EEC in 1967?

Table 3.6: The number of strikes and working days lost through industrial disputes 1951–70

Year	No. of strikes	Days lost	Year	No. of strikes	Days lost
1951	1719	1,694,000	1961	2686	3,046,000
1952	1714	1,792,000	1962	2449	5,795,000
1953	1746	2,184,000	1963	2068	1,755,000
1954	1989	2,457,000	1964	2524	2,277,000
1955	2419	3,781,000	1965	2354	2,925,000
1956	2648	2,083,000	1966	1937	2,398,000
1957	2859	8,412,000	1967	2116	2,787,000
1958	2629	3,462,000	1968	2378	4,690,000
1959	2093	5,270,000	1969	3116	6,846,000
1960	2832	3,024,000	1970	3906	10,980,000

page 63). Wilson did this in the face of his party's continuing uncertainty on the issue. He feared that Britain would be left behind financially and economically by 'the six' unless it joined them. Preliminary discussions with the EEC took place against the background of the sterling crisis that had led to devaluation.

Fully backed by the Conservatives and the Liberals, but opposed by 36 Labour MPs, the government made its formal request. Again, on the same grounds as in 1963, the belief that Britain would be an obstructive member of the EEC, French President De Gaulle vetoed the UK's application. On this occasion, the annoyance of the other five members of the EEC with the French became quite open. However, this was of little consolation to Wilson; he had suffered the same humiliation that had befallen his predecessor, Harold Macmillan.

'In Place of Strife' 1969

Failure over Europe strengthened Wilson's determination to bring the unions into line. The climax of his campaign to make them accountable came in 1969 with the publication of a **White Paper**, 'In Place of Strife', a set of proposals aimed at preventing future strikes.

The central proposal in the White Paper was for the introduction of a series of legal restrictions on the right of workers to strike. Members of a union would have to be balloted and would have to agree by a clear majority on industrial action before a strike would be recognised as legal. Proposals were also included in the paper that obliged employers to keep to agreements and to consult the unions when major decisions were being contemplated. However, the unions were not fooled; they saw the supposed restrictions on employers as obvious attempts to make the strike controls more palatable to the employees.

'In Place of Strife' never got beyond the White Paper stage. When it was put before the Cabinet by **Barbara Castle**, the Employment Secretary, it created immediate and deep divisions. The left asked bitterly why the government was contemplating a measure that undermined the principles for which the Labour Party was supposed to stand – protection of the unions. The party

Key dates

UK's second EEC membership application rejected: 1967

'In Place of Strife' introduced for discussion: 1969

Key term

White Paper
A preliminary parliamentary statement of the government's plans in regard to a bill that it intends to introduce.

Key figure

Barbara Castle 1910–2002
MP, 1945–79; Minister for Overseas Development, 1964–5; Minister of Transport, 1965–8; Minister of Labour; 1968–70; Minister for Social Services, 1974–6.

had come into being to resist restrictive laws on the workers and now it was being suggested the laws should not be relaxed but tightened. There were allusions to the irony of Barbara Castle, a convinced left-wing Bevanite in her younger days, introducing the type of measure that one would expect from the Tories.

It was the moderate James Callaghan, the Labour Party treasurer as well as the Chancellor of the Exchequer, who finally killed off any chance of 'In Place of Strife' proceeding by stressing the dangers to the party and government of alienating the trade unions, which still provided the bulk of Labour's funds.

The record of the Wilson government 1964–70

In 1970, at the end of Harold Wilson's first government, there was a general feeling that it had not lived up to expectations. The sharpest sense of disappointment was among traditional Labour supporters. They felt that the government had promised much but delivered little. It had entered office claiming to be a modernising reforming government, but in practice had differed from its Conservative predecessors only in style not in content. There had not been substantial change. Although certain sections of industry had been improved, it could not be said that the streamlining of British industry overall had been achieved. A leading social analyst, Peter Townshend, dismissed Labour's attempts at reform as 'hot compresses on an ailing body politic'.

Key question
Why did Wilson's government prove a disappointment to many of its supporters?

Social reforms

While the government may have done nothing really new on the economic and industrial front, the same could not be said of its social reforms. In retrospect, these appear groundbreaking.

Key question
How progressive were Labour's social reforms in this period?

Race Relations Acts 1965 and 1968

These Acts:

- prohibited racial discrimination in public places and in areas such as employment and housing
- made incitement to racial hatred an offence
- set up a Race Relations Board with the power to investigate complaints of racial discrimination
- set up the Community Relations Commission to promote inter-racial understanding.

In 1968, the race issue had been highlighted in a dramatic way, not by the government but by a prominent figure in the opposition, **Enoch Powell**.

Powell was an able but maverick Conservative politician. A fervent nationalist, he came to regard unlimited immigration as a threat to the character of the UK. Ironically, it was while he was Minister of Health in Macmillan's government that he had presided over the recruitment of Commonwealth immigrants as nurses and hospital workers. However, in a notorious speech in 1968, he gave his nightmare vision of a future Britain sundered by racial conflict. Quoting the *Aeneid*, he prophesied: 'As I look ahead, I am filled with foreboding. Like the Roman, I seem to see

Enoch Powell 1912–98
MP, 1950–87; Treasury Secretary, 1957–8; Minister of Health, 1960–3.

Key figure

Race Relations Act: 1965 and 1968

Key date

Aeneid
An epic poem by the Roman writer Virgil (70–19BC).

Key term

"the River Tiber foaming with much blood".' The speech was condemned from all political sides and Edward Heath, the Conservative leader, felt obliged to dismiss him from the shadow cabinet. Although the speech made Powell popular with some working-class groups, such as the London dockers, it effectively ended any possibility of his holding high office again.

The Abortion Act 1967

The Act permitted the legal termination of pregnancy where two doctors certified there was a serious risk to the physical or mental health of the mother, or a strong possibility that the child would be born with serious abnormalities. It was a highly controversial measure. Some moralists saw it as the state's sanctioning of the murder of the innocent, but most feminists hailed it as a major step in the liberation of women since it gave them 'the right to choose'. The controversy became more intense over the succeeding decades; by 2005, the number of terminations had passed over five million, a figure that anti-abortionists condemned as a '**holocaust**' of deaths.

The Sexual Offences Act 1967

The measure was based on the recommendations of the Wolfenden Report of 1958. It permitted male homosexual acts in private between 'consenting adults'. Female homosexuality was not mentioned in the Act, since this had never been illegal.

The Office of Ombudsman created 1967

A special parliamentary officer was appointed to whom ordinary citizens could appeal if they felt they had suffered from an abuse of authority by a government department.

Commonwealth Immigration Act 1968

The Act prohibited new immigrants from settling in Britain unless they had family connections already established. Since the Act built upon a previous measure introduced by the Conservatives in 1962, it was clear that both major parties had concluded that limitations on entry into Britain were necessary in the interests of good race relations. To make that point, the Labour governments introduced Race Relations Acts in 1965 and 1968.

Theatres Act 1968

This measure effectively ended theatre censorship by removing the antiquated system by which plays had to be submitted to the Lord Chamberlain for approval before they could be performed.

Abolition of the death penalty 1969

The Act ending death sentences made permanent a measure passed in 1965 that had suspended the operation of the death penalty for an experimental four years. It removed the five remaining categories of offence for which the death sentence had been imposed.

Key dates

Abortion Act: 1967

Sexual Offences Act: 1967

Appointment of Ombudsman: 1967

Immigration Act: 1968

Death penalty abolished: 1969

Key term

Holocaust
The murdering of six million Jews in Nazi-occupied Europe.

Divorce Reform Act 1969

The Act allowed couples to divorce on the grounds of the 'irretrievable breakdown' of their relationship.

The Open University 1969

This new higher education institution was established to enable previously unqualified students to read for degrees by studying courses broadcast on radio and television. Harold Wilson later claimed this was his greatest achievement as Prime Minister.

Open University established: 1969

Key date

Roy Jenkins as Home Secretary

The reforms listed above, particularly those relating to abortion, divorce, homosexuality, censorship and the death penalty, may be said to mark an important stage in the modernising of British social attitudes. They were largely the work of Roy Jenkins, Home Secretary between 1965 and 1967, who left such a mark on the Home Office that James Callaghan who succeeded him simply continued with the programme that had been laid down.

The measures were not always Jenkins' direct initiative. The abortion law, for example, was introduced by the Liberal MP David Steel. But it was Jenkins' support and encouragement of progressive social thinking that helped to create an atmosphere in which reform became acceptable.

Jenkins personified the tolerant, sophisticated attitudes that he wished to see become predominant in Britain. He was, of course, dealing with controversial issues. There were many in the population who were unhappy with these expressions of what became known as the 'permissive age'. They argued strongly that permissiveness could easily become an encouragement to socially irresponsible behaviour. Jenkins' response was to suggest that a more appropriate term for the times might be not the 'permissive' but the 'civilised age'.

Jenkins himself acknowledged that if one were looking for a starting date for the permissive age it would be appropriate to begin with the 'Lady Chatterley' case in 1960. It was in that year that Penguin Books had been prosecuted for publishing an obscene text, D.H. Lawrence's 1928 novel, *Lady Chatterley's Lover*, which contained four-letter words and explicit descriptions of sexual activity, including sodomy. The trial became a test case and there are certainly grounds for regarding the not-guilty verdict as the beginning of the permissive age in literature.

Criticisms of Wilson's first government

Even those who accepted the value of social reforms tended to see them as isolated achievements. It was the left of the Labour Party, and the young people who had had the highest hopes of Harold Wilson, who by 1970 were the most disillusioned. The specific charges of the left-wing critics are worth listing. They complained that Wilson's government had either introduced or presided over:

- rising unemployment
- growing inflation

Profile: Roy Jenkins 1920–2003

1920	– Born near Pontypool, Monmouthshire
1948–77	– Elected MP for Southwark, London
1965–7	– Home Secretary
1967–70	– Chancellor of the Exchequer
1974–6	– Home Secretary
1977–81	– President of the European Commission
1982–3	– Leader of the Social Democrat Party
1982–7	– MP
2003	– Died

Although Jenkins was Home Secretary for only two years initially, he had a profound effect on social attitudes. It is arguable that his liberal approach, which continued that of R.A. Butler (see page 45), set the pattern for the rest of the century. A man of refinement and high culture, a connoisseur of fine wines and a distinguished historian, who wrote major biographies on Gladstone and Churchill, Jenkins was less liberal and more orthodox in his economic polices as Chancellor of the Exchequer.

Never happy with the way the left tried to impose what he regarded as their dated concepts on the Labour Party, Jenkins was one of the so-called 'gang of four' who broke away in 1981 to form the Social Democratic Party. It has been said that Roy Jenkins was New Labour (see page 140) before New Labour actually came into being. Had he stayed in the Labour Party rather than breaking from it to form the SDP he could have been a formative influence in the shaping of New Labour.

- wage controls
- attempted restriction of trade union freedoms
- immigration controls
- Britain's failed attempt to join Europe,
- retention of Britain's nuclear weapons
- support of the USA's involvement in the Vietnam War.

Vietnam War 1963–75

In an attempt to restrict the spread of Communism in Asia, the USA became mired in a long-drawn out struggle in Indo-China. Britain did not become directly involved in Vietnam, but throughout the conflict, Labour and Conservative governments consistently gave their diplomatic backing to the USA. Left-wing protests led to a violent riot outside the US embassy in London's Grosvenor Square in March 1968.

The end of Britain's 'east of Suez' role' 1967–71

What found more favour with the left was the government's decision to end Britain's **east of Suez** stance. In 1967, Denis Healey, the Defence Minister, announced plans for the withdrawal of British troops from their bases in Borneo, Malaya, Singapore and the Persian Gulf. This was planned to take effect by 1971. The withdrawal went ahead against the protest of the host

Key term

East of Suez
A traditional shorthand way of referring to Britain's military and naval bases and commitments in the Middle East and Asia.

governments, who lost both income and protection. The USA also strongly disapproved, arguing that Cold War tensions required a greater not a lesser commitment to the defence of the world's strategic areas. But a number of considerations combined to make Wilson's government determined to proceed with the withdrawal:

- The sheer cost of maintaining expensive bases was difficult to justify in a time of financial and economic difficulty at home.
- Exhausting military engagements in the 1950s and 1960s in Malaya, Cyprus, Kenya and Aden, although largely successful, had stretched Britain's military resources to the limit.
- The Suez crisis had undermined Britain's confidence in playing the role of world policeman.
- The process of giving up its former colonies and the abandonment of the vestiges of its Empire (see page 57) made it wholly logical for Britain to withdraw from many of its military bases.
- Since Britain was still committed to the development of its nuclear weapons, it could still claim to be a world power, notwithstanding its military cutbacks.

It was this last point in the list that continued to anger the left and divide the Labour Party. Significantly, although the Conservatives had criticised the undermining of Britain's east of Suez role, Edward Heath's government after 1970 made no attempt to reverse the staged withdrawal that the Labour government had begun.

The 1970 election

Despite internal party unrest and the loss of a number of seats in by-elections, Wilson believed that Labour's basic support remained solid. The result of the election he called in 1970 took him by surprise. He had not realised that his undistinguished economic policies, and his apparent failure to control the unions, had lost his government a significant degree of support among moderate voters.

A particularly odd, not to say disturbing, factor was that, although Enoch Powell had been dismissed from the party following his 'rivers of blood' speech (see page 88), his stand on immigration gained the Conservatives 2.5 million votes. The **psephologist** R.W. Johnson went so far as to claim that Powell won the 1970 election for the Conservatives. 'Of all those who had switched their vote from one party to another in the election, 50 per cent were working class Powellites. Not only had 18 per cent of Labour Powellites switched to the Tories but so had 24 per cent of Liberal Powellites.'

Key date

Heath became Prime Minister following Conservatives' election victory: 1970

Key term

Psephologist
An expert on election trends and voting patterns.

Table 3.7: Election results 1970

Political party	No. of votes	No. of seats	Percentage of vote
Conservative	13,145,123	330	46.4
Labour	12,179,341	287	43.0
Liberal	2,117,035	6	7.5
Others	903,299	7	3.1

The five per cent swing from Labour to Conservative was enough to put Edward Heath into office with a Commons' majority of 30 seats.

Summary diagram: Harold Wilson's governments 1964–70

Wilson's narrow election victory

- Conservative failings – tired and ageing image
- Wilson out-debates Douglas-Home
- Labour's young and enterprising image

Labour's economic difficulties

Britain in transition:
- Manufacturing industries shrinking
- Service and finance industries expanding
- Rejection of UK's EEC application
- Union resistance to reform
- 'In Place of Strife' abandoned
- Inflation
- Unemployment
- Wilson devalues the pound

Social reforms

- Abortion Act 1967 liberalises abortion law
- Sexual Offences Act 1967 decriminalises homosexuality
- Ombudsman office created, 1967, to protect ordinary citizen
- Theatres Act 1968 ends censorship of plays
- Abolition of the death penalty 1969
- Divorce Reform Act 1969, allows 'irretrievable breakdown' as grounds
- The Open University 1969, provides higher education through radio and TV

Role of Roy Jenkins ushers in the permissive age

Social unrest

- Government responds to racial violence with restrictive Commonwealth Immigration Act 1968

Overseas

- Costs and changing attitude to policeman role leads to abandoning of Britain's east of Suez position
- UK gives diplomatic support to USA

Shortcomings of the Wilson years

- Rising unemployment
- Growing inflation
- Conflict with trade unions
- Immigration controls
- Failure to join Europe

1970 Election defeat

- Undistinguished economic policies
- Failure to control the unions
- Devaluation
- Powell factor

Key question
What new style of government did Heath try to adopt?

2 | The Edward Heath Government 1970–4

Edward Heath's position in 1970 was similar to Harold Wilson's six years earlier; he entered office with the aim of following expansive policies. He declared that he was adopting 'a new style of government' and that he intended 'to reduce the rise in prices, increase productivity and reduce unemployment'. Where Heath differed from Wilson was in his intention to break with the consensus that had broadly operated since 1945 in regard to state intervention in economic and social matters.

This attitude was summed up in the term '**Selsdon man**'; it referred to the new type of Conservatism, sometimes called the

Key term

Selsdon man
An imaginary anti-Keynesian, pro-market, individual.

Profile: Edward Heath 1916–2005

1916	– Born in Broadstairs, Kent
1950–2001	– Elected MP for Bexley, London
1965–75	– Leader of the Conservative Party
1970–4	– Prime Minister
2001	– Retired from Parliament
2005	– Died

Grammar-school educated, Heath was one of the talented young Conservatives who helped to regenerate the party in the early 1950s. In 1960 Harold Macmillan gave him the task of negotiating the UK's entry into the EEC (see page 63). This work became the defining characteristic of his career.

In 1965 Heath became the first elected leader of the Conservative Party. However, this democratic distinction did not prevent his only period as Prime Minister, 1970–4, from being widely regarded as a failure. After two election defeats in 1974 (he lost three elections out of four within a space of nine years) he was beaten in the party's 1975 leadership contest by Margaret Thatcher with whom he had strained relations for the rest of his long career. He did not hold office again but remained in politics as a backbench MP. In tribute to him after his death, Margaret Thatcher commented that he had helped to change the character of Conservative leadership 'by his humble background, by his grammar school education and by the fact of his democratic election'.

'new right', that Heath had advocated in the run-up to the 1970 election. At a party strategy conference at Selsdon Park in January 1970, the Conservatives had agreed to promote a largely hands-off approach in matters of government direction and to encourage the people to use the new freedom to promote their own interests.

The change of approach was intended to be a liberating form of politics, but the Labour Party was quick to brand it as a return to right-wing reaction. Harold Wilson memorably declared a month later: 'Selsdon man is designing a system of society for the ruthless and the pushing, the uncaring. His message to the rest of us is: you're out on your own.'

A key feature of Heath's break with consensus was his decision to abandon an incomes policy; his government would not seek to impose a wage and salary freeze or interfere with pay settlements. Instead, **market forces** would be allowed to operate, allowing free bargaining between employers and workers. However, to make such bargaining genuine and fair it was important not to permit the trade unions to have unfair advantages. That was the reasoning behind the introduction of the 1970 Industrial Relations Act by Robert Carr, the Minister of Labour.

Market forces
The natural laws of supply and demand operating without interference by government.

Key term

Key date

Industrial Relations
Act: 1971

Industrial Relations Act 1971

The Act was an extension of 'In Place of Strife', the measure which Wilson's government had considered in 1969 but had withdrawn in the face of party and trade union opposition (see page 87):

- It restricted the right of workers to strike by introducing a new concept of 'unfair industrial practice'.
- A National Industrial Relations Court (NIRC), with authority to judge the validity of strike action, was created.
- Unions were required to put themselves on a government register if they wanted to retain their legal rights.

It was with the same object of giving freer rein to market forces that Heath appointed John Davies to head the new Department of Trade and Industry (DTI). Davies was not a conventional politician; he came from outside Parliament having been director-general of the **CBI**. One of his first statements was that he would strongly advise the government against helping 'lame ducks', referring to companies and businesses which, not having performed well, expected public money to be spent on helping them out.

A further example of the 'new right' approach was the policy followed by Anthony Barber as Chancellor of the Exchequer. Barber replaced Iain Macleod, whose death in 1970, after being at the Treasury for only a few weeks deprived the government of arguably its ablest minister. Barber's early measures included income tax cuts, reductions in government spending and the scrapping of the Prices and Incomes Board. Whatever thanks Barber may have gained from the workers for lifting the restrictions on wage bargaining was more than lost by his tax concession to the wealthy and the cuts in government spending whose effects included a rise in council house rents following the reduction in the subsidies paid to local authorities.

One particular cut that made the government unpopular was the withdrawal of free milk for school children. This measure was piloted through by Margaret Thatcher, the Education Minister, which led to opponents chanting, 'Margaret Thatcher, milk snatcher'. Whatever the economic argument might have been for such measures, they were a failure in public relations. The opposition seized the opportunity to condemn Heath's government for:

- abandoning the mixed economy
- weakening the welfare state
- undermining the principle of full employment
- putting economic calculation before social improvement.

These may have been exaggerated charges, but there was no denying that Heath's government had provided sufficient ammunition for Wilson to claim that he had been right in his interpretation of 'Selsdon man' as an essentially reactionary force in politics.

Key term

CBI
Confederation of
British Industry.
Represented
Britain's leading
manufacturers and
industrialists.
Officially it was
politically neutral,
but it tended to side
with the
Conservatives.

Heath's U-turn

The opposition had even more reason to mock when, within 18 months of attempting his new style of government, Heath had had to turn 180 degrees. Inflation, which had risen to 15 per cent by the end of 1971, and declining industrial output destroyed the government's confidence that they could continue with their original policy. In 1972 the government announced that in an attempt to counter inflation it was returning to a policy of controlling prices and incomes.

By then it had also abandoned the notion of government non-interference in industrial matters. Contrary to John Davies' warning that the government would not help out lame ducks, the DTI began to do precisely that. One of Britain's most famous companies, Rolls-Royce, had hit hard times. Its orders were falling and it was haemorrhaging money at an alarming rate. Rather than see the company, which historically was a beacon of British industrial genius and managerial expertise, go under, the government nationalised it in 1971. It was now going to be sustained by government grants.

Subsidies were also granted to other private companies in difficulties, a major one being the Upper Clyde Shipbuilders. The threat that this company might be forced to close led to a determined resistance from the workers. Fearing that the industrial action, skilfully organised by Communist unionists, of whom Jimmy Reid was the most prominent, might spill over into violence, the government backed down and authorised a subsidy of £34 million to be paid to keep the company going.

Mounting problems with the unions

Having had to abandon his original hands-off policy, Heath now appealed to the unions to sit down with him and the CBI and solve their common problems together. But it was too late for co-operation; too much had happened. The unions were suspicious and hostile; with good reason, they claimed. They asked the obvious question: why, if the government genuinely wanted partnership had it introduced the 'union bashing' Industrial Relations Act in the first place?

As soon as the Act had been passed in 1971, the TUC had resisted by formally voting not to co-operate with the government's measures and calling on the individual unions to refuse to register. None of the unions did register. Such a blanket rejection made it impossible to enforce or apply the Act. It made Heath and his Cabinet appear both incompetent and unrealistic and encouraged the more combative unions to increase their demands, something that was evident in the number of strikes that marred Heath's four years in government (see Table 3.8).

It was the National Union of Miners (NUM) that forced the issue. In 1972, in a joint bid to gain a wage increase and to highlight the increasing number of pit closures that threatened its members' livelihood, the NUM, led by **Arthur Scargill**, called a strike during which it effectively used **flying pickets** to bring the

Key question
In what ways did Heath reverse his earlier policies?

Key dates

Government pay freeze reintroduced: 1972

Miners' strikes: 1972

Key figure

Arthur Scargill 1938–
Hated by the right and adored by the far left, he was a committed Marxist who, it was later alleged, had received secret funding from the Soviet Union.

Key term

Flying pickets
Groups of union members ready to rush to areas where strikes had been called to add their weight in persuading workers not to go through the factory gates.

Table 3.8: Strike record during the Heath years 1971–4

Years	No. of strikes	Working days lost
1971	2228	13,551,000
1972	2497	23,909,000
1973	2873	7,197,000
1974	2922	14,750,000

movement of coal to a standstill. This seriously disrupted fuel and electricity supplies and reduced industrial production.

The three-day week introduced 1973

Rather than give in to the miners, Heath hoped to defeat them by imposing severe limits on the use of fuel thereby enabling the government to resist the NUM's attempted blackmail. Heath calculated that the government would be able to survive the strike longer than the miners. In December 1973, he announced that from the end of the year 'most industrial and commercial premises will be limited in the use of electricity to three specified days a week'. The situation could hardly have been more serious. The restrictive measures introduced by the government recalled the austerities of wartime and the late 1940s. The government was locked in battle with a group of workers that required it to resort to desperately restrictive measures such as electricity blackouts which interfered with industrial production and left ordinary people without light and heating for long periods. Sitting in candlelight and unable to cook, listen to the radio or watch television, most people were well disposed neither to the miners nor to the government.

When the miners' dispute was eventually settled, the NUM gained a 21 per cent wage increase: a figure nearly three times the amount that the employers had originally offered. The whole affair, the strike and its settlement, marked a major defeat for Heath and his government.

Emboldened by its success, the NUM again went on strike early in 1974 in pursuit of a further wage demand. This was too much for Heath. He called an immediate election on the issue of who ran the country: the miners or the government. The answer of the electorate was not what he had expected.

The February 1974 election

The election results showed that many voters judged Heath to be a failure; his government had achieved none of the economic goals it had set itself on taking office four years earlier:

- Rapid inflation had made the holding down of prices impossible.
- The wage demands of the unions, which in the majority of cases were accepted by the employers, and the large number of days lost through strikes, resulted in a decline rather than a growth in productivity.

Key dates

A 'state of emergency' led to three-day working week: 1973

Miners went on strike again: 1974

Heath government defeated in election: 1974

- Unemployment had not been reduced. Indeed, 1972 marked the highest figure for joblessness since the depression in the 1930s.
- The resort to the three-day week in 1973 showed how far the government had fallen short of its aims.

There was a sense of hopelessness and desperation about it all that conveyed itself to the electorate. The number of voters who felt disillusioned with the government was sufficient to give the Labour Party a narrow victory. The Conservatives gained a higher aggregate vote but the more telling figure was that their support had slipped by nearly seven points. The Labour Party also lost ground electorally. Despite winning four more seats than the Conservatives, its popular vote dropped by six per cent. The impressive performance was by the Liberals, who increased their vote by over four million. Their 14 seats were small reward for gaining well over half the vote achieved individually by the Conservative and Labour parties.

Table 3.9: Election results February 1974

Political party	No. of votes	No. of seats	Percentage of vote
Conservative	11,868,906	297	37.9
Labour	11,639,243	301	37.1
Liberal	6,063,470	14	19.3
Northern Irish parties	717,986	12	2.3
Scottish Nationalists	632,032	7	2.0
Plaid Cymru	171,364	2	0.6
Others	260,665	2	0.8

The election gave Labour a majority of four over the Conservatives. With the support of the 14 Liberal MPs, Harold Wilson was able to embark on his second period of government. But before turning to consider Wilson's second term in office, there are three other features of the Heath years which demand attention: local government reform, Britain's joining the EEC and the international oil crisis.

Local government reforms 1972–3

In terms of the scale of its effects, one of the most significant measures of the Heath years was the Local Government Act (passed in two stages in 1972 and 1973), prepared and introduced by Peter Walker, the Environment Minister. This proved to be the most sweeping reform of its kind yet attempted; in reshaping the structure of local government, the measures destroyed many historical administrative landmarks. Whole areas were subsumed into newly created regions and many place names disappeared. There were protests, particularly from Conservatives on the right, that Walker's reforms amounted in many cases to an attack on local identity. Arthur Marwick has captured the essence of the traditionalists' objections by noting as typical of the measures that they: 'recognised the great conurbations (e.g. Merseyside, Strathclyde) as metropolitan counties, abolished

Local Government Act: 1972

Key date

historic Rutland, and redesignated the City and Royal Burgh of Edinburgh a mere district'.

Britain's entry into Europe 1973

Key question
Why was Britain able to enter the EEC at the third attempt?

Following De Gaulle's retirement in 1969, the EEC had invited Britain to reapply. Britain duly did so; in 1972, it signed the treaty of accession and became a full member of the EEC on New Year's Day 1973. There is little doubt that in his own judgement Edward Heath regarded the greatest achievement of his four years in office to be his taking Britain into the EEC.

Since the late 1950s when Macmillan had asked him to be the UK's special negotiator with Europe, Heath had committed himself to achieving Britain's entry. It became the defining characteristic of his political career. He had staked his reputation on it. That was why he was willing for Britain to enter at any price.

Having been invited to apply by 'the six', Heath rushed to comply with their conditions of entry. Although he tried to give the impression that Britain was negotiating from strength and would strike a hard bargain, it is now known that Heath told his team of officials to accept any terms; he assured them they could always sort it out after Britain had joined. That was a fateful decision that shaped Britain's relations with Europe ever after.

The weakness of Britain's bargaining position

The hard fact in 1972 was that Britain's economic difficulties made it not so much a welcome guest but a beggar at the European feast. 'The six' knew that, nothwithstanding Heath's

A cartoon published in the *Observer* newspaper, 20 February 1972. Pompidou, the French President, says to Prime Minister Heath: 'I was going to ask about all that technological know-how Britain will bring into Europe.' How has the cartoonist mockingly linked Britain's industrial troubles with its negotiations to join the EEC?

personal ambitions, Britain had requested membership because it judged it could not survive economically on its own. This remains a highly controversial viewpoint. There are those who now argue that membership of the EEC, far from helping Britain, has been a brake on its progress. But at the time the majority view prevailing in government circles, though not in the Conservative or Labour parties, was that Britain could not afford to remain outside.

However, Britain could not negotiate from strength in 1972. The EEC's terms and structure had already been set by the six founding states. Britain had had no say in the setting up of the EEC and the existing members were not going to allow Britain as a 'Johnny-come-lately' to redefine the character and workings of the system they had created. One of the most significant EEC demands that Britain accepted was that Commonwealth food and goods would no longer enter Britain on preferential terms. Produce, for example, from Australia and New Zealand now had a European tariff placed on it that made it no longer profitable for those countries to sell to Britain or beneficial for Britain to buy from them.

It was true the EEC did permit a transition stage so that Britain and the Commonwealth countries could adjust to these changes, but the position was now clear. Britain had had to sacrifice its economic relationship with the Commonwealth. There is a strong argument for regarding Britain's accession into Europe as an irreversible moment. Joining the EEC meant that it turned its back on its old allies and partners. With that decision there disappeared the last chance that the Commonwealth could be turned into the world's first truly multiracial, global, economic block. The decision was made in a strange atmosphere of post-imperial apathy and fear. Britain seemed resigned to the fact it was a declining economic force whose only chance of survival was as a member of a protectionist European union.

Advantages to Britain of joining the EEC:

- It gained access to European markets.
- As part of a European block, it stood a better chance of attracting foreign business.
- British regions were entitled to European development grants.
- British workers had the right to work in other EEC countries.

Disadvantages to Britain of joining the EEC:

- Britain was no longer able to buy cheap food from the Commonwealth.
- At the time of entry, Britain was classified as an advanced industrial economy. This meant that it had to make higher contributions to the EEC budget than it received in grants from Europe. By the early 1980s Britain was paying 20 per cent of the revenue raised by the EEC but was receiving only eight per cent of the expenditure. An illuminating contrast was the position of Ireland, which joined the EEC at the same time as Britain. Classed as an agricultural economy, Ireland was a net

receiver of European funds; this largely explains why Ireland experienced an economic boom in the last quarter of the century.

- As victims of CAP's dear food policy, British consumers found themselves paying inflated prices, reckoned in 1980 to be an average of £1000 per family per annum.
- The Common Fisheries Policy severely restricted Britain's right to fish in its customary grounds and led to the virtual destruction of the UK's fishing industry.
- As a condition of entry, Britain had to impose value added tax (VAT) on most of the commodities which British consumers bought; VAT began in 1973 at eight per cent and later more than doubled to 17.5 per cent.
- In entering the EEC Britain had joined a protectionist organisation that was already beginning to look dated now that the world was entering the era of global markets.

Prime Minister Heath had hoped that by joining Europe his government would be able to claw back some of the economic ground Britain had lost since 1970. But he was mistaken. Europe did not hold the key to British recovery. By a cruel twist, the UK's entry into the EEC in 1973 coincided with the onset of an international crisis that showed that however Britain and, indeed Europe, might organise themselves they were dangerously susceptible to events in the outside world over which they had no control.

Key dates

UK formally joined the EEC: 1973

Beginning of oil price crisis: 1973

The international oil price rise 1973

Until the early 1970s large multinational companies had controlled the production and distribution of oil and had supplied the Western world with a steady supply of relatively cheap fuel. However, from the early 1960s **OPEC** members began to establish greater control over their own oil industries. How strong OPEC had become was shown dramatically in 1973 when its Arab members chose to use oil as a weapon in their long-running conflict with Israel.

In retaliation for the West's support of Israel in the Arab–Israeli war fought in October 1973, the Arab members of OPEC drastically reduced their oil supplies to those Western countries which they believed had sided with Israel. At the same time, OPEC sharply raised the price of its oil exports. Between 1973 and 1980 the cost of oil increased from $2 to $35 per barrel. The main target was the United States, but all the other Western states whose economies were heavily dependent on oil suffered. It was not simply fuel that increased in price, but all the many oil-based products, such as plastics, became greatly more expensive. The result was rapid and severe inflation throughout the industrial world. In the decade after 1973 Britain suffered a severe recession.

Key term

OPEC Organisation of Petroleum Exporting Countries. Formed in 1961, this body came to represent all the leading oil-producing nations, including the strategically important Arab states of Bahrain, Iraq, Kuwait, Libya and Saudi Arabia.

Economic effects

The economic effects in Britain of the oil price rise included the following:

- the balance of payments deficit rose to £1 billion
- the annual inflation rate rose to 16 per cent
- the value of sterling dropped from $2.00 to $1.57
- the interest rate was raised to 15 per cent
- a record budget deficit occurred
- between 1974 and 1976 the unemployment figures more than doubled to 1.44 million and remained high for the rest of the decade.

The unemployment statistics in Table 3.10 illustrate that although the oil crisis began during the Heath's time in office, it was to be the Labour government of 1974–9 that suffered the full force of these developments.

Table 3.10:
UK unemployment figures 1970–9

Year	No. unemployed
1970	628,000
1971	868,000
1972	929,000
1973	785,000
1974	628,000
1975	1,152,000
1976	1,440,000
1977	1,567,000
1978	1,608,000
1979	1,464,000

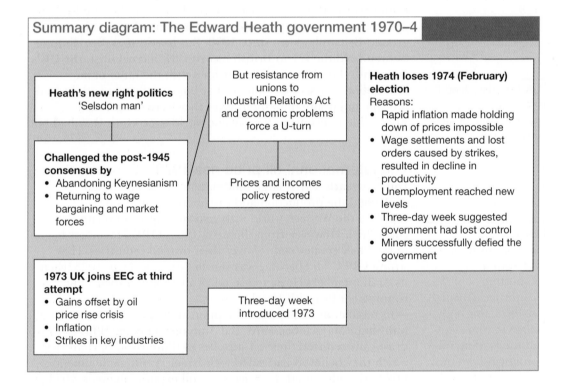

Summary diagram: The Edward Heath government 1970–4

Heath's new right politics
'Selsdon man'

Challenged the post-1945 consensus by
- Abandoning Keynesianism
- Returning to wage bargaining and market forces

1973 UK joins EEC at third attempt
- Gains offset by oil price rise crisis
- Inflation
- Strikes in key industries

But resistance from unions to Industrial Relations Act and economic problems force a U-turn

Prices and incomes policy restored

Three-day week introduced 1973

Heath loses 1974 (February) election
Reasons:
- Rapid inflation made holding down of prices impossible
- Wage settlements and lost orders caused by strikes, resulted in decline in productivity
- Unemployment reached new levels
- Three-day week suggested government had lost control
- Miners successfully defied the government

3 | Labour in Office 1974–9

From the beginning, the Labour governments of 1974–9 suffered from three crippling restrictions:

- the narrowness of Labour's overall majority in the Commons
- the grim effects of the rapid inflation that followed the oil price rise of 1973
- the struggle with the trade unions.

Key question
What problems confronted the Wilson and Callaghan governments between 1974 and 1979?

Table 3.11: Election results October 1974

Political party	No. of votes	No. of seats	Percentage of vote
Labour	11,457,079	319	39.2
Conservative	10,464,817	277	35.8
Liberal	5,346,754	13	18.3
Northern Irish parties	702,094	12	2.4
Scottish Nationalists	893,617	11	2.9
Plaid Cymru	166,321	3	0.6

Key dates

Wilson became Prime Minister: 1974

Lib–Lab pact: 1977

IMF crisis: 1976

Key term

Lib–Lab pact
A deal made by James Callaghan and David Steel in March 1977, committing the Liberals to vote with the government in the Commons in return for the government's agreement to consult the Liberals on key issues. The pact lapsed in the autumn of 1978.

Labour's narrow Commons' majority

Although the second election in 1974 gave Labour a majority over the Conservatives of 42, its overall majority throughout its five years in office was never more than three seats. This tight margin made the government heavily dependent on the Liberal MPs, and gave the Liberal Party an influence, eventually formalised in the 1977 **Lib–Lab pact**, that it had not enjoyed for half a century. There was some justice in this, since, in the two elections in 1974, the Liberals had won nearly 20 per cent of the popular vote.

Inflation

The second problem was that the Labour governments of 1974–9 held office at a time when Britain began to suffer the worst effects of the rapid inflation that followed the oil price rise of 1973. The decline in the value of money and the growing debit in its trade balance threatened to make Britain bankrupt. In March 1976, for the first time in its history, the pound dropped below $2 in exchange value.

The IMF crisis 1976

In September 1976, the Chancellor of the Exchequer Denis Healey had to begin negotiating a loan of £3 billion from the IMF. The terms of the loan required Britain to make major cuts in its public expenditure. This outraged the left and the unions, who threatened to make trouble. In October, Healey had to delay a flight to Manila where the IMF negotiations were held, to rush to the Labour conference in an effort to preserve party unity. He was only partially successful. A number of delegates jeered him when he appealed to them to show realism and accept that cuts in public expenditure were necessary in the country's interests.

Healey's rough reception showed that the long-running feud between the left and centre-right of the Labour Party was as fierce as ever. The left complained that the government was following policies which were indistinguishable from those of the Conservatives; it was trying to fight Britain's financial and economic ills by policies shaped round the demands of international financiers. The centre-right counter-claimed that the government by appearing so feeble in the face of threats from the trade union extremists was in danger of losing its power to govern independently and was detaching itself from the ordinary voters of Britain.

Callaghan, who succeeded Wilson as Prime Minister in 1976, continued to try to face the left down. By 1979, the government, in line with the IMF demand, had reduced its spending programme by £3 billion. This helped to stabilise the financial situation but at the cost of increased unemployment which reached 1.6 million in 1978. Commentators on both the left and right regarded these concessions to the IMF demands as marking a critical stage in the Labour Party's development. Tony Benn, for example, later claimed that the Cabinet's decision to give in to the demands of international bankers deprived a supposedly socialist government of the moral high ground and so opened the way for the Thatcher revolution of the 1980s (see page 117). Many others saw the IMF loan as a further measure of Britain's decline.

Labour and the unions

The government's failure to handle its economic problems without recourse to very large loans from the IMF related very closely to Labour's third abiding problem: its struggle to come to terms with the unions. The cuts in public expenditure and the consequent rise in unemployment that followed the IMF agreement embittered the trade unions and weakened their traditional loyalty to the Labour Party.

The credit the government had gained from repealing the Industrial Relations Act in 1974 was lost by its inability to persuade the workers to co-operate consistently with it. In many respects this was a repeat of the troubles that had stalked the Heath government (see page 96). The bitter aspect for Labour was that for a time after 1974 Wilson had seemed to be on co-operative terms with the unions. His good relations with Jack Jones, the moderate leader of the influential TGWU, promised much. There was frequent reference to a '**social contract**' between the government and the unions, but it produced little in the way of direct results. There were certainly few examples of unions restricting their wage claims in accordance with it.

Key term

Social contract
An agreement in 1972 between Wilson and Vic Feather, the TUC General Secretary, to the effect that when Labour was returned to power the unions would follow a wage restraint policy in return for the adoption of pro-worker industrial policies by the government.

The 1975 referendum on Europe

It was to improve his relations with the unions that Wilson, in one of the major moves of his years in office, opted to renegotiate the terms of Britain's membership of the EEC. The left wing of the Labour Party and the trade unions remained deeply suspicious of the Common Market. They regarded it as a capitalist club necessarily hostile to socialism. 'The Durham miners don't like it', was the essence of their argument. In 1972, to quieten the left, Wilson began renegotiations in regard to agriculture, budget payments and the special provisions for Commonwealth imports. Callaghan took the role of the government's chief representative in this.

The whole exercise was largely a gesture since it produced no major changes. But able now to claim that he was offering the people a real voice in the shaping of their destiny, Wilson called a

Key question
What was the outcome and significance of the 1975 referendum?

Referendum on EEC membership: 1975

Key date

Key figure

Tony Benn 1925–
Born Anthony
Wedgwood Benn,
the heir to Lord
Stansgate. However,
he renounced his
peerage and
remained a
commoner and an
MP. He was a
minister under both
Wilson and
Callaghan but
despite gaining a
loyal following on
the left of the party
was never able to
convert his
popularity into a
successful bid for
the leadership.
Moderates regarded
him with suspicion
and the tabloid
newspapers
portrayed him as
part of the 'loony
left'.

national referendum in 1975, the first consultation of its kind in British history. In the campaign that preceded the referendum, the politicians showed more enthusiasm than the people. With the MPs under no instruction from their parties as to which side to take, there was an interesting cross-party divide. The bulk of Labour members were for coming out, the majority of Conservatives and Liberals for staying in. Prominent Labour pro-Europeans were Roy Jenkins and Shirley Williams who shared a platform with Edward Heath and other leading Conservatives. The most conspicuous Labour opponents of Europe were **Tony Benn**, Michael Foot, Barbara Castle and Peter Shore.

When it came to the actual referendum, the electorate, in historian Martin Pugh's words, 'voted more out of fear of the consequences of leaving than out of enthusiasm for remaining in'. It was no great surprise that the results showed a large majority for Britain's staying in the Community.

Table 3.12: Results of the British referendum on EEC membership, June 1975

Country	Total votes	'Yes' vote (%)	'No' vote (%)	Turnout (%)
England	21,772,222	68.7	31.3	64.6
Scotland	2,286,676	58.4	41.6	61.7
Wales	1,345,545	64.8	35.2	66.7
Northern Ireland	498,751	52.1	47.9	47.4
UK total	29,453,194	64.5	35.5	64.5

Opponents of the 'yes' vote claimed that the whole affair had been a betrayal of democracy. They argued that the referendum should have preceded Britain's entry, not followed it; Britain was voting on a *fait accompli*, not making a free choice. They also pointed out that, funded by the EEC, the 'yes' lobby had been able to spend twice as much on the campaign as the 'no' lobby, proportions which exactly matched the vote distribution.

In the referendum campaign little mention was made by the pro-Europeans of the political implications of EEC membership. Stress was laid on the economic advantages that Britain would gain. But these proved illusory. The international oil price rise that began in 1973 had such a restrictive effect on the British economy (see page 102) that whatever gains might have accrued from being a member of the EEC were far outweighed by the inflation and economic downturn of the 1970s.

It was also the case that in the period between 1958 and 1973, the year in which Britain formally joined the EEC, British exports to the EEC countries had more than doubled as a share of national income. Ironically, British exports to Europe declined after 1973. Thus, having joined Europe in the hope of improving its economic status, Britain found that the net effect of its membership was greatly increased financial costs with no real trade benefits.

The British people were never given the full story. As even pro-Europeans later admitted, on one of the biggest issues of the day,

Britain's relations with Europe, the people were kept in the dark. They were constantly told that there were no political implications attaching to Britain's joining, that it was purely an economic arrangement, involving trade agreements. British sovereignty was not in question.

It must be stressed that the deception was not Europe's fault. The members of the EEC made no attempt to hide the truth. They never denied that to join a federal union necessarily involved a loss of freedom. Jean Monnet had spelt that out clearly as early as 1948: 'Only the establishment of a *federation* of the West, including Britain, will enable us to solve our problems quickly enough, and finally prevent war.' Robert Schuman had re-emphasised this point in 1950: 'Europe must be reorganised on a federal basis.'

Wilson's retirement in 1976

Despite his achievement in leading his party to victory in the two elections of 1974, Harold Wilson was in office for only two years. He resigned in March 1976 to be succeeded by James Callaghan as Labour Prime Minister. From time to time there have been suggestions that Wilson's surprising decision to step down so early was because he wanted to leave office before the economic situation got worse or because he was threatened with blackmail by the Soviet secret service over an affair he was supposedly having with Marcia Williams, his personal secretary. The less dramatic but more likely explanation is that the strains of office and leadership led him to keep to an earlier resolution that he had made to retire at the age of 60.

In 1970, Wilson had led the nation to believe that Labour would break from the 'stop–go' economic policies associated with the Conservatives. But the effects of the 1973 oil price crisis destroyed any hopes he had of doing that. Callaghan fared no better after he took over. The industrial unrest that followed in the wake of the IMF crisis of that year set a pattern that was to continue throughout Callaghan's three years as Prime Minister. There was a scarcely a month in which a strike did not occur somewhere; even the more moderate unions became involved. Angered by such moves as Callaghan's sudden announcement in December 1977 of a compulsory five per cent ceiling on wage rises, the unions became more sweeping in their demands and more aggressive in their methods.

It was around this time that foreign journalists coined the term the 'British disease' to describe the combination of bad

> Callaghan succeeded
> Wilson as Prime
> Minister: 1976
>
> **Key date**

Table 3.13: Strike record during the Wilson and Callaghan years 1974–9

Year	No. of strikes	Working days lost
1974	2922	14,750,000
1975	2282	6,012,000
1976	2016	3,284,000
1977	2627	9,985,000
1978	2349	9,306,000
1979	4583	29,474,000

employer–worker relations and constant industrial stoppages. How disturbed industrial relations were was evident from the strike figures.

Among the most disturbing industrial actions were:

- the firemen's strike in 1977 which led the Prime Minister to announce a state of emergency
- a year-long strike beginning in 1977 at the Grunwick photographic works in north London involved mass picketing and violent clashes with the police
- the workers at all 23 plants of Ford Motors went on strike in September 1979; the dispute was settled only by the Ford management giving in and granting a 17 per cent pay rise
- a lorry drivers' strike, called for January 1979, threatened the nation's food supplies; it was called off after the drivers had gained a 20 per cent wage rise.

The winter of discontent 1978–9

Key date

Winter of discontent: 1978–9

Key terms

Winter of discontent
The term comes from the familiar first line of Shakespeare's *Richard III*: 'Now is the winter of our discontent'.

NUPE
National Union of Public Employees.

COHSE
Confederation of Health Service Employees.

A particularly significant development was increased militancy among the public sector workers. Not wishing to miss out on the large pay settlements being achieved by many unions in the private sector, public service unions began to make demands. They felt they had a strong case since they were the ones who felt most victimised by the government's cuts in public expenditure. It was their sense of grievance that intensified the industrial troubles and led to what became known as the 1978–9 '**winter of discontent**'. Taking their cue from the success of the haulage drivers, an alliance of public service unions, including the influential **NUPE** and **COHSE**, called for a day of action. On 22 January, around 1.5 million workers responded by coming out on strike.

Following this impressive success, selective strikes were organised in areas calculated to attract the greatest media attention. The school meals service was disrupted, mounds of refuse were left to pile up uncollected and, perhaps most dramatic of all, industrial action by the grave diggers left dead bodies unburied. The media had a field day with all this, but their depiction of a collapsing, rotting Britain was not all exaggeration. The Wilson and Callaghan governments had failed to meet their own expectations and the hopes of others. They had alienated large sections of their natural supporters and given encouragement to the opposition.

It may be claimed that the economic problems they faced were beyond their powers and resources, and would have overwhelmed any government. Yet it has to be said that Callaghan made matters worse during his period of government by appearing to allow things to drift. One example was his failure to call an election in the autumn of 1978, at a time when opinion polls showed that his government was picking up support. By waiting, he lost any room for manoeuvre, since there had to be an election no later than the autumn of 1979. His relaxed style of leadership had its attractions, but it was not ideally suited to a desperate situation where a more dynamic approach seemed necessary. When he was asked by reporters in January 1979 as to how he intended to deal with the chaos facing the country, Callaghan simply denied there was a crisis. This may have been a deliberately flippant response but it was felt by many to capture his reluctance to engage fully with the issues confronting his government.

The 1979 election

By the time Callaghan belatedly called the election in 1979, his government had been gravely damaged by:

- economic and financial crises
- rising unemployment
- belligerent trade unionism
- political misjudgements.

Of the government's political misjudgements, the most serious was its treatment of the minority parties on whom its continuation in office had come to depend. In the autumn of 1978 it allowed the Lib–Lab pact to lapse (see page 103). With its tiny majority practically wiped out by by-election losses, Callaghan's government was now dependent on the support of the Scottish Nationalist Party (SNP) in the Commons. However, when a referendum in Scotland in March 1979 failed to provide a clear mandate for **devolution**, the government dropped its proposal to introduce it. The SNP MPs immediately withdrew their support. The outcome was that on 28 March the government, with its majority gone, was defeated on a vote of no confidence. Obliged by this to call an election, Callaghan's government ended its years in office in parliamentary failure. The Labour Party thus went into the election campaign in a low state of morale. The

Devolution
Granting to Wales and Scotland a considerable degree of control over their own affairs by the creation of a separate Parliament or national assembly. This form of home rule stopped short of complete independence from the UK.

Key term

The Conservative's main election poster of 1979, voted 'the poster advertisement of the century' by the advertising trade magazine *Campaign*. How would you explain the poster's effectiveness as political propaganda?

Key date

Labour lost election: 1979

government's errors provided the opportunity for the Conservatives, under their new leader, Margaret Thatcher, who had ousted Edward Heath in 1975 (see page 119), to challenge Labour's hold on power.

Since she was to be in office for the next 11 years, it is easy to overlook how critical the 1979 election was for Margaret Thatcher. She had to win it. The Conservative Party has been always very unforgiving of its leaders who fail. It was doubly difficult for her; it was highly unlikely that as a woman she would be allowed a second chance. Fortunately for her, it was not so much a matter of the Conservatives winning the election as Labour losing it. One of the most effective campaign posters in modern electioneering showed a long winding unemployment queue with the caption 'Labour isn't working'. For a significant portion of the electorate, this was an accurate assessment of Labour's record.

The Labour government was not swept from power by an angry electorate; indeed it very nearly held its 1974 position in terms of votes and percentage support (see Table 3.14). But there was sufficient disillusion among the electors for them to give the Conservatives an eight-point increase in their 1974 showing and an additional three million votes. This provided the Conservatives with a comfortable majority of 70 seats over Labour and a majority overall of 43 seats. It was enough to allow Mrs Thatcher to take office and embark on a revolution.

Table 3.14: Election results 1979

Political party	No. of votes	No. of seats	Percentage of vote
Conservative	13,697,690	339	43.9
Labour	11,532,148	269	36.9
Northern Irish parties	695,889	12	2.2
Liberal	4,313,811	11	13.8
Scottish Nationalists	504,259	2	1.6
Plaid Cymru	132,544	2	0.4

Summary diagram: Labour in office 1974–9

Underlying problems
- Small Labour majority in the Commons
- The grim effects of the oil price rise of 1973
- The struggle with combative trade unions

1975 EEC referendum confirmed UK's membership of EEC

Callaghan succeeded Wilson in 1976, but
- 1976 IMF crisis deepened divisions in government and party
- Growing number of strikes 1977–9
- Industrial action by public sector unions led to 'winter of discontent'
- Labour government badly weakened by its failures to control the crisis
- End of Lib–Lab pact proved disastrous for Labour
- Door opened to Mrs Thatcher's Conservatives

Study Guide: AS Questions

In the style of Edexcel

Source 1

From: the political memoirs of John Cole, As It Seemed To Me, *published in 1995. Cole was a journalist working for the* Observer *newspaper during the 1979 election campaign.*

Margaret Thatcher's campaign, like the manifesto, was light in policy detail. The Callaghan government had gone through such a debilitating period since the IMF public spending crisis of 1976, and again during the winter of discontent, that she was dining out on the public mood. To win votes, detail was neither needed nor offered. Margaret Thatcher knew she was going to win.

Source 2

From: a poster published by the Conservative Party in summer 1979.

Source 3

From: Martin Pugh, State and Society, *published in 1994.*

Many [Conservatives] felt uncertain whether they would in fact recover power under Mrs Thatcher. No one knew whether the country was yet prepared to accept a woman as Prime Minister. James Callaghan continued to enjoy a big lead in terms of personal popularity. Mrs Thatcher was clearly lucky. Had Callaghan held an election in the autumn of 1978 he might well have won. Delay, and the industrial chaos of the winter of 1978–9, gave Mrs Thatcher her opportunity. Even so, the Conservatives won only 43 per cent of the vote, not one of their better performances. But it was enough to deliver a parliamentary majority.

Use Sources 1, 2 and 3 and your own knowledge.
Do you agree with the view that the 'industrial chaos of the winter of 1978–9' primarily accounts for Mrs Thatcher's election victory in 1979? Explain your answer, using Sources 1, 2 and 3 and your own knowledge. (40 marks)

Exam tips

The cross-references are intended to take you straight to the material that will help you to answer the question.

The view you are considering is contained in Source 3 which suggests:

- James Callaghan was personally more popular than Margaret Thatcher
- Callaghan might well have won if the election had been held in the autumn of 1978
- the industrial chaos of 1978–9 was the decisive factor.

You can use your own knowledge gained from Chapter 3 to develop each of these points, the text on pages 107–9 will also help you to answer this question. Note, too, that Source 1 confirms the damage inflicted on Labour by the 'winter of discontent'.

However, Sources 1 and 2 both suggest that longer term problems were also significant contributors to Labour's electoral weakness. You can use material from the sources and your own knowledge to consider:

- The problems of unemployment and the damage that did to the government's popularity. Note the effectiveness of the advertising (Source 2).
- The damage done to the government by the IMF crisis of 1976.

In addition, your own knowledge gained from Chapter 3 will allow you to consider the weakening effect of the problems of inflation and the difficulties of governing with a very small majority.

So what is your overall conclusion? How significant was the 'winter of discontent' in accounting for Thatcher's election victory?

In the style of OCR A

To what extent was the power of the trade unions the **main** problem facing Wilson's governments of 1964–70?   (50 marks)

Exam tips

The cross-references are intended to take you straight to the material that will help you to answer the question.

The problem given in the question (union power) must be taken seriously (whether you are going to agree or not) and weighed against the other problems Wilson faced, and a judgement should be made about its relative importance ('… the **main** problem …'). That means that you must put those problems into a rank order, deciding which was/were more important than the rest, and explain why. (A claim not backed up with hard evidence won't get you many marks.) While you are thinking, ask yourself 'main problem' for whom – the country or the government? The answer is not necessarily the same.

   Under the unions, look at their impact on industry, the economy and the country (e.g. industrial relations and strikes, opposition to wage controls, contribution to the trade deficit and to devaluation (pages 84–8). But look deeper, considering Wilson's belief that Marxist groups were using the unions to undermine the nation. Consider the issues around 'In Place of Strife' and examine its failure ever to be implemented, but also examine whether Wilson overestimated the problem. For alternative 'main' problems, you could consider economic weakness (e.g. manufacturing decline, inflation), immigration (including Powell's 1968 speech), EEC membership, social change and social instability (does Jenkins' broad raft of reforms show the very high importance of this area as a problem?). Whatever you decide, argue clearly one way or the other – and justify your lines of argument with firm evidence.

In the style of OCR B

Answer **both** parts of your chosen question.

(a) Why did the 1960s provide conditions conducive to the social reforms of Wilson's second government?
[Explaining ideas, attitudes and states of affairs]   (25 marks)

(b) Why did Wilson hold a referendum on EEC membership?
[Explaining circumstances and motives]   (25 marks)

Exam tips

The cross-references are intended to take you straight to the material that will help you to answer the questions.

Revise the General Introduction at the start of the Exam tips in Chapter 1 (page 33).

(a) The prompt in the brackets directs you to start in empathetic mode and then switch to a causal explanation. You could approach this question the other way around, but since its focus is so firmly on the mood of the time, a primary emphasis on attitudes and ideas will probably be more effective. Do not simply list the reforms: that will not get you many marks. Instead, build your circles of explanation by showing how the reforms of the 'swinging sixties' not simply reflected but were produced by changes in post-war British society. Exactly what you see as a 'social reform' is left to you to decide, but your essay should aim to include legislation changing the law on censorship, the death penalty, homosexuality, divorce and abortion. Social change must be rooted in something broader so your explanations need also to place these liberalising, tolerant reforms in the context of: (i) the long-term social changes that resulted from the Second World War, and (ii) the relative economic prosperity of the 1950s and 1960s that made such relaxations in morality possible. For further context, link the Acts of 1967–9 to party politics: they were the work of, or supported by, a Labour government championing 'progress'. Your conclusion could pull things together by reference to the Open University, a landmark in educational opportunity. As with the other changes/innovations, the conditions for its creation did not exist before the 1960s (pages 81–3 and 88–93).

(b) Start with a causal explanation and then expand into an explanation of motives (or vice versa). You might start by raising a problem: since Labour had opposed Britain's entry in 1973 and continued its hostile attitude in both 1974 elections, why did not Wilson just pull Britain out? Your search for an explanation to that conundrum will take you to the heart of this question. You will need to set out two circles of explanation that link together Wilson's situation: (i) official policy on a subject that badly divided his party, and (ii) trouble with the trade unions. These you can link together because his problems were overwhelmingly political. His ploy in 1972 to renegotiate membership terms having failed, the unions and the left wanted withdrawal. But while most Labour MPs were anti-EEC, a large number of ministers were pro. The party was split and, with a minute majority in the House of Commons, Wilson was very vulnerable. Europe was an issue that would bring down the government. Those are the circumstances. Wilson's genius (or deviousness, depending on your point of view) was to see that via a referendum he could solve the problem without splitting the party. The referendum was a tactic by a skilled party manager hoping to keep his fragile government in business (pages 61–5 and 86–7).

Study Guide: A2 Question

In the style of AQA

'Edward Heath's government of 1970–74 was an utter disaster.'
Examine the validity of this view.   (45 marks)

Exam tips

The cross-references are intended to take you straight to the material that will help you to answer the question.

This question invites a balanced response. Clearly Heath's government was a disaster in many respects and you will need to explain the failures, but there are also points that can be made to suggest that 'utter disaster' is too strong a view. Before writing, choose your line of argument and ensure you keep to it throughout the essay. Remember to introduce different points in different paragraphs and to support the points you make with specific examples.

Among Heath's failures were:

- the attempt to abandon an incomes policy (pages 94–5)
- the outcry over the withdrawal of free school milk (page 95)
- the problems with the unions: the miners' strike and the three-day week (pages 96–7)
- the apparent 'lack of control' by 1974 and Heath's election loss (pages 97–8).

Against these can be set:

- the local government reforms (you may consider these failures or successes depending on your viewpoint) (pages 96–7)
- Britain's entry into Europe (which Heath regarded as his greatest achievement) (pages 99–101).

4 The Thatcher Revolution 1979–90

POINTS TO CONSIDER

The final 20 years of the twentieth century were dominated by the two main political developments – Thatcherism and New Labour. Thatcherism broke the consensus that had operated in Britain between 1945 and 1979 and profoundly altered many aspects of economic and political life in Britain. New Labour was a movement that began as an attempt to accommodate itself to the changes that this revolution had brought. This chapter deals with the major elements in the story:

- The Thatcher Revolution: the first stage 1979–86
- The Falkland's War 1982
- The miners' strike 1984–5
- The Thatcher revolution: the second stage 1986–90
- The Labour Party during the Thatcher years 1979–92

Key dates

1979	Margaret Thatcher became Prime Minister
1980	Monetarism adopted
1981	Riots in a number of cities
	Serious slump occurred
1982	Falklands War
1983	Mrs Thatcher's second election victory
	Neil Kinnock became leader of Labour Party
1984–5	Miners' strike
1984	IRA Brighton bombing
1985	Further riots in major cities
	Kinnock's ground-breaking speech at Labour Party conference
1986	Westland affair
	Supply-side economics adopted
1987	Mrs Thatcher's third election victory

Key question
What was
Thatcherism?

Key dates

IRA Brighton
bombing: 1984

Margaret Thatcher
became Prime
Minister: 1979

Key terms

**Conviction
politician**
Someone with
strong opinions
who acts out of
principle rather
than political
expediency.

New right
A broad
conservative
movement in the
USA and Britain in
the 1980s which
combined an attack
on Keynesian
economics and
growing state power
with an emphasis
on the need to
maintain traditional
social values.

Key figure

**Keith Joseph
1918–94**
A leading
Conservative
thinker at this time,
who introduced
Thatcher to the
ideas of Von Hayek
and encouraged her
to adopt monetarist
policies.

1 | The Thatcher Revolution: The First Stage 1979–86

Margaret Thatcher gave her name to a new form of politics: Thatcherism. She was a striking example of a **conviction politician**. She had a strong aversion to the consensus politics that had developed in Britain since the Second World War. As early as 1968 she had attacked it as being devoid of principle:

> There are dangers in consensus: it could be an attempt to satisfy people holding no particular views about anything. It seems more important to have a philosophy and policy which, because they are good, appeal to a sufficient majority.

Her Methodist upbringing and the influence of the ideas of Friedrich Von Hayek and **Keith Joseph** gave Mrs Thatcher a set of beliefs that inspired her actions. Von Hayek was an Austrian economist and major critic of the Keynesian economic policies followed by most Western governments. He came to prominence with the publication of his book, *The Road to Serfdom* (1944), in which he attacked the notion of state direction of the economy. 'The more the government plans', he wrote, 'the less can an individual plan, and when the government plans everything the individual can plan nothing'. He argued that the proper role of the state was not to involve itself in the welfare of its citizens but simply to provide the conditions of liberty in which individuals were free to make their own choices. He was a strong supporter of the free market (see page 121), which he believed was the best guarantee of economic and political liberty. He had a particular distrust of trade unions whose power he regarded as a direct cause of unemployment and as a destroyer of democratic freedoms.

Mrs Thatcher's government may be regarded as part of the '**new right**'. Her 11 years in office ended the consensus politics that had operated since 1945 and which she regarded as a form of creeping socialism. Her belief was not simply that the Labour governments had increased the power and control of the state, but that the Conservatives had fallen into the same trap. Conservative governments had encroached upon the free market, subsidised private and public companies, and permitted the undemocratic growth of trade union power. Mrs Thatcher was angry with Heath for having abandoned his new right policies (see page 96) and reverting to the unimaginative, unproductive Keynesianism that had damaged Britain after 1945.

As she saw it, the result of all this was inefficiency and low growth, made worse by a welfare system which undermined personal responsibility and created a dependency culture (see page 157). The nation was suffering from a malaise under which the hard-working members of society were subsidising the workshy. Initiative was being stifled.

Profile: Margaret Thatcher 1925–

1925	–	Born Margaret Roberts, the daughter of a shopkeeper in Grantham, Lincolnshire
1943–7	–	Read chemistry at Oxford
1947–50	–	Trained as a lawyer
1950–1	–	Stood unsuccessfully as a Conservative candidate
1950	–	Married Denis Thatcher, a millionaire businessman
1959	–	Elected Conservative MP for Finchley
1964	–	Became opposition spokeswoman on pensions
1970–4	–	Secretary of State for Education and Science under Heath
1975–90	–	Leader of the Conservative Party
1979	–	Became Prime Minister after election victory
1982	–	Declining popularity was reversed by the Falklands victory
1983	–	Won second election victory
1987	–	Won third election victory
1990	–	Resigned as Prime Minister and party leader
1992	–	Became Lady Thatcher of Kesteven

Margaret Thatcher was the first woman in British history to become a party leader and a Prime Minister. Her three election victories in a row, 1979, 1983, 1987, meant that she held office continuously for 11 years from 1979 to 1990, the longest unbroken period for any Prime Minister in the twentieth century. Arguably the most controversial Prime Minister since Lloyd George, she was like him in being a 'populist'; that is, she claimed to have a special understanding of ordinary people that by-passed party politics. One example of this that she often quoted was her experience as a young woman helping to run her father's grocery shop; this, she felt, had given her an insight into the problems of the housewife having to make ends meet every week without getting into debt. She regarded this as appropriate training for running the national economy.

It is not easy to give exact definition to her politics. Some critics dismiss her simply as a right-wing Tory ideologue, but her strong belief in financial probity – the nation paying its way and balancing the books – made her much more a traditional liberal. So, too, did her wish to reduce the power of the state and give greater opportunity for people to live their lives without government interference.

She became an extraordinary leader in war. After Britain's victory over Argentina and the recovery of the Falkland Islands, she was likened by some observers to Winston Churchill in her ability to rouse the nation. Others who believed that she had deliberately provoked the war found her triumphalism after the British victory in 1982 repellent. However, her calm behaviour after the IRA tried to assassinate her in the Brighton bombing in 1984 enhanced her reputation.

As a staunch anti-Communist, she sided with US President Reagan in his condemnation of the Soviet Union as the 'evil empire'. The mutual liking and respect between her and Ronald Reagan redeveloped the special relationship between the USA and Britain. Republicans in the USA suggested that her uncompromising attitude helped to bring about the end of the Cold War. Interestingly, for many people in the Soviet bloc countries, she became a symbol of freedom. In Poland, for example, chapels and shrines were dedicated to her. This was in gratitude for her support of 'Solidarity', the Polish anti-Communist trade union movement. There was a bitter irony in this for those in Britain who believed she had trampled on the rights of trade unionists at home.

'One small step for woman – a giant leap for womankind.' A cartoon from the *Daily Mail* celebrates Margaret Thatcher's success in defeating Edward Heath by 130 votes to 119 in the final vote in the Conservative leadership contest in February 1975. Heath took his defeat badly; he regarded her standing against him as an act of disloyalty. Ever after, in what a journalist called 'the longest sulk in history', he remained cool towards her, declining to serve in any of her Cabinets. The other candidates depicted are (in descending order) Willie Whitelaw, James Prior, Hugh Fraser, Geoffrey Howe and Edward Heath. How effectively does the cartoonist convey the idea of Margaret Thatcher competing in a male-dominated party?

Ending the post-war consensus

The Conservatives' overall majority of 43 seats after the 1979 election was large enough to allow Mrs Thatcher to embark on a policy of radical change. Her intended solution to the problems she inherited was a return to the principle of individual accountability. The state, she believed, should no longer reward the incompetent and the half-hearted. It was false economics and bad social practice. In her memoirs she defined the harm she believed had been done to Britain by a consensus politics that had allowed the state to play too large a part in people's lives:

> The Labour Party gloried in planning, regulation, controls and subsidies. It had a vision of the future: Britain as a democratic, socialist society, third way between east European collectivism and American capitalism.
>
> The Tory Party was more ambivalent. At the level of principle, rhetorically and in Opposition, it opposed these doctrines and preached the gospel of free enterprise with very little qualification. But in the fine print of policy, and especially in government, the Tory Party merely pitched camp in the long march to the left. It never tried seriously to reverse it.

She was especially critical of Edward Heath, the man she had replaced as Conservative leader, whom, she claimed, had pushed Britain further towards socialism than even the Labour governments had:

> Ted Heath's government proposed and almost implemented the most radical form of socialism ever contemplated by an elected British government. It offered state control of prices and dividends, and the joint oversight of economic policy by a tripartite body representing the TUC, the CBI and the government, in return for trade union acquiescence in an incomes policy. We were saved from this abomination by the conservatism and suspicion of the TUC which perhaps could not believe that their 'class enemy' was prepared to surrender without a fight.

Mrs Thatcher's economic revolution

On taking up office in 1979 Margaret Thatcher set herself three economic objectives. In her memoirs she defined these as:

> First, everything we wished to do had to fit into the overall strategy of reversing Britain's economic decline. This led on to the second point: all policies had to be carefully costed, and if they could not be accommodated within our public expenditure plans they would not be approved. Finally, we had to stress continually that, however difficult the road might be and however long it took us to reach our destination, we intended to achieve a fundamental change of direction. We stood for a new beginning, not more of the same.

Her intention was nothing less than to change the economic basis on which Britain was run. This was part of her programme to end

Key question
What did Mrs Thatcher understand by the post-war consensus?

Key question
In what sense was Mrs Thatcher an economic revolutionary?

Key term

Free market
An economic system in which the forces of supply and demand are allowed to operate naturally without regulation by the government.

Key question
In what ways was Thatcherism a reversal of Keynesianism?

Key dates

Monetarism adopted: 1980

Serious slump occurred: 1981

Key question
What impact did monetarism have?

Key term

PSBR
Public Sector Borrowing Requirement. The public sector includes the whole of national and local government activity and the nationalised industries. The cost of running these has to be met from government revenue. If the revenue is insufficient the difference is made up by borrowing. The gap between government revenue and government needs is known as the PSBR.

the consensus politics that had allowed Britain to slip into harmful social and economic habits. Among those she identified as the most serious were:

- high levels of government spending which led to borrowing, excessive taxation and inflation
- unnecessary government interference in the running of the economy
- the growth of bureaucracy which meant that civil servants and officials increasingly intruded into people's lives
- a combination of weak managements and powerful unions which had resulted in a continual increase in wages and salaries but a decline in productivity; this had led to inflation and lack of competitiveness.

Margaret Thatcher's economic policy is best understood as an attempt to reverse the harmful trends, which, she believed, successive governments since 1945 had allowed to develop. The basis of all her efforts to achieve this was the restoration of the **free market** to replace the Keynesian system that British governments had followed since 1945. (Interestingly, her predecessor James Callaghan had previously hinted that he believed Keynesianism was dead.) She expressed this as 'taking government off the backs of the people'. Before any of this could be done, however, it was essential to tackle the major problem confronting Britain – inflation.

Monetarism

To bring inflation under control, Margaret Thatcher's government chose to adopt monetarism, a financial theory particularly associated with Milton Friedman, an influential US economist. Friedman taught that the root cause of inflation was government spending. It followed, therefore, that in order to control inflation governments had to restrict the amount of money in circulation and reduce public expenditure.

In keeping with Friedman's notions, Mrs Thatcher began to cut government spending, hoping that this would reverse the position in which Britain's **PSBR** was always in deficit. To control inflation further, interest rates were kept at a high level in order to deter irresponsible borrowing and keep the pound strong on the international financial market. The success of these measures was indicated by the fall in the rate of inflation from 19 per cent in 1979 to five per cent in 1983.

However, while monetarism was successful in reducing inflation it did so at the price of job losses. As Table 4.1 (on page 122) shows, unemployment rose at a disturbing rate every year after 1980. This might have been acceptable had the drop in inflation been accompanied by economic growth. But the opposite was happening. In 1981, falling orders for manufactured goods had seen the start of an economic recession. On top of all this, serious rioting had occurred in parts of London, Bristol, Manchester and Liverpool.

Social unrest

In April 1981, in Brixton in south London, hundreds of predominantly black youths went on the rampage, burning shops and looting property. It was only with the greatest difficulty that the police eventually contained the trouble. In July similar violence occurred in:

- the St Paul's region of Bristol
- the Toxteth area in Liverpool
- Moss Side in Manchester.

Although local conditions helped to explain the disturbances, they were in a general sense a reaction against Mrs Thatcher's tough monetarist policies that had led to increased unemployment. The common factors which combined to ignite the troubles were:

- poor job prospects in the deprived inner-city areas
- alienation of young black people who felt they were discriminated against by the authorities, particularly the police
- the high incidence of unemployment among school leavers.

The government did not always see the rioters as helpless victims of social and industrial change. There was a strong feeling on the right that the disturbances were deliberately started or whipped up by political troublemakers. Comparing his father in the 1930s with the layabouts of the 1980s, Norman Tebbit, the Minister for Employment, told applauding delegates at the 1981 Conservative Party conference: 'He didn't riot; he got on his bike and looked for work, and he went on looking until he found it.'

Tebbit was one of the tough guys in the Cabinet. Portrayed in the satirical television programme *Spitting Image* as a leather-clad, chain-bedecked, cosh-wielding enforcer, he was certainly one of Mrs Thatcher's staunchest supporters, who urged her not to allow the riots to deflect her from her policies. Such support certainly strengthened her resolve to keep to the promise made at the Conservative Party conference in 1980 when she had declared, to loud acclaim, 'the lady's not for turning'. This was a calculated act of defiance against the **'wets'**, ministers such as Francis Pym (Defence), James Prior (Employment) and Peter Walker (Agriculture) who, worried by the effects of monetarism, had urged that the policy be slowed down or modified.

However, by 1982 the mounting, social and economic problems had begun to threaten Mrs Thatcher's continuance in office. Opinion polls showed the Prime Minister's personal popularity and that of her government had declined significantly. Such developments led some Conservatives to doubt that they could win the next election. But in 1982 dramatic events took place that reversed all this: Britain went to war with Argentina over the Falkland Islands.

Table 4.1:
UK unemployment in Britain 1980–90

Year	No. unemployed
1980	2,244,000
1981	2,272,000
1982	3,097,000
1983	3,225,000
1984	3,284,000
1985	3,346,000
1986	3,408,000
1987	3,297,000
1988	2,722,000
1989	2,074,000
1990	1,850,000

Riots in a number of cities: 1981

Key date

'Wets'
Used during the Thatcher years as a description of those in the government and Conservative Party who opposed or were uncertain about the tough measures that Mrs Thatcher adopted.

Key term

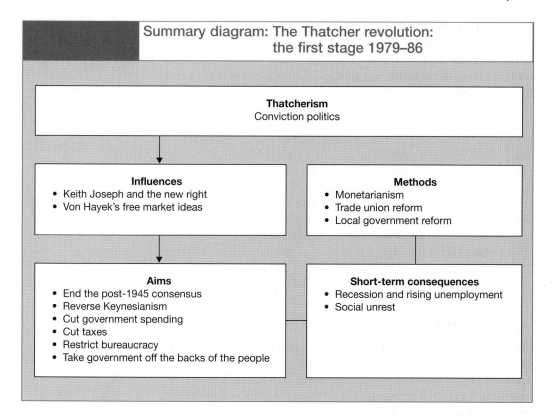

Summary diagram: The Thatcher revolution:
the first stage 1979–86

Thatcherism
Conviction politics

Influences
- Keith Joseph and the new right
- Von Hayek's free market ideas

Methods
- Monetarianism
- Trade union reform
- Local government reform

Aims
- End the post-1945 consensus
- Reverse Keynesianism
- Cut government spending
- Cut taxes
- Restrict bureaucracy
- Take government off the backs of the people

Short-term consequences
- Recession and rising unemployment
- Social unrest

Key question
Why did Britain go to war over the Falklands in 1982?

2 | The Falklands War 1982

The crisis over the Falklands Islands provided Margaret Thatcher with an opportunity, which nobody could have foreseen, least of all herself, to reveal a facet of her character that otherwise would have remained hidden. She became an outstanding war leader. Her commanding conduct and demeanour during the Falklands conflict so added to her reputation that she regained a popularity (sometimes referred to as 'the Falklands factor') that enabled her to stay in office until 1990, winning the elections of 1983 and 1987 along the way.

The Anglo-Argentinian dispute

The legal ownership of the islands had long been disputed between Argentina and Britain. The historical arguments over who had sovereignty were complicated. Britain's position was that the Falklands had legally been a British Dependency since 1833. What was not in dispute in 1982 was that 98 per cent of the population of some 2000 islanders wished to remain under the British flag. This was the point constantly emphasised by Margaret Thatcher. It gave her the justification for insisting that 'sovereignty is not negotiable'.

Interestingly, Mrs Thatcher's government had at first been willing to discuss a compromise with Argentina. Nicholas Ridley, a minister at the Foreign Office, had proposed a 'leaseback' agreement by which Britain, while maintaining ultimate sovereignty over the Falklands, would allow Argentina to administer the region as its own. However, any chance of a settlement on these terms was destroyed by Argentina's decision to take the islands by force.

In a precipitate move on 2 April 1982, General Galtieri, the Argentine dictator, eager to make his four-month old regime acceptable to the nation, ordered the seizure of the Falklands. Some 4000 troops invaded the islands and quickly overcame the resistance of the garrison of 80 Royal Marines. This act of aggression was condemned by all parties in Britain, but whereas the Labour opposition wanted the British response to be channelled through the United Nations, which formally condemned the Argentine invasion, Mrs Thatcher was adamant that it was entirely a matter for Britain to resolve. Its sovereignty had been affronted and its people in the Falklands put under occupation. It was therefore entitled to take action. She immediately ordered the retaking of the Falklands.

The conflict, April–June 1982

On 8 April, a British task force, having been rapidly assembled in four days, sailed from Portsmouth and Southampton. On 25 April, South Georgia, which Argentina had also seized, was recaptured. Air strikes began on 1 May against the occupying Argentine forces on the Falklands.

Having placed a 200-mile exclusion zone around the islands, Britain began its naval campaign on 2 May. In an action that caused considerable controversy in Britain, the Argentine cruiser *Belgrano* was sunk by a British submarine. Opponents of the war asserted that Mrs Thatcher had personally ordered the *Belgrano* to be torpedoed even though it was sailing out of the exclusion zone at the time it was struck. The accusation was that she had done this deliberately to wreck the efforts of the UN Secretary-General to bring about a negotiated settlement of the conflict. Mrs Thatcher's defence was that, in a war situation, the *Belgrano*, regardless of its position and heading, remained a real threat to British personnel. Ships, she pointed out, can always turn round.

Two days after the *Belgrano* had been sunk, HMS *Sheffield* was destroyed by an Argentine Exocet missile. In subsequent engagements, two British frigates were also destroyed and others damaged in air attacks. However, the Royal Navy had prepared the way effectively for British troop landings to begin on 21 May. By the end of the month the two key areas of San Carlos and Goose Green had been recaptured.

The climax came with the liberation of the capital, Port Stanley, on 14 June. Argentina then surrendered. The conflict had claimed the lives of 255 British and 665 Argentine servicemen. Although some found it tastelessly jingoistic, Mrs Thatcher's cry of 'rejoice, rejoice' at the news of the task force's victory found an echo with the population at large who read the tabloid press. People likened her to Churchill in her ability to inspire the nation in wartime.

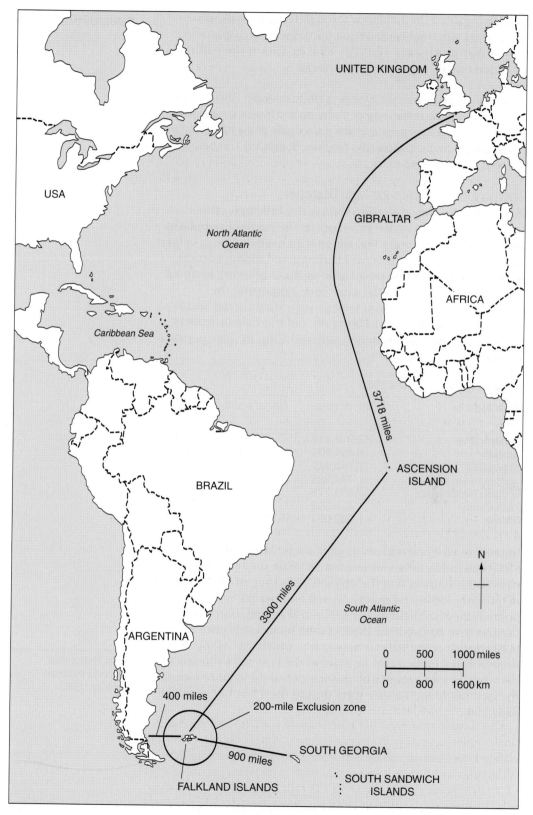

Figure 4.1: Map showing the location of the Falkland Islands and the route of the task force.

Having regained the Falklands through force of arms, Britain established a permanent garrison on the islands to guarantee their security. Margaret Thatcher let it be known she had no intention now of negotiating them away:

Falklands War: 1982

Key date

> Our men did not risk their lives for a UN trusteeship. They risked their lives for the British way of life, to defend British sovereignty. I do not intend to negotiate on the sovereignty of the islands in any way except for the people who live here. That is my firm belief. These islands belong to us.

The political benefits for Mrs Thatcher

The reward for her leadership during the Falklands crisis came in the 1983 election. Carried to victory by the surge of popularity that the war had brought her, she won an overwhelming victory. In contrast, the opposition who had opposed military action found themselves in the unenviable position of trying to attack the government while at the same time supporting the servicemen and women who were actually fighting the war. It proved an impossible act to bring off and the Labour leaders, Michael Foot and Neil Kinnock, suffered a dip in their personal standing.

Table 4.2: Election results 1983

Political party	No. of votes	No. of seats	Percentage of vote
Conservative	13,012,315	397	42.4
Labour	8,456,934	209	27.6
Liberal/SDP	7,780,949	23	25.4
Northern Irish parties	764,925	17	2.6
Scottish Nationalists	331,975	2	1.1
Plaid Cymru	125,309	2	0.4
Others	232,054	0	0.5

Impressive electoral success though it was, Margaret Thatcher's achievement has to be put in context. What she had done was to recover the support that the opinion polls suggested she had lost in the early 1980s and restore herself and her party to the position they had held in 1979. The real explanation for the Conservative landslide in 1983 was the remarkably poor performance of the Labour opposition, which saw its total vote drop by three million and its share of the vote fall by nearly nine per cent. To understand why this happened we need to examine the fortunes of the Labour Party during the Thatcher years (see page 138).

Mrs Thatcher's second election victory: 1983

Key date

(see page 138)

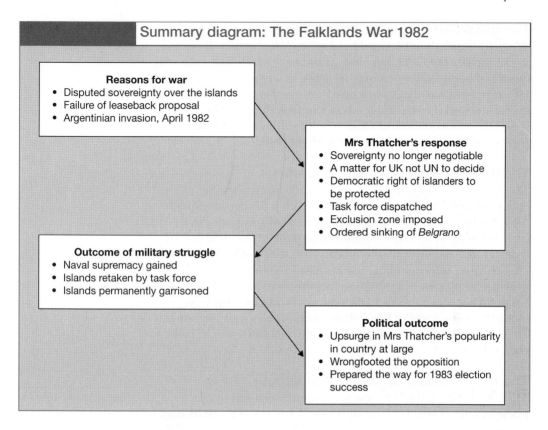

Summary diagram: The Falklands War 1982

Reasons for war
- Disputed sovereignty over the islands
- Failure of leaseback proposal
- Argentinian invasion, April 1982

Mrs Thatcher's response
- Sovereignty no longer negotiable
- A matter for UK not UN to decide
- Democratic right of islanders to be protected
- Task force dispatched
- Exclusion zone imposed
- Ordered sinking of *Belgrano*

Outcome of military struggle
- Naval supremacy gained
- Islands retaken by task force
- Islands permanently garrisoned

Political outcome
- Upsurge in Mrs Thatcher's popularity in country at large
- Wrongfooted the opposition
- Prepared the way for 1983 election success

Key question
What circumstances brought about confrontation between the Thatcher government and the miners?

3 | The Miners' Strike 1984–5

Margaret Thatcher's insistence on the nation's paying its way meant that subsidies would not normally be used to shore up ailing industries, a practice for which she had sharply criticised Edward Heath. Her argument was that, while sympathy might lead one to help enterprises that were experiencing hardship, it had always to be remembered that public subsidies by definition came from the public purse. This meant that some other area would be deprived of resources to pay for the failing ones. Robbing Peter to pay Paul made no sense economically if Peter was productive and Paul unproductive. This merely rewarded the inefficient at the expense of the efficient. It was such arguments that lay at the heart of the government's dispute with the miners, which came to a head in 1984.

Throughout the century the British coal industry had been in recurrent crisis. The basic fact was that coal was increasingly costly and difficult to mine. Nationalisation in 1948 had not altered this (see page 16). Indeed, there was a case for saying that a lack of government investment since then had added to the problem. For some time, Britain had been importing coal from abroad. With the exception of a few pits producing particular types of coal, British mines by the 1970s were running at a loss.

The government's case for pit closures

The government under Mrs Thatcher declared its unwillingness to put further public money into an industry which had little real chance of being able to recover its place in a competitive market. Her argument was that not to take hard measures when necessary simply delayed the inevitable. Better to face the situation now and lessen the consequences of closure by generous redundancy settlements than pretend things could get better.

The miners' case against closures

The miners' unions and other analysts advanced a strong counter-argument. They asserted that, with a proper investment programme backed by a genuine government commitment to coal as a long-term power source, large parts of the British coal industry still had a profitable future. Nor, they pointed out, was it only a matter of economics. The social consequences of widespread pit closures would be catastrophic. In areas such as South Wales, Yorkshire and Durham, coal was not simply an industry; it was a way of life. Whole communities were dependent on it. If the local mine closed, the local community would cease to exist.

The role of personalities in the dispute

These opposing points of view became personalised in the leading protagonists in the coal strike of 1984–5. The **NCB** had recently appointed as its chairman Ian McGregor, an unsentimental Canadian manager, whose remit was to cut out the non-profitable parts of the coal industry. He was faced by the equally uncompromising National Union of Mineworkers' leader, Arthur Scargill, the man who had brought down Edward Heath in 1974 (see page 96), who was equally determined to resist pit closures.

> **Miners' strike: 1984–5** | Key date

> **NCB**
> The National Coal Board, the body with overall responsibility for running the industry. | Key term

Although the government claimed to be neutral in the dispute and concerned solely with upholding law and order, it fully backed McGregor and the NCB. Indeed, it is arguable that the government deliberately encouraged a showdown with the miners as part of its campaign to bring the trade unions to heel. Anticipating a prolonged strike, the government had made careful plans. Its strongman, Norman Tebbit, the Employment Minister, had already steered through two Employment Acts in 1980 and 1982, intended as the first steps towards reducing union power. The measures:

- forbade mass picketing
- outlawed the 'closed shop', the requirement that all workers in a particular plant or factory had to be union members
- declared industrial action illegal unless the workers had voted for a strike in a formal union ballot.

In addition to weakening the miners' legal defences, the government had taken the practical step of stockpiling coal and coke at power stations and drafting emergency plans for importing further stocks should the need arise. The strike, which

Key terms

Battle of Orgreave
In 1984, strikers tried to prevent coke lorries leaving a British Steel coking plant in Orgreave, South Yorkshire. An estimated 6000 pickets struggled for hours against some 5000–8000 police before finally being overcome. Ninety-three arrests were made, and 51 strikers and 72 policemen were injured.

Print workers
Until the 1980s, among the highest paid workers in British industry, they were reluctant to accept new work practices based on new technology since this would threaten their job security and high earnings.

began in 1984, lasted a year and saw violent clashes between striking miners and the police, the worst occurring in June at the '**Battle of Orgreave**'. But Scargill's NUM never had any real hope of success. Weakened by breakaway miners who remained at work, and by the refusal of key unions, such as power-station workers, to join the struggle, the strike petered out early in 1985, leaving a legacy of bitterness and recrimination.

Reasons for the defeat of the strike included the following:

- Arthur Scargill's abrasive manner alienated other unions within the mining industry with the result that the strike was never solid. The notable example was the Nottinghamshire miners who defied Scargill's appeals and threats and continued working throughout the strike.
- Scargill's persistent refusal to hold a ballot of the NUM members made it appear that he was undemocratically forcing his union into a strike.
- Few other trade unions were willing to support the strike.
- Although the strikers claimed it was heavy-handed police action that started the violence, the broad public perception was that it was the strikers who were most at fault. Public opinion became largely pro-government.
- The government, which backed the NCB throughout, had made careful preparations to maintain essential fuel stocks and supplies.
- The Labour opposition did not perform well. Although some on the left wholly supported the striking miners, Neil Kinnock as leader tried to take a middle path, condemning violence but being sympathetic towards the strikers' cause. It was unimpressive and did not convince voters that Labour had a logical response to the strike.
- Norman Tebbit's Employment Acts gave the NCB and the government powerful restraints against the strikers.
- The police forces involved were largely successful in enabling strike-breakers to get into work and delivery lorries to get through picket lines.
- Coal was no longer the vital fuel source for ordinary people the way it had been in previous generations. The strike, therefore, never made the impact the strikers had hoped.
- Since coal was of declining industrial importance there was a sense in which the strike was a hopeless act. It seemed to belong to an age that had passed.

The miners' defeat marked a major success for the government's anti-union campaign and encouraged other employers to begin resisting union demands. Worker power was on the decline. This was clearly evident in 1986 in the failure of the **print workers**, despite prolonged and desperate efforts, to prevent Rupert Murdoch, a press baron and the proprietor of the *Times* Newspaper Group, from obliging them to accept new technology and modern work practices. Murdoch followed the tactics of Eddie Shah, a newspaper owner in Manchester, who in 1982 had used the legal powers granted to employers under the new

Employment Acts to break the power of the unions. Since the miners and the print workers were arguably the strongest unions in Britain their defeat marked a major success for Mrs Thatcher's industrial policies. It also strengthened her resolve to overcome the other forces in Britain, such as irresponsible local governments, which she regarded as undemocratic and economically wasteful.

Impact of the miners' strike

The impact of the strike was much wider than just in the mining industry and regions:

- The scenes of violence between strikers and police regularly seen on television shocked the nation and divided public opinion. Polls suggested that 65 per cent of people supported the government and the police, 35 per cent the miners. Commentators suggested that these figures reflected the divide in the nation at large between the people who lived and worked in the areas of declining industry and those (the majority of the population) whose livelihoods no longer depended on the old staple industries. In simplified terms, the divide was between the two nations, the north and the south.
- Social commentators suggested that the violent clashes that frequently accompanied the strike stimulated a general lawlessness in Britain as evidenced by further riots in some of Britain's cities in 1985.
- The failure of the strike allowed the planned closures to go ahead at greater speed. The result was job losses, redundancy, social disruption and the decline of traditional mining communities.
- The violent nature and the ultimate failure of the strike convinced the majority of people that action of this kind was no longer an appropriate way of settling industrial issues in modern Britain.
- The failure of the miners gave heart to employers who wanted to convert their workers into accepting modern ways and new techniques.
- Since the NCB's victory was really the government's victory, Margaret Thatcher was encouraged to think that other opponents could be defeated if the government kept its sense of purpose and determination.

Further riots in major cities: 1985

Key date

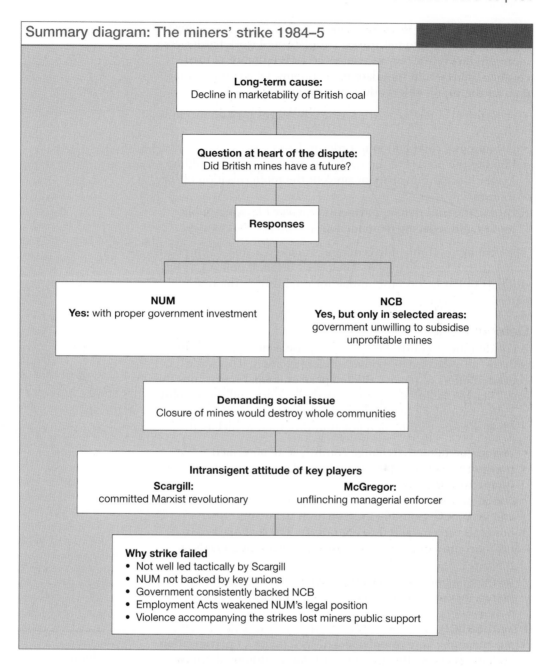

Summary diagram: The miners' strike 1984–5

Long-term cause:
Decline in marketability of British coal

Question at heart of the dispute:
Did British mines have a future?

Responses

NUM
Yes: with proper government investment

NCB
Yes, but only in selected areas:
government unwilling to subsidise
unprofitable mines

Demanding social issue
Closure of mines would destroy whole communities

Intransigent attitude of key players
Scargill:
committed Marxist revolutionary

McGregor:
unflinching managerial enforcer

Why strike failed
- Not well led tactically by Scargill
- NUM not backed by key unions
- Government consistently backed NCB
- Employment Acts weakened NUM's legal position
- Violence accompanying the strikes lost miners public support

---

Key question
What were the
essential features of
supply-side
economics?

Key date

Supply-side
economics adopted:
1986

4 | The Thatcher Revolution: The Second Stage. Supply-side Economics

Despite Margaret Thatcher's impressive victory in the 1983 election and her earlier declaration that she was 'not for turning', the severity of the recession obliged the government to modify its financial policies. Although monetarism was never formally dropped as a policy, from the mid-1980s it was in practice largely abandoned. In its place the government began pursuing 'supply-side economics'. This approach was based on the belief that Keynesian policies had distorted the operation of the economy by attempting to create demand artificially. Supply-side economists argued for a return to incentives; people would work harder and more productively if they were allowed to keep more of their earnings. This would stimulate the economy. Chief among the policies the supply-siders advocated were:

- reducing taxation so as to provide employees with an incentive to work
- encouraging competition in order to lower prices
- limiting the powers of the trade unions so that they could no longer block productivity or prevent the modernisation of industry
- cutting wasteful welfare payments as a way of saving public money and reducing dependency.

The turning to supply-side economics marked a shift of emphasis rather than a basic change in Thatcher's original policies. It was still part of her broad programme for establishing the free-enterprise economy.

Deregulation

A critical move towards the free-enterprise economy was made with the introduction of a policy of deregulation. This was a concerted effort to remove the financial and legal restrictions that Mrs Thatcher believed had prevented efficiency and profitability in many areas of social and economic activity.

Chief measures in the deregulation programme included:

- finance: credit and exchange controls were abolished
- transport: bus companies were deregulated to encourage competition
- education: schools were entitled to opt out of the state sector and become responsible for their own financing
- hospitals: were required to operate an 'internal market' by taking control of their own finance and matching needs to resources
- housing: council house tenants were given the right to buy the homes they were renting.

Privatisation

These measures were complemented by a policy of **privatisation**. As well as providing the Treasury with large additional funds, the policy aimed at increasing 'popular capitalism' by giving a much greater number of ordinary people the chance to become **shareholders**. Between 1979 and 1990 the number of shareholders in Britain rose from three million to nine million.

Of the 50 enterprises sold off during the Thatcher years the largest were:

- British Airways
- British Steel
- British Coal
- Cable and Wireless

Key terms

Privatisation
The selling of nationalised (government-owned) concerns fully or in part to private buyers and investors.

Shareholders
Investors in companies or public utilities, such as electricity and gas.

Table 4.3:
Government revenue
derived from
privatisation 1979–89

Year	Value
1979–80	£377 million
1985–6	£2600 million
1988–9	£7000 million

- British Telecom
- regional electricity and water boards.

Table 4.3 shows how much revenue was raised by this policy.

Financial deregulation encouraged banks and building societies to advance larger loans to their customers. A significant part of the money borrowed was then spent on consumer goods from abroad. The result was that between 1980 and 1989 Britain's balance of payments deficit rose from £16 billion to £47 billion.

North Sea oil

One of the most contentious privatisation measures was the selling off of North Sea oil. In 1976 the Labour government had established the British National Oil Corporation (BNOC) as a means of keeping **North Sea oil** under public control. However, beginning in 1982, Mrs Thatcher's government sold off its majority shareholdings to the private sector. The government's argument was that despite the considerable revenue gains for Britain since 1976, world oil prices in the 1980s had entered a period of long-term decline.

Key term

North Sea oil
This resource had come on tap in the late 1970s and turned Britain from a net importer to a net exporter of oil.

Critics rejected this argument. They complained that Mrs Thatcher's government had squandered a national asset for short-term gain. They saw deregulation as part of a broader irresponsibility on the government's part that threatened to destroy large parts of Britain's industrial economy. Weight appeared to be given to this argument by the figures showing a marked fall in the numbers of those employed in British manufacturing industries (see Table 4.4).

Table 4.4: Number of
industrial workers in
Britain 1970–90

Year	Number
1970	9 million
1980	7 million
1990	4 million

The debate over deregulation and privatisation

The figures in Table 4.4 do not necessarily prove decline. Indeed, the government's defenders claimed the opposite. They argued that the shift in employment, although obviously painful for those experiencing redundancy, was part of a necessary modernising process. The firm measures adopted by the Thatcher governments obliged British industry to shed the wasteful practices and overmanning that had formerly hindered it. Streamlining and cost-effective techniques resulted in higher productivity since fewer workers were involved.

Such arguments, of course, were of little comfort to those who had lost their jobs. They were unimpressed by the figures which revealed that between 1979 and 1989 manufacturing productivity grew at an annual rate of 4.2 per cent, the highest growth rate in British industrial history and also some way ahead of Britain's European partners. Some writers, such as Alan Sked, have gone so far as to suggest that Britain in the 1980s, like Germany in the 1960s, had achieved an economic 'miracle'. This claim should be examined in the light of Tables 4.5–4.7 (see page 134) indicating some of the key aspects of economic performance in the period 1979–90.

Table 4.5: A comparison of GDP growth rates 1950–89

Per capita GDP	Britain	European average
1950–79	1.8%	3.9%
1979–89	2.1%	1.9%

Table 4.6: Rise in real wages of workers in the period 1979–94

Britain	France	West Germany	USA
26%	2%	3%	–7%

Table 4.7: Job creation in UK 1979 and 1989

	1979	1989
No. of firms	1,890,000	3,090,000
No. of self-employed	1,906,000	3,497,000

The growth of small businesses in Britain is part of the explanation why by 1990 it had much lower unemployment rates than the other countries of the European Union. This was in spite of the industrial recessions Britain experienced in 1981 and 1987 that produced a serious balance of payments deficit by the late 1980s.

Table 4.8: UK's balance of payments record (in £ millions) 1978–90

Year	Amount	Year	Amount
1978	1162	1985	2888
1979	–525	1986	–871
1980	3629	1987	–4983
1981	7221	1988	–16,617
1982	4034	1989	–22,512
1983	3336	1990	–18,268
1984	1473		

A factor that needs to be stressed is that throughout the period of the Thatcher government North Sea oil brought billions of pounds into the Treasury. Arguably it was this rather than genuine economic growth that funded the unemployment and benefit payments that the recession of the 1980s necessitated. Critics of Thatcherism claimed that it was this revenue that made possible the income tax cuts in which the government took great pride. A combination of North Sea oil and privatisation saved Thatcher's government from bankruptcy, enabling it to overcome the recessions that its monetarist policies had created.

Figure 4.2 shows that the highest point of oil income came in 1985, but governments continued to draw considerable revenue from North Sea oil until 2007 when income began to decline following the realisation that the natural supplies were beginning to dry up.

Taxation under Mrs Thatcher

One of the government's proudest boasts was that the Thatcher years were a period of low taxation. However, it is clear from Table 4.9 that although there certainly was a significant reduction in income tax rates during Mrs Thatcher's years in office, the

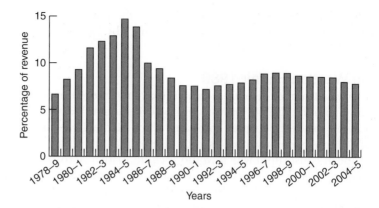

Figure 4.2: Proportion of UK revenues from oil and gas 1978–2005.

overall tax bill for ordinary people had not greatly altered. This was because of increases in indirect taxes such as National Insurance contributions, VAT and local rates.

Table 4.9: Percentage of gross income taxed for people on average earnings in 1979 and 1990

	Single person		Married man with two children	
	1979	1990	1979	1990
Income tax	25.0	20.3	18.8	12.9
National Insurance	6.5	8.0	6.2	8.0
VAT	2.7	5.1	2.5	5.0
Indirect taxes	8.1	7.1	8.1	7.1
Rates/poll tax	3.1	2.4	2.8	4.9
Totals	45.4	42.8	38.4	37.9

Thatcherism and the USA

In 1987, a feature film was released in the United States called *Wall Street* which, while not being explicitly about Thatcherism, was widely interpreted as a critique of the prevailing mood of the times in **Reagan's America**. The film's main character was an unscrupulous financier who, in his pursuit of personal wealth, rode roughshod over anyone who got in his way, destroying incomes and livelihoods. He justified his behaviour in these terms:

> Greed, for lack of a better word, is good. Greed is right; greed works. Greed clarifies, cuts through, and captures the essence of the evolutionary spirit. Greed, in all of its forms, greed for life, for money, for love, knowledge – has marked the upward surge of mankind.

Opponents of Thatcherism seized on this statement as being a precise description of the amorality of a system that allowed the powerless in society to be abused and exploited by the powerful. Defenders responded by pointing out that the film was fiction made by people of the political left intent on putting the worst interpretation on Thatcherism. Their reply was that, far from being exploitative, Thatcherism had given the powerless the opportunity to regain control over their lives by loosening the grip of the state over them.

The Westland affair 1986

In 1986, a Cabinet dispute indicated that there were times when total unanimity did not prevail in the government. Westland was an ailing British helicopter company which Michael Heseltine, the Defence Secretary, proposed to save by making it part of a European consortium which would include British Aerospace, a recently privatised company. However, Leon Brittan, the Industry Secretary, put forward an alternative package which involved the takeover of Westland by a US company, Sikorski. When Mrs Thatcher chose to back the Sikorski option, Heseltine stormed out of the Cabinet. His resignation on 9 January was followed two weeks later by Brittan's when it was revealed that his Department of Industry had put pressure on British Aerospace to withdraw from the European consortium. Nobody came out of the affair with credit. Critics suggested that the whole thing showed up two unattractive aspects of Mrs Thatcher's style of government: her bullying of the Cabinet and her subservience to President Reagan and the USA.

Key dates

Westland affair: 1986

Mrs Thatcher's third election victory: 1987

The 1987 election

The internal squabble over Westland did not greatly harm the government's standing with the voters. The year 1987 witnessed Mrs Thatcher's third consecutive electoral victory. Although the results showed some recovery by the Labour Party from its disastrous performance in the 1983 election (see page 140), the government maintained its share of the popular vote and despite losing 22 seats still had an overall majority of 100 in the Commons.

Key question
How did Mrs Thatcher interpret the result of the 1987 election?

Table 4.10: Election results 1987

Political party	No. of votes	No. of seats	Percentage of vote
Conservative	13,763,747	375	42.2
Labour	10,029,270	229	30.8
Liberal/SDP	7,341,275	22	22.6
Northern Irish parties	730,152	17	2.3
Scottish Nationalists	416,873	3	1.4
Plaid Cymru	123,589	3	0.3
Others	151,517	1	0.4

Local government reforms

Margaret Thatcher interpreted the election success as a mandate for pressing on with her reforming policies, particularly in regard to local government. In 1988, a series of changes in local authority finances were introduced:

• A system of Standard Spending Assessments (SSAs) that enabled the central government to control local government expenditure levels.

- Councils were also required to adopt 'compulsory competitive tendering' (CCT), that is, to contract out their services to the companies that could provide the best service at the lowest price.

The government hoped that these measures would be welcomed by the general public, who would see that the financial changes would create 'more gainers than losers'. For Mrs Thatcher, the financial adjustments were a further step in her plan to bring local government into line with her ideas of public accountability. She believed that public institutions, whose primary purpose after all was to serve the public, had to be made more responsive to the needs of the people. This was especially true of local government. She knew that many local authorities were unpopular. Only a minority of people (sometimes fewer than 25 per cent) voted in local elections. This had allowed extreme socialist groups to dominate areas such as the London boroughs and the city councils in Liverpool and Manchester. These were among the high-spending 'loony left' Labour authorities that she had successfully attacked by breaking up the metropolitan councils and abolishing the Greater London Council (GLC) in 1983.

Education

Margaret Thatcher also regarded her 1987 election victory as a mandate for the most significant educational reform since the 1944 Butler Act (see page 11). The Education Reform Act of 1988 had essentially the same purpose as her local government reforms; namely, to make the service provider, in this case the schools, more efficient and responsive to the needs of the consumer, in this case the children and their parents. Introduced by Kenneth Baker, the Education minister, the principal provisions of the 1988 Act were:

- The principle of Local Management of Schools (LMS) was introduced, under which schools were entitled to free themselves from direct financial control by the Local Education Authority. School budgeting could now be taken over by the head teacher and the school governors.
- Primary and secondary schools could also opt to become Grant Maintained Schools (GMS) which allowed them to become independent of their Local Education Authorities and be financed directly by central government.
- Secondary schools could restore some element of selection at 11 plus.
- A National Curriculum was introduced, containing 'core' subjects, such as English and maths, and 'foundation' subjects, such as geography, history and art.
- In their teaching, schools were to cover a set of 'Key Stages', aimed at achieving a number of prescribed learning aims.
- Where local conditions allowed, parents could specify which school they wanted their children to attend.
- League tables, showing the examination results achieved by schools, were to be published.

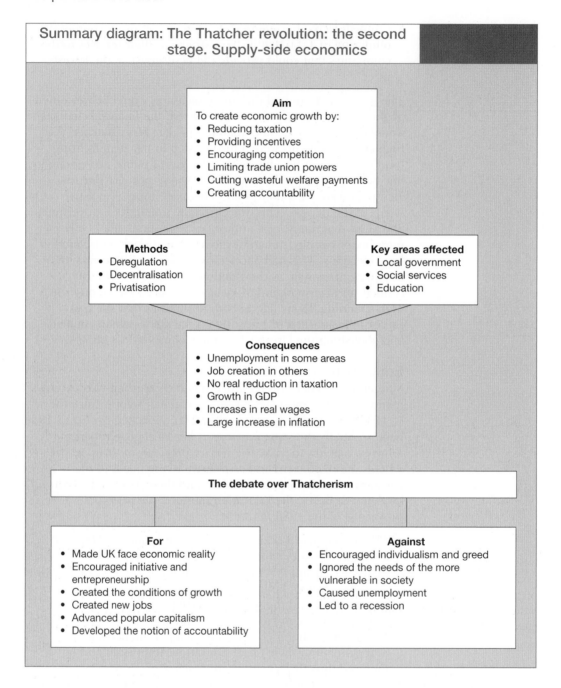

Summary diagram: The Thatcher revolution: the second stage. Supply-side economics

Aim
To create economic growth by:
- Reducing taxation
- Providing incentives
- Encouraging competition
- Limiting trade union powers
- Cutting wasteful welfare payments
- Creating accountability

Methods
- Deregulation
- Decentralisation
- Privatisation

Key areas affected
- Local government
- Social services
- Education

Consequences
- Unemployment in some areas
- Job creation in others
- No real reduction in taxation
- Growth in GDP
- Increase in real wages
- Large increase in inflation

The debate over Thatcherism

For
- Made UK face economic reality
- Encouraged initiative and entrepreneurship
- Created the conditions of growth
- Created new jobs
- Advanced popular capitalism
- Developed the notion of accountability

Against
- Encouraged individualism and greed
- Ignored the needs of the more vulnerable in society
- Caused unemployment
- Led to a recession

5 | The Labour Party During the Thatcher Years

If Margaret Thatcher had a profound effect on her own party, her impact on the Labour Party was hardly less significant. The 1980s were a disastrous decade for the Labour Party:

- Between 1979 and 1992 it lost four elections in a row.
- The final year of James Callaghan's administration in 1978–9 witnessed the 'winter of discontent', a series of damaging strikes by public service workers (see page 107).

Key question
Why was the Labour Party unable to mount an effective challenge to Thatcherism?

Key figure

Michael Foot 1913–
A man of strong socialist opinions, a distinguished essayist and a powerful orator, lacked the common touch. He was never able to establish an easy relationship with the ordinary voter. His three-year period as leader saw the Labour Party lose touch with the electorate. Politically, he proved no match for Thatcher.

Key question
How had the SDP come to be formed in 1981?

Key term

Militant Tendency
A Marxist group founded in 1964 with the aim of infiltrating Labour and forcing revolutionary policies on it. It had considerable success at local level becoming a dominant force in 1970s and 1980s in the councils of Merseyside.

- The Labour Party's strong links with the unions were seen by the voters as a contributory factor to the industrial strife, and to Labour's inability to govern. This view prevailed between 1979 and 1992. The electorate no longer seemed to regard Labour as a party of government.
- In many respects Labour was its own worst enemy in this period. It presented an image of a divided party more concerned with its own internal wrangles than with preparing itself for government.
- A major problem was the split between the left and right of the party. Callaghan had been a moderate but he was followed as leader in 1980 by **Michael Foot**, whose election marked a success for the left-wing backbench MPs.

Tony Benn (see page 105) had interpreted Labour's defeat in 1979 as a sign not that the party was too left wing, but that it was not left wing enough. He urged the party to embrace genuinely socialist polices instead of tinkering with capitalist ideas. As a step towards achieving this, he led a campaign to change the party's constitution. At Labour's 1980 and 1981 conferences, the left forced through resolutions that required all Labour MPs to seek reselection by their constituencies. The aim was to give greater power to left-wing activists who, although being a minority in the party overall, were disproportionately stronger in the constituencies.

The Social Democratic Party (SDP)
Benn hailed the changes as a victory for party democracy, but for Labour moderates it signalled the takeover of the party by extremist groups, such as the '**Militant Tendency**'. Believing that the party was allowing itself to be divorced from people's real needs by pursuing an unrealistic political agenda, a number of Labour MPs broke away in 1981 to form a new Social Democratic Party (SDP). The most prominent among these were Shirley Williams, David Owen, William Rodgers and Roy Jenkins, known as the 'gang of four'. Although they had all held posts in the Labour governments of the 1970s, none of the four had been happy with what they perceived to be the Labour Party's domination by the trade unions and its anti-Europeanism. They had stifled their feelings and gone along with the main policies of Wilson and Callaghan. But Labour's defeat in 1979, the election of Foot as leader in 1980, and the constitutional changes that pushed the party still further to the left, convinced them the time had come for a complete break.

The SDP leaders' claim was that the new party would be a radical, but not a socialist, force in British politics. Their hope was that it would attract disaffected members from both the Labour and Conservative parties. In alliance with the Liberals, the SDP gained a quarter of the popular vote in the 1983 election. But, despite such early success, it was never able to establish itself as a credible alternative to the major parties. By the early 1990s the SDP had formally merged with the Liberal Party to form the Liberal Democrats.

The 1983 election

Led by Michael Foot, the Labour Party suffered a humiliatingly heavy defeat in the 1983 election. The reasons are clear:

- Foot led the party and the campaign in a doddering, uninspiring way.
- The party was weakened by its serious internal disputes.
- The party's ill-thought-out manifesto was largely a concession to its left wing and in particular to CND. Among its vote-losing pledges was the promise to abandon Britain's independent nuclear deterrent and reintroduce nationalisation. A Labour MP, Gerald Kaufman, wittily, if despairingly, described the manifesto as 'the longest suicide note in history'.
- Margaret Thatcher was riding high on the Falklands factor (see page 126).
- The apparent pacifism of Foot and Kinnock during the Falklands War made Labour Party look unpatriotic at a time of national crisis.

Key question
Why did Labour perform so poorly in the 1983 election?

Kinnock's reforms

Michael Foot was replaced as party leader in 1983 by Neil Kinnock. This was to prove a turning point in Labour's fortunes. Although Kinnock had earlier been on the left of the party he was realistic enough to appreciate that the hard left path was unlikely to lead Labour back to power. He began a wide-ranging policy review that rejected many of the programmes, such as unilateralism, which the party had saddled itself with under Foot. A key moment came in 1985 at the annual party conference when Kinnock denounced the Militant Tendency councillors, such as those in Liverpool and Manchester, whose extreme activities had earned the contempt of the electorate. He told the party it had to adapt to the real world or it would be condemned to permanent powerlessness:

Key question
How did Kinnock try to reform the Labour Party?

Neil Kinnock became leader of Labour Party: 1983

Kinnock's ground-breaking speech at Labour Party conference: 1985

Key dates

> Implausible promises don't win victories. I'll tell you what happens with impossible promises. You start with far-fetched resolutions. They are then pickled into a rigid dogma, a code, and you go through the years sticking to that, outdated, misplaced, irrelevant to the real needs ... I'm telling you, you can't play politics with people's jobs and people's services.

There is a strong argument for regarding Kinnock's conference speech in 1985 as having destroyed the SDP. By advancing the notion of a party wedded to reform but determined to avoid extremes, he had stolen the SDP's clothes. A reformed, but still radical, Labour Party meant there was no need for an SDP. It has also been suggested that had the 'gang of four' shown patience and waited they would have found that New Labour perfectly fitted their ideas.

Yet in battling with the left and laying the base for the modernisation of the Labour Party, Kinnock had sacrificed his own party political future. He had, in effect, to execute a series of

U turns, on nationalisation, on the nuclear issue, and on Europe. These were courageous moves on his part and unavoidable if his party was to progress, but the consequence for Kinnock personally was that he was never again fully trusted by either his party or the electorate. He stood down after his second election defeat in 1992. His successor, John Smith, was very popular in the party but had little time to build on this before his premature death in 1994. Smith was succeeded as leader by another able Scotsman – Tony Blair (see page 170).

Summary diagram: The Labour Party during the Thatcher years

Difficulties of its position

- Took time to live down the memory of the 'winter of discontent'
- Internal divisions between left and right a continual source of weakness
- Michael Foot a disappointment as a leader – unable to inspire the party or engage with the electorate
- Angered by the prevailing influence of CND, Militant Tendency and the unions, a section of the party split away to form the SDP in 1981
- The party came badly out of the Falklands War in 1982 – its objection to military intervention was read by the electorate as lack of support for those fighting the war
- The party's disastrous performance in the 1983 election showed how out of touch the party had become

Kinnock's reforms

- Began the painful process of trying to reshape the party to win the centre ground
- His 1985 speech a landmark in the evolution of what was to become New Labour
- Helped to nullify the SDP
- But in making the necessary policy adjustments was seen as abandoning his previous principles
- The distrust this excited was evident in the election defeats of 1987 and 1992

Study Guide: AS Questions

In the style of Edexcel

Source 1

From: The Benn Diaries, *published in 1994. In 1984 Tony Benn was a leading member of the Labour Party and the MP for Chesterfield, a mining area.*

The strike was the culmination of a long conflict between the Conservative Party and the mineworkers' union. The strike in 1973–4 which led to the defeat of Edward Heath's government still rankled with the Conservatives when Mrs Thatcher came to power. The government was determined that trade unions would never again have such influence. In order to break their power, the Conservative government decided to take on the NUM, the strongest and most political union.

Detailed preparations were made to renew the conflict against the NUM. The overall strategy was produced in 1978 before the Thatcher government had come into power. A Conservative government would provoke a strike with the coal industry and build up maximum coal stocks.

Source 2

From: the memoirs of Margaret Thatcher, The Downing Street Years, *published in 1993.*

As an industrial dispute the coal strike had been wholly unnecessary. The NUM's position throughout the strike – that uneconomic pits could not be closed – was totally unreasonable. Only in a totalitarian state could the coal industry have functioned irrespective of financial realities and the forces of competition. But for people like Mr Scargill these were desirable things. The coal strike was always about far more than uneconomic pits. It was a political strike.

Source 3

From: A. Seldon and D. Collings, Britain Under Thatcher, *published in 2000.*

Although the strike cost the country over £2 billion, Nigel Lawson (the Chancellor of the Exchequer) believed that 'it was necessary that the government spent whatever was necessary to defeat Arthur Scargill'. The government had wanted to exorcise the myth, present since the defeat of Heath, that even a democratically elected government could not govern without the support of the NUM.

Use Sources 1, 2 and 3 and your own knowledge.
Do you agree with the view that the prime cause of the miners' strike in 1984 was the Conservative government's determination to reduce trade union power? Explain your answer, using Sources 1, 2 and 3 and your own knowledge.　　　　(40 marks)

Exam tips

The cross-references are intended to take you straight to the material that will help you to answer the question.

Tony Benn in his diaries (Source 1) is convinced of a long-term plan to destroy trade union power. What evidence do you have of this in Source 1? And what weight will you give to his views? He is closely involved, but very partisan. Note, however, the elements of Source 3 which support his view and which suggest a determination to 'defeat Arthur Scargill'.

Margaret Thatcher in Source 2 is strongly of the view that the blame for the strike lies with Scargill. How does she convey that opinion? And what weight will you give to her view? She like Benn is both knowledgeable and partisan. Source 2 provides evidence of political as well as economic disagreements between the NUM and the government. How does Source 3 lend support to this point?

As you can see, the package of source material for this (b)-type question provides you with sharply differing views. You will need to consider the authorship of the sources as part of the process of coming to a conclusion. In order to arrive at an overall conclusion, you will also need to use your own knowledge gained from Chapter 4.

You should consider:

- Thatcher's view that public money should not be used to prop up ailing industries (pages 117–27)
- the government case for pit closures (page 128)
- the miners' arguments against pit closures (page 128)
- the personalities and attitudes of Arthur Scargill and Ian McGregor (page 128)
- evidence that the government deliberately 'engineered a showdown' (pages 128–30)
- evidence of measures prior to the strike which were designed to weaken trade union power: the Employment Acts of 1980 and 1982 (page 128)
- the stockpiling of fuel and the plans to import stocks in an emergency (page 128).

Where does the balance of evidence lie in your view? Remember that you will need to argue a case. It is not enough to assume that the government engineered the clash simply because you have evidence of planning for fuel shortages. A sensible government which feared that a strike would result from the dispute between the NUM and the NCB would make contingency plans.

So, what is your overall conclusion? Do you agree with the view that the prime cause of the miners' strike in 1984 was the Conservative's government's determination to reduce trade union power?

In the style of OCR A

'The Conservatives won the 1983 general election because their opponents were so weak.' How far do you agree?   (50 marks)

Exam tips

The cross-references are intended to take you straight to the material that will help you to answer the question.

The question asks you to examine the reasons for the Conservative victory (pages 126 and 138–40). It also asks you to put them in order of importance ('… How far do you agree?') so a core task in your essay must be weighing one against another to work out their relative significance. You also have two basic sides to consider: positive reasons to explain Conservative success as well as negative reasons that denied their opponents the chance of victory. Given the wording of the question, start with those negatives. Labour was in a mess and the new SDP–Liberal alliance rode high in the opinion polls even if only temporarily. The alliance was quite strong, winning 25 per cent of the vote, but that vote was spread evenly across the country so it won almost no seats. It could not 'break the mould'. Against them in the anti-Tory campaign, Labour shrank by 10 per cent and won only two per cent more than the Alliance, but its geographically concentrated vote won it 32 per cent of the seats. The net effect was clear: these two sizeable (if very different) blocks split the anti-Tory vote and the Conservatives swept through with 58 extra seats. The opposition was divided, but the consequences were exaggerated massively by the British electoral system.

Turning to look at Mrs Thatcher's government (pages 120–30), it made radical changes that challenged the post-war consensus. Whether these were good for the country is not what you have been asked. Your focus needs to be, rather, on how popular they were: did monetarism and the free market economics bring in votes in 1983? What about inner-city riots? Was 'get on your bike' a vote winner? The Thatcher government was deeply unpopular in 1981–2. Having weighed the evidence, make your answer clear. Note that the Conservative vote in 1983 was 1.5 per cent lower than in 1979 so the increased Commons majority did not reflect popular support. Don't forget two other possibilities:

- Was Labour split because it didn't know how to deal with Thatcher?
- Was the Falklands War the real influence on the 1983 election result? This is a major factor to consider.

In the style of OCR B

Answer **both** parts of your chosen question.

(a) Why was Mrs Thatcher determined to confront the miners
in 1984?
[Explaining motives, intentions and actions]   (25 marks)
(b) How is Mrs Thatcher's overthrow in 1990 best explained?
[Explaining attitudes, motives and circumstances]   (25 marks)

Exam tips

*The cross-references are intended to take you straight to the material
that will help you to answer the questions.*

Revise the General Introduction at the start of the Exam tips in
Chapter 1 (page 33) and pages 117–30.

(a) You could start your first circle of explanation with the recent
context: the unions had broken Heath's government and the
miners were the great symbol of the British union movement. But
saying that on its own does not explain anything. You need
several circles of explanation that put that fact in the context of
how Thatcherite economic thinking affected the mining industry.
Do not wander off into a long survey of her economic policies.
Rather, use your understanding to pick out key features to help
your explanation: the coal industry had not been profitable for
years but Mrs Thatcher believed that companies/industries must
pay their own way and government subsidies must end (which,
in turn, would help Thatcherite policy to cut taxes). Your next
circle needs to focus on a core question: why was the NUM's
counter-case rejected out of hand? Could the mines have been
made profitable, and mining communities secured? Thatcher
said that was unrealistic, but was her judgement an economic or
a political decision? Here you can bring in the great clash of
personalities between Mrs Thatcher, Scargill and McGregor that
made confrontation inevitable. From there, use your next circle
to consider to what extent the confrontation was of Mrs
Thatcher's making (or, at least, whether she encouraged the
NCB into a showdown). The struggle with the miners may have
been a follow-on from her Employment Acts, but does the Battle
of Orgreave show that Scargill was just too tempting a target for
Thatcher? In determining the elements in her thinking, you must
decide whether her fundamental motive was economic or
political.

(b) The text in Chapter 5 (pages 149–55) considers this subject.
Your answer must deal with motives, intentions and causes and
should link the three elements together. You might start your first
circle by explaining Mrs Thatcher's apparent political strength
that followed from her three election victories. Had her success
led to her regarding herself as invincible, thereby losing a sense
of reality and allowing Labour, which had begun to reform itself,

to gain ground? Your next circle could examine the significance of the two policies that so damaged her in 1988–90: the new poll tax and her hardening attitude to the EU. Do not tell the story of either. Take each and show how it weakened her position.

That could take you to a next circle which considers whether Mrs Thatcher was a lucky politician whose luck started running out, or was it a case of her legendary commitment to conviction politics becoming a liability rather than an asset? Democratic politicians need to be flexible, but the rising chorus of critics within her party saw her as increasingly inflexible. Might these two be linked? Remember she was toppled in a coup by her own ministers. What worried them so much? The four by-election defeats of 1989–90 and the Conservatives' position in the opinion polls were crucial in opening their eyes to the possibility of defeat in the next general election. But was it a strike for the sake of the party?

Your last circle could consider the significance of divisions within the Cabinet. Yes, Thatcher had succeeded in alienating key heavyweights, but how do we interpret Heseltine's leadership challenge? She had been weakened, but did his political ambition finally bring her down?

Study Guide: A2 Question

In the style of AQA

'Success in the Falklands War ensured Margaret Thatcher's election victory of 1983.' Assess the validity of this view.

(45 marks)

Exam tips

The cross-references are intended to take you straight to the material that will help you to answer the question.

A successful answer to this question will balance the effects of the Falklands War against other factors contributing to Thatcher's electoral victory of 1983 (pages 123–6 and 140). The essay should consider a variety of factors and sustain an argument as to what was the most important reason for the 1983 election success.

In support of the importance of the Falklands War, you might argue:

- overwhelming victory increased her popularity with the public
- the victory weakened the position of those who had opposed military action
- victory undermined the authority of Kinnock and Foot who appeared pacificist and unpatriotic.

Other factors which may have contributed to Thatcher's success at the polls:

- economic factors
- Labour Party weaknesses through their association with the unions and the activities of extremists (and the breakaway Social Democratic Party)
- Foot's leadership
- arguments over disarmament and nationalisation, i.e. the direction of the party and the direction of the party manifesto.

5 From Thatcherism to New Labour 1990–9

POINTS TO CONSIDER
It has been said that all political careers end in failure.
Certainly Mrs Thatcher's fall in 1990 brought her down from
the heights of power and popularity she had enjoyed earlier.
So remarkable had her 11 years in office been that they left
a legacy that could not be ignored. It would not be an
exaggeration to say that she had made a revolution. The
question then arose: how would those who came after her
handle the legacy she had bequeathed? After an interlude
in which John Major extended the period of Conservative
government to 18 years, New Labour came to power under
its young leader Tony Blair, who was to take Britain into the
new millennium. These developments are treated as the
following themes:

- The fall of Margaret Thatcher 1990
- Thatcher's legacy
- John Major's government 1990–7
- New Labour 1994–9

Key dates

1986	The Single European Act
1988	Mrs Thatcher's Bruges speech
1989	Leadership challenge of Anthony Meyer defeated
1990	Poll tax crisis
	UK joined ERM
	Howe's resignation speech
	Mrs Thatcher resigned after failing to win leadership contest
	John Major became Prime Minister
1991	Citizen's Charter
	Coalition forces liberated Kuwait
1992	Maastricht Treaty signed
	UK withdrawal from ERM
1993	Euro rebellion over ratification of Maastricht Treaty
1994	Tony Blair became Labour Party leader
1995	Major won party leadership election
	NATO intervention in Bosnia
1997	Election victory for Labour
1999	NATO intervention in Kosovo

1 | The Fall of Margaret Thatcher 1990

Key question
What issues led to Thatcher's downfall in 1990?

Key date

Poll tax crisis: 1990

Margaret Thatcher's extraordinary 11 years in office came to an end in 1990. By a fascinating irony, the problems which finally brought her down were largely of her own making. This can be read as a sign that after all the years in office she was losing her political touch. The problem was made worse by her having been deprived of the avuncular advice of Willie Whitelaw, the Deputy Prime Minister who retired from politics in 1987 after suffering a stroke. She once said in all innocence, 'every Prime Minister needs a Willie', referring to the invaluable common sense that Whitelaw applied to all issues.

The problems that were to destroy her position were the **poll tax** and Britain's relations with Europe.

The Poll tax 1989–90

Key question
Why did the introduction of poll tax arouse such bitter controversy?

Key terms

Poll tax
A flat-rate levy to fund local services, to be paid by all the adults resident in the local area, not just owners of property; introduced into Scotland in 1989 and into England and Wales in 1990.

Hubris
Punishment for arrogance.

Adam Smith Institute
A Conservative 'think-tank', which challenged the idea that the state should redistribute resources in society by taxing the rich and providing for the poor; it argued that the free play of market forces was the best way of fulfilling people's needs.

Margaret Thatcher believed that the general public would continue to support her as she continued with her drive for accountability in local government. It was such thinking that led to the community charge, which was introduced into Scotland in 1989 and a year later into England and Wales. The poll tax, as it was better known, has been described as **hubris** and 'a reform too far'. Few issues in modern times have excited such public anger. Yet it was never intended to be so dramatic; it was meant to be a rationalising of the existing system of raising money through rates, which nearly everybody agreed was unfair. For, example a single pensioner living alone might well be charged the same rates as a household of four wage-earners living in a property of equal value. The plan was now to tax people not property.

The idea of a community charge or poll tax in place of the rates came originally from the **Adam Smith Institute**, which suggested that, since there would be 38 million poll-tax payers, compared with only 14 million ratepayers, payment for local services would be much more evenly and justly spread. Moreover, if everybody had to pay for local services then everybody would become much more conscious of the quality of the services provided.

Impressed by this reasoning Mrs Thatcher judged that the community charge would help make local authorities answerable to their 'customers', who would be the people now paying for the services. Her hope was that local electors would embrace the poll tax and then go on to vote out high-spending Labour councils and vote in responsible Conservative ones. This was a serious miscalculation. The opposite happened. The poll tax created fury in the country at large, provided a cause around which her opponents rallied, and alienated some of the Conservative Party's staunchest supporters.

Opposition from within the party: the 'one-nation Conservatives'

There were a number of Conservative MPs, Edward Heath and Michael Heseltine being the most prominent, who had become unhappy with Mrs Thatcher's approach. They argued that the government should use redistributive taxation to help the disadvantaged members of society. For these 'one-nation Conservatives', as they were called, the poll tax's main disadvantage was that it was a regressive tax; that is, as a flat rate levy it bore hardest on the poorest. They believed that the rioting in various English cities in the 1980s held a message (see page 122). Although the disturbances had complex causes, they could be interpreted, at least in part, as an expression of the disaffection of many people, particularly the young unemployed, from Thatcherite Britain.

Unfolding events showed that the government had misjudged the situation. The financial merits that the poll tax might have had meant little to a public who saw it as a new tax imposed by a grasping government intent on trapping everybody in the same net. The government did, in fact, list a large number of exemptions from payment for poorer people, but these concessions were lost in the furore that the tax aroused. Opposition to the charge when it was introduced into Scotland in 1989 and England and Wales in 1990 was immediate and organised. Millions of people refused or avoided payment.

Opposition spreads

The significant feature of all this was that opposition came from across the political spectrum. The far left group, Militant Tendency, which had caused such trouble to the Labour Party in the early 1980s (see page 139), revived itself to form the All-Britain Anti-Poll Tax Federation. The Scottish National Party (SNP) ran a successful 'can't pay, won't pay' campaign. Although the Labour Party and the Liberals did not openly encourage non-payment, they lost no time in savaging the government on the issue.

More disturbing for Mrs Thatcher was the reaction of many in her own party. She had had a forewarning of this in 1988 when several Conservative backbench rebellions against the poll tax had occurred, the most worrying arising from an amendment by Michael Mates to modify the proposed tax in the interests of 'fairness'. When the charge came into force in England in March 1990, it was on average double the original estimate. At this, even the respectable middle classes, previously Margaret Thatcher's strongest allies, began to protest. The most serious disturbance came with a violent anti-poll tax demonstration in London's Trafalgar Square on 31 March.

The cost of collection

A further irony was that, owing to the resistance it aroused, the poll tax cost two-and-a-half times more to collect than the rates had. In an effort to keep down poll tax levels, the government 'charge-capped' a number of authorities (mostly Labour, but also some Conservative). This involved compelling them to reduce their budgets even if it meant cutting services, a result that stood on its head the original notion of improving local government services in the interest of the 'customer'. Critics had strong grounds for asserting that the whole exercise had been aimed not at encouraging greater local democracy but at imposing the will of the central government on the local authorities. The poll tax was withdrawn in 1991, and substituted by a new council tax, based on the value of a home within eight assessment bands.

Key question
What was Thatcher trying to achieve in her struggles over Europe?

Margaret Thatcher and Europe

When Margaret Thatcher came into office in 1979 she had been confronted by the record of Britain's poor economic performance in the 1970s, caused in part by the difficult adjustments that had had to be made on entering the EEC. She later claimed that she had not been initially anti-EEC, but, when she realised how much waste and inefficiency there was in the Brussels bureaucracy and how much Britain was disadvantaged, she felt compelled to speak out. The centralising, bureaucratic character of Europe ran counter to the revolution she was trying to bring about in Britain. Her main concerns were:

- Protectionism, the principle on which Europe operated, was outmoded in an age of economic globalism.
- Europe was obsessed with a dated concept of centralisation when that polity was clearly collapsing in the wider world (e.g. in the Soviet Union).
- The disparity between the budget payments made by the separate member states rewarded the inefficient nations and penalised the efficient and productive ones.

The issue of federalism

Mrs Thatcher's response was to emphasise the virtues of national sovereignty and free enterprise. She was also disturbed at a deeper level by the threat that European federalism held for Britain:

- She stressed how young the European institutions were; none of them pre-dated 1945 whereas Britain's governmental system had evolved over centuries.
- She felt that Europe could easily become the prey of creeping socialism and bureaucracy because in the final analysis the EEC was not subject to genuine democratic control.

These fears were not new. They had shaped the attitude of both Labour and Conservative Parties as early as the 1950s when the first moves were taken towards European union (see page 62). What made Margaret Thatcher appear particularly hostile was her manner. She carried over into her discussions with European ministers the adversarial style of debate which she had learned in British politics. But this was out of place in a European context. Direct confrontation was rare between European ministers and officials. They tended to get things done by compromise, concession and private agreements. Such techniques irritated Mrs Thatcher and she was not reluctant to show it.

The issue of Britain's budgetary contributions

The ground on which Mrs Thatcher chose to defend the British position most strongly was that of Britain's disproportionately high payments to the EEC budget. In her memoirs, she defined her position:

> Britain's unique trading pattern made her a very large net contributor to the EC [European Community] budget – so large that the situation was indeed unacceptable. We traditionally imported far more from non-EC countries than did other community members, particularly of foodstuffs. This meant that we paid more into the community budget in the form of tariffs than they did. By contrast, the community budget itself is heavily biased towards supporting farmers through the common agricultural policy. ... The British economy is less dependent on agriculture than that of most other community countries; consequently we receive less in subsidy than they do.
>
> (*The Downing Street Years* by Margaret Thatcher, 1993)

Her battling had some success, the EC reluctantly authorising a reduction in Britain's budget payments. But Thatcher's dislike of the centralising process within Europe remained. She was at her most forthright in attacking the notions of **Jacques Delors** whom she regarded as typical of the unelected and unaccountable bureaucrats who were making the rules for Europe. In a landmark speech in Bruges in Belgium in 1988 she condemned 'the erosion of democracy by centralisation and bureaucracy':

> **Jacques Delors 1925–**
> EU President from 1985 to 1995 and a strong federalist.
>
> *Key figure*

> It is ironic that just when those countries, such as the Soviet Union, which have tried to run everything from the centre, are learning that success depends on dispersing power and decisions away from the centre, some in the community seem to want to move in the opposite direction. We have not successfully rolled back the frontiers of the state in Britain only to see them reimposed at a European level, with a Brussels super-state exercising a new dominance from Brussels.

Her speech was widely regarded as a rallying cry to all those who wished to prevent the absorption of national identities into a centralising Europe. It was a piece of populism; she was trying to appeal over the heads of Europe's bureaucrats to the ordinary people in France and Germany as well as to the British.

> Mrs Thatcher's Bruges speech: 1988
>
> Single European Act: 1986
>
> *Key dates*

Britain's deeper absorption into Europe

Yet, despite her fighting words, the great paradox was that it was Mrs Thatcher who presided over the process by which Britain was drawn ever closer into Europe. It was she who in 1986 accepted the Single European Act, which marked the biggest step towards a centralised Europe that had yet been taken. The main terms of the Act were:

- The signatory countries committed themselves to closer monetary and political union.
- The principle of supra-nationality (the subordination of individual member states to the EU) was established.
- The right of individual member states to veto majority decisions was abolished.

The exchange rate mechanism

Key term

ERM
Exchange rate mechanism. A precursor to monetary union within the EU.

Key dates

UK joined the ERM: 1990

Howe's resignation speech: 1990

Margaret Thatcher was also in office when Britain agreed to enter the **ERM** in October 1990. She had been told by her financial experts that it would provide a means of fighting inflation. In the event it did the opposite and in 1992 a monetary crisis obliged Britain to withdraw from the ERM (see page 165).

Mrs Thatcher claimed later that she had been misled into entering the ERM in 1990 by her former Chancellor of the Exchequer, Nigel Lawson, and her Foreign Secretary, Geoffrey Howe. Both ministers were to play an important role in the weakening of Thatcher's position as Prime Minister and party leader. In 1989 Lawson had resigned when he found that the Prime Minister was taking more notice of Alan Walters, whom she had appointed her special economic adviser, than she was of him as Chancellor. Howe, a pro-European, made a similar charge, claiming that the Prime Minister's aggressive anti-Europeanism was distorting his attempts as Foreign Secretary to smooth Britain's entry into the ERM.

On 31 October 1990, on Mrs Thatcher's return from a top-level European meeting in Rome where she had openly declared that Britain would never join the single currency, she stated emphatically to the Commons:

> The President of the Commission, M. Delors, said at this conference that he wanted the European Parliament to be the democratic body of the community, he wanted the Commission to be the Executive, and he wanted the Council of Ministers to be the Senate. No, No, No!

Howe's momentous speech, November 1990

It was in the wake of this that Howe, feeling his position had been made untenable, resigned. In his resignation speech in the Commons on 13 November 1990, he revealed the serious divisions within the Conservative Party over Europe. Those who witnessed it said the speech took its power from its understatement. Read in Howe's characteristically flat unemotional tones, which expressed sorrow rather than anger, it amounted to a devastating criticism of the Prime Minister for her obstructive attitude towards European development, and her undermining of his position. In a cricketing metaphor, he likened himself to a batsman arriving at the wicket only to find that his bat had been broken by the team captain. Howe's measured criticism of Margaret Thatcher proved devastating. It was the prelude to the leadership struggle that led to her resignation in November 1990.

The fall of Margaret Thatcher

Given the anger and disappointment aroused by the government's inept handling of the poll tax, it was no surprise that the Conservatives lost all the four by-elections held in 1989 and 1990. In April 1990, opinion polls showed that Labour had gained a 20-point lead over the Conservatives. The polls also revealed that Mrs Thatcher's personal popularity rating was lower than at any other time in her 11 years as Prime Minister. Such developments led a growing number in her party to question whether they could win the next general election if she were still their leader. This feeling was intensified by the disagreements within the Cabinet over the economy and Europe, as evidenced by the Lawson and Howe resignations.

It was in this atmosphere that Michael Heseltine, who had been bitter towards the Prime Minister ever since the 1986 Westland affair (see page 136), decided in November to mount an open challenge for the leadership. Mrs Thatcher had easily survived a challenge in 1989 when a pro-European backbencher, Sir Anthony Meyer, had formally stood against her. Yet the fact that 33 MPs voted against her and 25 others abstained suggested to some, including Heseltine, that her popularity was beginning to wane and that a heavyweight in the party, such as he, might be able to unseat her should the opportunity arise.

The leadership contest, November 1990

The poll tax and the Lawson and Howe resignations appeared to have provided that opportunity. Heseltine announced his candidacy for the leadership of the party. Although in the ensuing contest Margaret Thatcher won the first ballot by 52 votes she regarded the narrowness of the margin as evidence that she had lost the confidence of two out of five of the Conservative MPs. She took an individual sounding of her Cabinet colleagues. With a few exceptions, they all told her, some openly weeping, that her time was up. So, she withdrew from the second ballot and announced that she would resign as soon as her successor was chosen. By the time the second ballot was held John Major and Douglas Hurd had entered the race. This ended Heseltine's chances. He had gone a long way to removing Mrs Thatcher only to find that the majority of the parliamentary party did not really want him. They preferred the stolid John Major to the flamboyant Michael Heseltine.

The Conservative Party had decided that after 11 years of Margaret Thatcher they wanted a safer, even if a much duller, leader. Mrs Thatcher felt betrayed. She had not, she said, been dismissed by a vote of Parliament, still less by the people at an

Key dates

Leadership challenge of Anthony Meyer defeated: 1989

Mrs Thatcher resigned after failing to win leadership contest: 1990

John Major became Prime Minister: 1990

Table 5.1: Conservative Party leadership election results 1990

Date	Candidates and no. of votes		
20 November	Michael Heseltine: 152	Margaret Thatcher: 204	
22 November	Prime Minister announced she would resign		
27 November	Michael Heseltine: 131	John Major: 185	Douglas Hurd: 56

election, but by the ganging up against her of the leading Conservative MPs. 'It is something I will never forget and never forgive.'

Summary diagram: The fall of Margaret Thatcher 1990

Reasons for Thatcher's fall in 1990

- The poll tax crisis aroused fierce reactions over a wide cross-section of the population
- The economic recession of 1987 had begun to bite by 1990
- The rebellion over Europe led by Geoffrey Howe proved devastating
- After 11 years in office Thatcher was losing her political touch
- Leading conservatives believed that they could not win the next election with her as leader
- All four by-elections between 1989 and 1990 were lost by the Conservatives
- Opinion polls indicated that Thatcher's popularity had dropped to its lowest point since she became Prime Minister in 1979

Key question
Was Thatcherism a creative or destructive force in British politics and society?

2 | Margaret Thatcher's Legacy

The bitterness and recrimination that accompanied Mrs Thatcher's resignation in November 1990 did not alter the fact that her period in office had been of huge significance. She had changed the political, economic and social agenda of British politics. Deeply controversial though her policies were, the governments that came after her, those of John Major (1990–7) and Tony Blair (1997–2007), were profoundly affected by what she had done. It is worth listing the chief features of Thatcherism since all subsequent governments followed policies that were either a continuation of or a reaction against it:

- the abandonment of consensus politics
- replacing Keynesianism with the free market
- reducing the power of the state and giving greater opportunity for people to live their lives without government interference
- limiting the power of the trade unions
- making local government answer more directly to people's needs
- restoring the notion of social accountability, the idea that effort should be rewarded and lack of effort penalised.

The impact Thatcherism had made was thoughtfully described in the 1990s by two voices, one from the left and one from the right. Tony Benn observed that 'the Prime Ministers who are remembered are those who think and teach, and not many do. Mrs Thatcher influenced the thinking of a generation.' Patrick Minford, an economist and admirer of Thatcher, suggested:

The dozen years since Mrs Thatcher gained power in 1979 have constituted a peaceful revolution in the way the British economy is organised. Virtually no area of activity has remained untouched by the drive to reinstate market forces and reduce government intervention.

(*The Supply Side Revolution in Britain* by Patrick Minford, 1991)

It is true, of course, that Mrs Thatcher did not achieve all her aims. Her mistakes over the poll tax, when she misjudged the attitude of ordinary people, showed that her **populist** instinct could seriously let her down. There are also many fascinating paradoxes about her; what she wanted was sometimes contradicted by what she did. There are four particular examples:

Populist
A way of appealing directly to ordinary people that bypasses normal party politics.

- She intended to reduce taxes but in fact Britain's tax bill went up under her leadership (see page 135).
- Despite her determination to cut government spending, when she went out of office public expenditure was at record high levels, and in 1992 the government was having to borrow heavily to finance a Public Sector Borrowing Requirement of nearly £30 billion. This was largely because her policies had led to unemployment and thereby increased the government's need to borrow to pay for social security and other welfare benefits.
- She promised to reduce the power of central government but in practice broadened and increased it, there being more government departments and more civil servants in 1990 than there had been in 1979.
- She appeared to be anti-European but she took Britain deeper into Europe (see page 152).

'A woman but not a sister'

Feminists have also pointed to another paradox. Some of Mrs Thatcher's strongest critics were women, who complained that she was 'a woman but not a sister', a reference to her unwillingness to support female causes. She certainly did little to promote women in politics, appointing only one woman to her Cabinet, Linda Chalker, as Minister for Overseas Development in 1986. It has been suggested that this was because as the lone woman she wanted to exploit her femininity among her male colleagues, free of competition from other females. A weightier charge is that in 11 years of government she made no effort to introduce structural changes to advance the role of women in politics and society.

Against that, it might be said that in the end what really mattered historically about Margaret Thatcher was not what she did but what she was. In 1966, only nine years before she became party leader, she had been one of only seven women Conservative MPs out of a total of 266. For a woman to lead a political party for 15 years, to be Prime Minister for 11, and during that time to be acknowledged internationally as an outstanding stateswoman were extraordinary achievements. She had successfully stormed the fortress of male dominance. After her, things would never be the same again.

Thatcherism and social attitudes

Mrs Thatcher's disinclination to support broad movements like feminism was consistent with her idea that social responsibility was an individual matter not a group affair. The rights of the

Key term

'If you want to stay living round here you're going to need loadsamoney!' A mocking comment on the **yuppy** world created by Thatcher's economic policies. The scene is set in London's dockland area, which in the 1980s was redeveloped as an expensive residential area. In the cartoon Mrs Thatcher is behaving in the manner of the character 'Loadsamoney', an aggressive yuppy, created by the television comedian Harry Enfield. How accurate is this depiction of the Prime Minister's financial and social aims?

Key term

Yuppy (or yuppie) Young upwardly mobile professional person.

individual and the family should take precedence over abstract notions of social good. In her social attitudes she was much more of a Victorian Liberal then a modern Conservative. She often expressed admiration for what she called 'Victorian virtues'. The wish to restrict the power of the state and to prevent the irresponsible spending of public money were key aspects of her approach. It was false sentiment to keep systems or institutions in being and spend public money on them once they had become wasteful and expensive.

'There's no such thing as society'

Margaret Thatcher aroused a storm when, in an interview printed in a woman's magazine in October 1987, she remarked, 'there's no such thing as society'. Her critics seized on this as evidence of her lack of compassion and her wish to encourage unbridled individualism. The passionately anti-Thatcher newspaper, *The Guardian*, reprinted the interview on its front page. Opponents said that her statement illustrated why she was willing to cut government spending on social welfare. She defended herself by quoting how her statement had continued:

> There are individual men and women, and there are families. And no government can do anything except through people, and people must look to themselves first. It's our duty to look after ourselves and then to look after our neighbour.

She claimed that her purpose had in fact been to emphasise self-reliance and the individual's responsibility towards society. She was defending the family as the basic social unit. In her memoirs published in the early 1990s Mrs Thatcher described the social ills she had had in mind:

> Welfare benefits, distributed with little or no consideration of their effects on behaviour, encouraged illegitimacy, facilitated the break-down of families, and replaced incentives favouring work and self-reliance with perverse encouragement for idleness and cheating.
> (*The Downing Street Years* by Margaret Thatcher, 1993)

It might be thought that such convictions would have made her government eager to reform the welfare state. It is true that certain steps were taken. To tackle what Mrs Thatcher called the 'why work?' problem, her reference to the **poverty trap**, the government introduced a measure taxing short-term income relief. It also imposed a five per cent cut in unemployment, sickness, injury, maternity and invalidity benefits.

However, the government's public-spending cuts were largely restricted to her first administration in the early 1980s. This was because unemployment remained so high during her 11 years in office that it necessitated not a decrease but a major increase in unemployment payments. The remarkable fact is that Mrs Thatcher's governments spent more on the NHS than any previous administration. As Figure 5.1 shows, between 1977 and 1994, government expenditure on social security and welfare rose by 60 per cent in real terms.

Poverty trap
The dilemma facing the low paid; if they continued working they were penalised by being taxed, which reduced their net income to a level little higher than if they simply drew unemployment benefit.

Key term

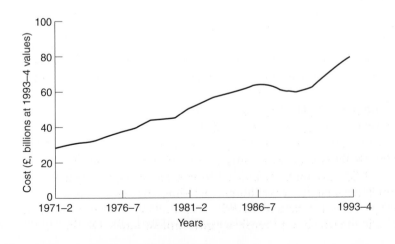

Figure 5.1: A graph showing the real growth in social security benefit expenditure 1971–94.

How greatly the Conservatives under Margaret Thatcher and her successor John Major were committed to financial provision for welfare services can be gauged from Tables 5.2 and 5.3, which illustrate the order of priorities in benefit provision and government spending.

Table 5.2: Principal non-contributory benefits paid by the state

Benefit	Target beneficiary
Income support	For those of working age who are unable to work, or to those who have inadequate pensions. It has been called 'the safety net of the welfare state'. In the late 1990s income support was costing over £13 billion annually
Invalidity benefit	For those medically certified as being physically or mentally unable to work. Between 1982 and 1998 the number of recipients trebled from 0.6 to 1.8 million, at a cost of £5.2 billion per year
Housing benefit	Rent and rate rebates for those on inadequate incomes
Child benefit (previously called family allowance)	A weekly amount paid to parents (usually the mother) for each child. This was a universal payment, i.e. there was no means testing. By 1998 this was costing £6 billion per year
Family income supplement	Provides a cash benefit for poorer families with children

Table 5.3: Government expenditure 1993–4

Area	Amount (£, billions)	Percentage of total expenditure*
Social Security	65.0	26.6
Environment	38.9	15.9
NHS	29.9	12.2
Local government	24.2	9.9
Defence	23.5	9.6
Scotland	13.9	5.6
Education	9.5	3.9
Northern Ireland	8.4	3.5
Wales	7.2	3.0
Foreign and overseas	6.5	2.7
Transport	6.4	2.6
Home Office	6.1	2.5
Employment	3.7	1.5
Trade and Industry	2.6	1.1
Agriculture	2.6	1.1

* Rounding means that the total does not add up to exactly 100 per cent.

Aspects of Thatcherism
Margaret Thatcher's unpopularity

Despite her government's large-scale welfare spending, Mrs Thatcher's 'no such thing as society' statement and her belief in public accountability largely explain her unpopularity in intellectual circles. Institutions, including universities, were subjected to the same demands of accountability as other areas of public life which were receiving government funds. On the grounds that her policies were undermining education, Oxford University, in a controversial gesture in 1983, voted to deny her the honorary degree that had traditionally been conferred on prime ministers.

There was a further aspect to this. Mrs Thatcher's distrust of those intellectuals who said much but did little made her the target of attacks from the 'chattering classes', a term denoting those broadsheet and television journalists who were strongly influenced by the 'welfarist' notions that had become the received thinking among social scientists. Such thinking had become an important part of the consensus that had dominated politics after 1945. In challenging that orthodoxy Mrs Thatcher aroused resentment among those academics and politicians who believed that the Beveridge Report and Keynesianism had become indispensable to Britain's social and economic well-being. Her questioning of these notions gave her an uncaring, hard-hearted image that damaged her reputation and lessened her popularity.

Foreign affairs

It is a remarkable fact that at the end of her period in government Mrs Thatcher was far more popular abroad than she was at home. This was because as a staunch anti-Communist, she had played no small role in bringing about the collapse of the Soviet Union and the end of the Cold War. Her populist instincts served her well in this regard. She sensed that Communism no longer represented the will of the people in those countries where Communist regimes were still in power. Although she was prepared 'to do business' with the Soviet Union in commercial matters and got on well personally with its leader, Mikhail Gorbachev, whom she met on a number of occasions, she never budged from her conviction that Communism as an ideology was the enemy of freedom.

'The iron lady'

As early as 1976 Margaret Thatcher's attitude had earned her the nickname 'the iron lady' in the Soviet press. The title was intended as a disparaging allusion to her opposition to Communism, but she delighted in it, viewing it as a recognition of her firmness of purpose. As Prime Minister, she made a number of visits to the Eastern bloc, including Poland, Hungary and the USSR itself. For many people in those countries Mrs Thatcher became a symbol of freedom. In Poland, for example, chapels and shrines were dedicated to her. This was principally because of her open support throughout the 1980s for 'Solidarity', the Polish trade union movement. Led by its chairman, Lech Walesa, Solidarity fought a running battle with Poland's Communist government, demanding recognition as an independent movement free from control by the authorities. Its successful resistance to attempts to crush it was a major factor in encouraging the anti-Communist, anti-Soviet movements throughout the Eastern bloc that culminated in the '**velvet revolution**' of the late 1980s.

Key question
How did Margaret Thatcher acquire the title 'the iron lady'?

Velvet revolution
In the face of popular nationalist opposition, the USSR abandoned its authority over the countries of Eastern Europe without a fight; this culminated in the collapse of the USSR itself in 1991.

Key term

There was some shaking of heads in Britain. Critics asked how the Prime Minister could reconcile being pro-trade union abroad and anti-trade union at home. Defenders suggested that it was all a matter of freedom; she was against trade unions when their actions threatened liberty, but for them when what they did promoted it.

Prime Minister Thatcher and President Reagan

Margaret Thatcher's powerfully expressed anti-Communism chimed well with the prevailing view in the United States. It so happened that her leadership of Britain in the 1980s coincided with the presidency of Ronald Reagan. The two leaders were soul mates. Reagan had been greatly impressed, as indeed had most Americans, by Thatcher's resolute handling of the Falklands War in 1982. Their liking for each other and their shared attitudes personalised the special relationship between Britain and the USA. The modern British historian Peter Clarke has neatly conveyed the personal, ideological and economic bonds between them:

> Nowhere was Thatcher more warmly received than in the USA. An idealised USA was held up by Thatcherites as a model of society based on the free market, minimal government, anti-Communism, the mighty dollar and Almighty God. After Ronald Reagan was elected President in 1980, Thatcher found a real ally, with her trenchant expositions of their common outlook complemented by his benignly bemused concurrence. This was indeed a special relationship which helped to inflate Thatcher's international standing.
>
> (*Hope and Glory Britain 1900–1990* by Peter Clarke, 1996)

While they might have disagreed over aspects of foreign policy, they were of one mind over the Cold War's big questions. They agreed that the West was fighting against the forces of evil and had to remain fully armed with nuclear weapons. One result of this was Britain's buying Trident missiles to replace the obsolete Polaris variety from the USA at an initial cost of £10 billion. In addition, Britain agreed in 1981 to allow the USA to install its Cruise missiles at the US airforce base at **Greenham Common** near Newbury, a decision that led to a major resurgence in the CND movement (see page 66).

While the left in both countries accused Reagan and Thatcher of crudely over-simplifying the issues, the effect of the Anglo-American unyielding front towards international Communism in the 1980s was to put great pressure on the Soviet Union, whose attempt to keep up in the **arms race** with the West exhausted it militarily and financially. This proved a major factor in the USSR's eventual disintegration in 1991. Thatcher had played a part in winning the Cold War for the West.

The special relationship that Thatcher had helped to renew was to prove a significant factor in the subsequent administrations of John Major and Tony Blair when Britain and the USA acted together in a number of critical international issues.

Key terms

Greenham Common
Became the site of a women's peace camp which picketed the US base from 1981 to 2000, a graphic example of the extraparliamentary protests against government policy that were a feature of late twentieth-century politics.

Arms race
In 1983 US President Reagan announced the development of a strategic defence initiative (popularly known as 'Star Wars') which when fully operational would give the USA complete protection against missile attack. This may have been exaggeration but it convinced the USSR that it could no longer keep pace with the West.

Photograph of a dinner at 10 Downing Street, held in honour of the US President in July 1988. It shows Reagan, Mrs Thatcher and George Shultz, the US Secretary of State. At the bottom of the picture Reagan had written: 'Dear Margaret – As you can see, I agree with every word you are saying. I always do. Warmest Friendship. Sincerely Ron.' Opponents of Thatcher and Reagan found such sentiments either comic or nauseating.

Summary diagram: Margaret Thatcher's legacy

Effects of Thatcherism

Political
- Had changed the political agenda by its challenging of the post-1945 consensus

Industrial
- Had legally restricted trade union powers

Economic
- Had challenged the Keynesian pattern of government – directed economic planning

Foreign affairs
- The iron lady committed to anti-Communism
- Heroine to Eastern bloc nationalists
- Special relationship renewed with USA
- Contributed to victory of West in the Cold War

Social
- Called for public accountability
- Called for individual responsibility: 'no such thing as society'

Paradoxes of Thatcherism

Aim:
to reduce taxes
Outcome:
UK's tax bill went up

Aim:
to cut government spending
Outcome:
expenditure increased to record levels

Aim:
to reduce the power of central government
Outcome:
more bureaucracy

Aim:
to resist European federalism
Outcome:
Britain taken deeper into Europe

Key question
How was John Major able to win the 1992 election?

3 | John Major's Government 1990–7

The path to Major's election victory in 1992

Margaret Thatcher had been the dominant political figure of her time, a leader capable of arousing both intense admiration and deep dislike. John Major was not in the same mould. For some this was his attraction. He did not have the abrasive, combative character of his predecessor. Yet personally likeable though he was, he was not an inspiring figure. Despite having held key ministries in the Thatcher government, he had not held them long enough to create a lasting impression. A satirical television puppet show, *Spitting Image*, portrayed him as a literally grey figure, boringly consumed with the unimportant details of life. This was a caricature but it did match the picture many people had of him. The historian John Keegan described the Major government as 'one of the dreariest administrations of the century'.

Key dates

Coalition forces liberated Kuwait: 1991

Citizen's Charter: 1991

Maastricht Treaty signed: 1992

The Gulf War 1991

Yet in one respect at least Major made an impressive debut. His conduct was statesmanlike during the crisis over Kuwait, when he co-operated effectively with the United States in creating a coalition invasion force. In 1991, this force, in keeping with UN resolutions, successfully ended the illegal occupation of Kuwait by the forces of Iraq's leader, Saddam Hussein. Major's decision to keep the opposition leaders, Neil Kinnock and Paddy Ashdown, informed on the key moves in the Gulf War won him considerable respect.

At home, knowing that an election had to be called within 18 months, Major made little attempt to modify the Thatcherite policies he had inherited. With only the slightest hint of criticism of his predecessor, he declared on taking office that he wanted to build 'a country that is at ease with itself'. The unpopular poll tax, which was already doomed before Thatcher had left office, was quietly withdrawn in 1991(see page 151), and in the same year Major announced that his government would base its approach on a new 'Citizen's Charter', which read as a watered down version of Thatcherism:

> The Citizen's Charter is about giving more power to the citizen. But citizenship is about our responsibilities – as parents for example, or as neighbours – as well as out entitlements. The Citizen's Charter is not a recipe for more state action; it is a testament to our belief in people's right to be informed and choose for themselves.
>
> (From 'The Citizen's Charter', 1991)

The Maastricht Treaty 1992

One issue over which the new Prime Minister did adopt a different approach from his predecessor was Europe. Major wished to show that he was a good European. He took a momentous step by signing up Britain to the Maastricht Treaty in February 1992, whose declared aim was 'to create an ever-closer union among the peoples of Europe'. His decision was to have long-lasting consequences (see page 198).

The main terms of the Maastricht Treaty were as follows:

- full European integration
- a common European foreign policy
- a common European defence policy
- a European Central Bank
- a single European currency, the euro, to be adopted by 1999: Britain obtained an opt-out clause, which it exercised in 1999
- the Treaty to come into effect in November 1993
- the European Community would become the European Union (EU).

The 1992 election

Until the week before polling day on 8 April 1992, it was generally assumed, even by some Conservatives, that, after 13 years in power, the government would lose. However, the Labour Party led by Neil Kinnock conducted a poorly judged campaign. Having in the early part of the campaign successfully promoted itself as the caring party, it assumed from the opinion polls that it was going to win. This was evident in an embarrassingly ill-conceived rally in Sheffield in the week before the election. Aping the razzamatazz style of American politics, the Labour campaigners put on an extravaganza with blaring music and announcements and spotlights picking out the members of the shadow Cabinet who walked to the platform through ranks of cheering admirers. The climax came with Neil Kinnock bounding up to the rostrum and exchanging with the audience cries of 'Right … well all right! … well all right!', as if he were at an American convention. Kinnock later reluctantly admitted that the triumphalism had been both premature and rather tasteless, although he disputed that it had lost Labour the election.

More seriously for Labour, it also got itself into a tangle by presenting a shadow budget that seemed to threaten large increases in taxation. John Major exploited this by literally standing on a soap-box and suggesting in a homely way that only the Conservatives could be trusted to run the economy. *The Sun* newspaper was sufficiently convinced to switch its support from Labour to Conservative. This defection to the Conservatives of one of the main leaders and shapers of popular opinion was a

Table 5.4: Election results 1992

Political party	No. of votes	No. of seats	Percentage of vote
Conservative	14,092,891	336	42.0
Labour	11,559,735	271	34.2
Liberal Democrats	5,999,384	20	17.9
Northern Irish parties	740,485	17	2.2
Plaid Cymru	154,439	4	0.5
Scottish Nationalists	629,552	3	1.9
Others	436,207	0	1.3

serious loss to Labour and explained the late and decisive swing to Major.

The result was much closer than in 1987. Labour increased its vote by 3.5 per cent and its number of seats from 229 to 271. But this was not enough to defeat the Conservatives who, despite losing 40 seats, still had a workable overall majority of 21.

Crises over Europe

Events soon challenged the notion that the Conservatives were in control of economic affairs. In late summer 1992, a crisis developed over the ERM. The ERM had been devised as a system for reducing inflation. This was to be done by creating parity between the various European currencies by pegging them to the value of the Deutschmark (DM), Europe's strongest currency, rather than let them find their market value. When Britain joined the ERM in 1990 (see page 153) the exchange value of the pound sterling had been DM2.95. This was unrealistically high and caused British exports to become over-priced.

Worse was to follow. In September 1992, international bankers, sensing that the pound sterling was overvalued, began to speculate against it on the money markets. The pound began to fall alarmingly. In a desperate attempt to maintain the pound at the level required by the ERM, the government resorted to desperate measures. These included Norman Lamont, the Chancellor of the Exchequer, raising interest levels from 10 to 15 per cent and selling off £30 billion's worth of Britain's foreign reserves to shore up sterling. It was all to no avail. The pressure on the pound was too great. Major's government did the only thing it could; on 16 September, known afterwards as 'Black Wednesday', it withdrew from the ERM.

The consequences of this withdrawal were as follows:

- Britain's case for becoming involved in European monetary union was weakened.
- The argument of the Eurosceptics against deeper integration with Europe was strengthened.
- The Conservatives' reputation for financial expertise was gravely damaged.
- Labour gained a 15-point lead in the opinion polls.
- Major's authority as Prime Minister was undermined.
- A deepening of the Cabinet split between **Eurosceptics** (principally Peter Lilley, Michael Portillo and Michael Howard) and pro-Europeans (principally Kenneth Clarke, Michael Heseltine and Douglas Hurd).

Remarkably, the longer term economic effects proved far less disastrous. Indeed, some observers have called the event 'White Wednesday', a reference to the fact that, freed from its artificial ties, the pound began to recover. By 1996, the exchange rate of the pound was DM3.00, a higher rate than when the pound was in the ERM. What was true of finance was also true of the economy overall. Britain's growth rate outperformed that of its European partners, as Table 5.5 indicates. It prompted the

Key question
What problems arose for the Major government over Europe?

Key date
UK withdrawal from ERM: 1992

Key term
Eurosceptics
Those who doubted that the UK's closer integration into Europe would serve British interests.

Eurosceptics to enquire yet again what precisely Britain was supposed to get from being in the European Community. Norman Lamont later remarked 'I know of no single benefit which has come to Britain solely because of its membership of Europe.'

Table 5.5: Comparative growth rates 1995–2005

Country	Percentage growth
France	1.5
Germany	2.0
Italy	1.3
EU average	2.0
Britain	2.7

However, these longer term effects were obviously of no immediate benefit to Major's government. The truth was that Black Wednesday left its mark on the remainder of his administration down to 1997. A divided Cabinet, greater uncertainty about Europe, a public who now doubted the government's economic financial competence, and a Labour Party recovering its political loss of confidence; these were the legacies of the ERM crisis.

The struggle over the Maastricht Treaty 1993

John Major's signing up to the Maastricht Treaty in 1992 (see page 163) had been only the beginning of the process. To become binding on Britain it had to be ratified by Parliament. The ERM fiasco had made this extremely problematical. Many in Major's own party, and a significant number of Labour MPs, were so concerned over the loss of sovereignty entailed by the Maastricht Treaty that they voted against the ratifying bills when they were introduced. The climax came in July 1993 when organised resistance by the **Eurorebels** defeated a key Bill necessary for the Treaty to come into effect in November 1993.

Having committed his government to Maastricht, Major was not prepared to accept the verdict of the Commons. In a hurried move, he reintroduced the proposal to accept the Maastricht Treaty and made it part of a formal vote of confidence in the government. In this way the proposal was forced through, since for the Eurorebel Conservative MPs to have voted against it would have brought down the government. But the desperate means Major had used gave strength to the growing number of Eurosceptics within and outside Parliament who claimed that Britain was being railroaded into European integration. They asserted that Europe and its supporters seemed frightened of democracy.

Calls for a national referendum, such as those held in Ireland, Denmark and France, were rejected by the government on the grounds that a referendum was 'unconstitutional'. The real reason was that the government knew it would lose a referendum, opinion polls indicating that the majority of the population were

Key dates

Euro rebellion over ratification of Maastricht Treaty: 1993

Major won party leadership election: 1995

Key term

Eurorebels
A large group of Conservative MPs, openly led by Bill Cash, and supported by most of the party's Eurosceptics, who fought against the ratification of the Maastricht Treaty.

Subsidiarity
The principle that in matters of special concern to a particular member state, that state should have the right to bypass European decisions.

Genocide
The planned extermination of a people or a race.

on the Eurosceptic side. Having been tricked into voting 'yes' in the 1975 referendum (see page 104), the British people were unlikely to be fooled again. Major's success later in 1992 in obtaining the European Community's agreement to the principle of **subsidiarity** had done little to lessen Eurosceptic fears.

Although the Labour Party (now led by John Smith following Neil Kinnock's resignation after the election defeat) officially accepted Maastricht, there was no doubt it derived great satisfaction from the government's embarrassments. But it was the opposition within his own party that most offended Major. In an unguarded moment, he was recorded describing his critics within the Cabinet as 'bastards'. Although he would not give names when further questioned about this, it was widely assumed that he was referring to Peter Lilley, Michael Portillo, John Redwood and Michael Howard. Clearly, a Prime Minister who does not have the full support of his Cabinet and party is in a very difficult position and this was the case for Major throughout his period of office, which ran its full term until 1997.

In July 1995, in an effort to end the backstabbing to which he felt he was continually subjected, Major called a leadership election, which he easily won, defeating John Redwood by 218 to 89. But small though the vote against Major was, if the 22 abstentions were added in, it showed that over 100 members were not fully committed to him as leader. This unwelcome fact burdened him throughout the remainder of his term as Prime Minister.

Foreign affairs
Bosnia 1995

NATO intervention in Bosnia: 1995

Problems for Major also arose in foreign affairs. A bitter and complex war civil war was fought in the early 1990s in the troubled Balkans where the break-up of the former federal state of Yugoslavia had left a set of fiercely competing national, religious and ethnic groups. Fighting had become so vicious in Bosnia between 1992 and 1995 that the international powers became involved in order to prevent the **genocide** of the largely Muslim Bosnians by the largely Christian Serb forces under Ratko Mladić. Douglas Hurd, who had been Foreign Secretary since 1989, had irritated the Americans by opposing European or US intervention. Much to the annoyance of President Clinton's administration, Hurd and other European ministers had previously declined to support the idea of NATO involvement on the grounds that outside interference would simply prolong the struggle.

European reluctance was eventually overcome and Britain contributed to a massive series of NATO aerial attacks on Serbian forces in August and September 1995. Over 3500 sorties were flown. 'Operation Deliberate Force', as it was code-named, brought the Serbs to the negotiating table. In the Dayton peace agreement signed in December 1995, the warring parties agreed to keep to certain designated areas, which were to be monitored by UN and NATO forces. Major had the satisfaction of being one of the signatories when the Dayton agreement was ratified in Paris in December by the major powers, the USA, Britain, France, Russia and Germany.

Major's satisfaction was somewhat diminished by a later development when it was alleged that Hurd's slowness to move against Serbia had been because of his commercial links with that country. The charge was largely based on the revelation that Hurd had subsequently gone to Serbia to meet Slobodan Milošović, the Serbian leader. In fact Hurd was representing the NatWest bank, a position he had taken up when he was no longer Foreign Secretary. However, some of the mud stuck. There was even a Bosnian accusation that Hurd had been complicit in the genocide. This may have been an absurd accusation, but the overall impression given to observers was that the government had not come well out of the episode.

'Sleaze'

In 1993 John Major, seeking a unifying theme for the nation, had appealed for a return to basics: 'It is time', he said, 'to get back to basics; to self-discipline and respect for the law; to consideration for others'. No doubt sincerely meant, his call for moral improvement came back to haunt him. By the time the general election came in 1997 his position had been gravely weakened by a press campaign determined to expose leading Conservatives as being guilty of sexual scandal corruption or '**sleaze**'. Among the most damaging of the many scandals uncovered were:

- The Heritage Minister, David Mellor, resigned in 1992 over an affair with a Spanish actress, which, according to *The People* newspaper, involved his wearing the Chelsea football team's strip when making love.
- The Environment Minister, Tim Yeo, resigned in 1994 after it was revealed that an affair he had had with a Conservative local councillor had produced a 'love child'.
- In 1994, a promising young Conservative MP, Stephen Milligan, accidentally throttled himself to death while engaging in an act of sexual self-strangulation.
- In 1994 the *Guardian* accused Neil Hamilton, a Corporate Affairs Minister, of having received brown envelopes stuffed with money from Mohamed Al Fayed, the billionaire owner of Harrod's store, who hoped to gain special commercial favours in return. Hamilton denied the allegations and a series of libel actions followed. In the 1997 election, Martin Bell, a BBC correspondent, stood as an independent against Hamilton in Tatton constituency with the calculated aim of highlighting the lack of probity in government circles. The Labour and Liberal Democrat parties agreed not to field a candidate, which resulted in Bell's winning by a majority of 11,000. The media attention given to the campaign was a great embarrassment to Major's government.

Key term

Sleaze
The term covered such activities as 'cash for questions', the practice whereby, in return for payment, MPs asked questions in the Commons that were intended to promote the interests of particular commercial companies.

Key date

Election victory for Labour: 1997

This mixture of the laughable, the disreputable and the tragic spread a lengthening shadow over Major's years in office and contributed significantly to his losing all the by-elections held during his time. The lowest point was reached in the general election of 1997 when his party suffered the heaviest defeat that any government had undergone in the twentieth century.

The following are some of the reasons for the Conservatives' defeat in 1997:

- the continuous divisions within the Cabinet and the Conservative Party between Eurosceptics and pro-Europeans
- the government's enforced withdrawal from the ERM undermined the Conservatives' reputation for responsible financial management
- the public's distaste for the unseemly squabbles over the undemocratic ratification of the Maastricht Treaty in 1992
- Major's uninspiring leadership, given that he was never able to win the total loyalty of his colleagues and party
- the Conservatives had already lost all the by-elections held since 1990
- throughout the 1990–7 period, the government had a very small majority, which had the inhibiting effect of making it do deals with the minority parties such as the Ulster Unionists
- the cumulative destructive effect of a long series of sexual and financial scandals involving government ministers and Conservative MPs
- the recovery in strength and confidence of the new Labour Party under Tony Blair, who presented a far more youthful and lively image than the Prime Minister (see page 172).

To the list should be added two other influential factors. With hindsight it can be seen that his unexpected victory in 1992 had been a mixed blessing for John Major. Long periods in government have a dispiriting and wearying effect on the holders. It might have been better for the Conservatives to have been defeated then, after 13 years in office. It would have given them a chance to refresh themselves. But the government ran its full term to 1997, leading to its facing mounting problems particularly within the Conservative Party itself. It was a tired and in many ways self-doubting party that went into the election of 1997.

The Conservatives had clearly outstayed their time. The 1997 result was a in a sense a delayed reaction against Thatcherism. Although it was seven years since Mrs Thatcher had been Prime Minister, the shattering defeat of the Conservatives in 1997 was, arguably, a rejection not just of Major's government but of 18 years of Thatcherite Conservatism.

Yet the results shown in Table 5.6 also offer a graphic example of how the imbalance in the electoral system now heavily favoured the Labour Party. There was a remarkable parallel with the great Labour victory of 1945. Despite its overwhelming number of seats, Labour was a minority government. The

Table 5.6: Election results 1997

Political party	No. of votes	No. of seats	Percentage of vote
Labour	13,518,167	418	44.4
Conservative	9,600,943	165	31.4
Liberal Democrats	5,242,947	46	17.2
Northern Irish parties	492,992	14	1.5
Scottish Nationalists	621,550	6	2.0
Plaid Cymru	161,030	4	0.5

disparity that the electoral system had produced is evident in the following figures:

- for each seat Labour won, it had polled 32,340 votes
- for each seat the Conservative Party won, it had polled 58,187 votes
- for each seat the Liberal Party won, it had polled 113,977.

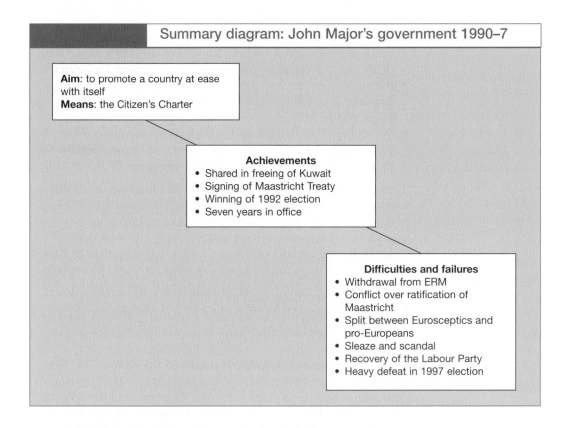

Summary diagram: John Major's government 1990–7

Aim: to promote a country at ease with itself
Means: the Citizen's Charter

Achievements
- Shared in freeing of Kuwait
- Signing of Maastricht Treaty
- Winning of 1992 election
- Seven years in office

Difficulties and failures
- Withdrawal from ERM
- Conflict over ratification of Maastricht
- Split between Eurosceptics and pro-Europeans
- Sleaze and scandal
- Recovery of the Labour Party
- Heavy defeat in 1997 election

4 | New Labour 1994–9

Tony Blair as New Labour leader

On the sudden death of John Smith in May 1994, Margaret Beckett briefly became the caretaker leader of the Labour Party prior to the election of Tony Blair in July. It was later claimed by various commentators that shortly before the leadership election

Key question
In what sense was New Labour new?

Key date

Tony Blair became Labour Party leader: 1994

Blair had done a deal with his chief rival, Gordon Brown, the shadow Chancellor of the Exchequer. The story was that at a meeting at the Granita restaurant in London, Brown had agreed not to stand against Blair in the leadership contest thus handing Blair the title since the only other contender, John Prescott, lacked sufficient support in the party. Blair, in return, agreed to give Brown a wholly free hand as Chancellor once Labour was in government; in addition, Blair promised to pass on the premiership to Brown no later than 2003. Although both men denied having made any such deal, the story was widely believed and certainly provides a credible explanation of their strained political relationship during Blair's 10 years as Prime Minister after 1997.

Despite its defeat in the 1992 general election, there were clear signs that the Labour Party's move away from the left, begun under Neil Kinnock (leader 1983–92) and continued by John Smith (leader 1992–4), had begun to find favour with the electorate. Tony Blair extended the process by which the party distanced itself from the dated policies that had deterred rather than encouraged support from the general public. As leader of the opposition during the final three years of Major's government, he skilfully and wittily played upon the tired character of the Conservatives, who had been too long in government and who had become associated with corruption and scandal.

Blair complemented his attack on the government with the development of his programme for **New Labour**. The chief features of this were:

Key term

New Labour
Began as a slogan at the 1994 Labour Party conference, the first held with Tony Blair as leader, and became the title by which the party was known from then on.

- Nationalisation (public ownership, see page 16) was to be abandoned as a party objective.
- Labour MPs and candidates were to avoid using the term 'socialist' in their public statements so as not to frighten the electorate.
- The City and the business world were to be wooed by the promise that capitalism would be safe in New Labour's hands.
- The legal restrictions on trade unions were to be maintained.
- Accepting that class-based politics were no longer relevant in Britain, New Labour would no longer present its policies in terms of class struggle.

These policies were intended primarily to appeal to middle-class Britain where the bulk of the electorate was to be found. By both avoiding extremes and adopting progressive ideas, New Labour hoped to win over uncertain Conservative and floating voters. It was a recognition that the old working class, which historically had been the main support of Labour, had greatly shrunk with the decline of large-scale industry in Britain. It was also an implicit acceptance that Thatcherism had made changes that could not be undone.

Profile: Tony Blair 1953–

1953   – Born in Edinburgh
1966–71 – Attended Fettes public school in Edinburgh
1972–5   – Studied law at Oxford University
1975–83 – Became active in left-wing politics
1983   – Elected as an MP for Sedgefield, near Durham
1994   – Became Labour Party leader
1997   – Became Prime Minister
2007   – Resigned after 10 years in office

Tony Blair came from a Scottish background. He was educated at
public school and at Oxford. A lawyer by training, he entered
politics, became an MP in 1983 and a shadow Cabinet member in
1988. As a young politician he was a member of CND and took a
left-wing stance on most issues. However, once in Parliament, he
moved to a centre position and aligned himself with Neil
Kinnock's programme for modernising the party. A great asset in
his rapid rise up the party ladder was his youthful style and
appearance. He looked younger than his years and his buoyant
personality was greatly to his advantage when contrasted with the
greyness of John Major. It was certainly a factor in Labour's
crushing victory in the 1997 election.

Not long after the election, at the time of Princess Diana's
death in a car crash in Paris in August 1997, Blair showed his
populist gift for assessing the public mood by touchingly saying
the things about her that most people wanted to hear.

In 2001, after four years in office, Blair was riding high in the
opinion polls. His own and his government's popularity rating
was 20 points ahead of William Hague, the Conservative leader
(1997–2001). Sceptics suggested that his popularity had been
earned too easily, that he was liked for his style rather than the
content of his policies, and that he relied too greatly on his public
relations team, which tried to make him appear to be all things to
all men. Blair watchers noted that his style and even his accent
changed to match the particular audience he was facing. He
declared on one television chat show that he wanted to be
thought of 'as a regular kinda guy'. It was not an expression that
one could imagine Clement Attlee or Harold Macmillan ever
using, but its colloquial style seemed perfectly fitted to its time.
Style and presentation mattered. Politics had become presidential
in style. There was no denying that he was in tune with his times.
A sign of this was that his popularity rating up to 2001 was at its
highest among young voters who were attracted by what they saw
as New Labour's progressive stance.

Blair's popularity declined somewhat in the new decade, but he
was still able to win comfortable victories in the 2001 and 2005
elections, although with a reduced majority each time. In foreign
affairs he skilfully juggled his sometimes contradictory
commitments to Europe and the USA. Arguably his greatest
political achievement was his contribution to the bringing about
of a peaceful settlement in Northern Ireland.

Three issues dominated the final four years of his premiership. One was the timing of his departure. Having held on to office longer than his obvious successor, Gordon Brown, had expected, he was the only modern Prime Minister to announce the date of his resignation a year before he intended to go. This gave his last year a lame-duck quality. Another issue was the 'cash for honours' scandal. Although a police investigation did not result in charges, the thought that the Blair administration was involved in shady dealings made a mockery of the party's great claim that its coming to power in 1997 marked the end of sleaze in government.

The most important issue was Iraq. Blair's taking Britain into war with Iraq in 2003 on the dubious grounds that Saddam Hussein had weapons of mass destruction was wilfully done in the face of strong domestic and international censure. It is likely that the final estimation by historians of the Blair years will rest on the outcome of the Anglo-American involvement in the Middle East.

Tony Blair campaigning in the Sedgefield constituency in the 1983 general election when he was first elected as an MP at the age of 31. Why by the 1990s had Tony Blair abandoned most of his earlier radical ideas?

Reaction of the left

This new line of approach naturally upset the socialist left of the party. They characterised it as a sell-out by the Labour Party to the forces of expediency. They were concerned that New Labour lacked a distinct, radical ideology. Instead, it presented itself to the electorate as wanting to do the same things as the Conservatives, only more efficiently. The response of the supporters of New Labour within the party was to point out that the world had changed. Loyalty to old Labour values and refusal to modify policy had simply made the party unelectable for 18 years. The argument was convincingly vindicated in the sweeping victory of New Labour in 1997.

Blair's style of government
Spin doctors

Tony Blair's style of government was well illustrated by his use of spin doctors. The term was borrowed from the USA in the late 1990s to describe the special advisers employed by politicians to present their policies in the best light possible. At its best, spin was essentially a form of public relations; at its worst it was telling lies. Blair relied on a team of advisers, most prominent of whom were **Alistair Campbell** and **Peter Mandelson**, to handle the media and help him judge the public mood, so that he could adjust his approach accordingly. The practice was not new. Margaret Thatcher, for example, had employed a well-organised press team, led by Bernard Ingham. What was different about Labour's spin doctors was the large degree of influence they appeared to have not simply on the presentation but on the shaping of government policy.

New Labour's progressive image

It was Blair's spin doctors who provided him with the 'buzz words' and sound bites that Blair and the party used to convey New Labour's approach. Among these were the following terms:

- 'cool Britannia': an already existing journalistic term appropriated by New Labour to describe how fashionable and in touch it was as a movement
- 'inclusiveness': referring to a society where nobody was left out, where there would be no 'social exclusion'
- 'stakeholder society': meaning in a practical sense ordinary people having state-protected investments and pensions, and in an abstract sense people feeling that they belonged collectively to society
- 'forces of conservatism': a blanket term, first used by Blair in a speech in 1999, to condemn everything that held back his idea of progress.

New Labour's economic policies

New Labour's first four years went well. The economy appeared healthy and Gordon Brown proved a major success as Chancellor of the Exchequer. One of his first moves was to give the Bank of

Key figures

Alistair Campbell 1957–
Blair's special adviser and chief spokesman from 1994 to 2003; although he held no official government post, he was so influential in presenting Blair and his policies to the public that some newspapers described him as the 'real Deputy Prime Minister'.

Peter Mandelson 1953–
Blair's highly successful 1997 election manager. He became Trade Minister in 1998, but resigned in the same year, then Northern Ireland Minister in 1999, but resigned in 2001. In both instances his resignation was brought about by allegations that he had been involved in irregular financial dealings. This did not prevent his being appointed Britain's European Trade Commissioner in 2004.

England the authority to set interest rates independently of government interference. This appeared to take an important financial issue out of the political arena, although those of a more suspicious turn of mind wondered whether it was not a subtle way of avoiding blame should mistakes later be made in the fixing of the rates. Brown also kept to a pledge, given before taking office in 1997, that Labour would keep within the spending plans the Conservatives had laid down. His prudent budgets swelled Britain's reserve funds while at the same time keeping inflation down.

Yet there is an argument that he could not have done this had he not inherited a strong economy. What is sometimes lost sight of is that the poor economic reputation Major's government had gained by 1997 was not entirely justified. Despite the fiasco of the ERM crisis of 1992, the fact was that once Britain had withdrawn from the ERM its financial and general economic situation considerably improved (see the figures in Table 5.5 on page 166). This, however, was not destined to last. By the time Gordon Brown moved from No. 11 to No. 10 Downing Street, it was clear that the success he had achieved in his early years as Chancellor of the Exchequer had not been sustained (see page 187).

Constitutional issues

In its election manifesto Labour had made a commitment to devolution, which it duly honoured by the creation of **Scottish Parliament** and a **Welsh Assembly**. Devolution was deliberately intended to fall short of full independence, which was something no Labour government could contemplate. The reason was one of survival. All the figures showed that historically Scotland and Wales voted Labour while England voted Conservative. If ever Scotland and Wales gained full separation it would destroy Labour's chance of holding power.

The House of Lords

The reform of the House of Lords, to which Labour was also committed, raised further problems for the government. Ending the right of unelected hereditary peers to sit in the upper house may have been sincerely intended to strike a blow for democracy. But the problem was what form the new chamber would take and what powers it would have. By 2001 Blair had created more life peers in his four years of government than the Conservatives had in their 18. Critics complained that it was part of his scheme for consolidating New Labour's authority by packing the House of Lords with his own appointees so that it would cease to be obstructive. Even some of his own side were unhappy at this. Tony Benn, in his role as Labour's conscience, described the process as going back 700 years to the time when monarchs got their way by surrounding themselves with placemen.

Key terms

Scottish Parliament Created in 1998 following a referendum in Scotland the previous year, in which, in a turn out of 60 per cent, three-quarters of the voters opted for a system in which Scotland, while remaining within the UK, would have its affairs run by a Scottish Parliament and a Scottish Executive with tax-raising powers.

Welsh Assembly Created in 1998 following a referendum the previous year which gave the pro-devolution voters a mere 0.6 per cent victory; initially the Assembly was simply a revising chamber examining UK measures that related to Wales, but later legislation gave Wales governmental powers, similar to those enjoyed in Scotland.

The continuity between New Labour and Thatcherism

What was particularly observable about Tony Blair's government was that though it was very different in style and tone from the Thatcher–Major Conservatism that it replaced, it made no substantial effort to undo what had been done in the previous 18 years. Margaret Thatcher's legacy proved a powerful one. She had weakened the trade unions, reintroduced the principle of accountability into the public services, and made the nation acknowledge that in economic matters nothing was for nothing. Although she was attacked for it in her time, the effectiveness of what she had done convinced those who came after her to follow much the same path. As the contemporary historian Peter Clarke put it:

> The fruits of her reforms were accepted by many long-standing opponents. Though their hearts might have bled for the miners, they did not propose to put the unions back in the saddle; although they might have been scornful of privatisation, they did not propose to go back to a regime of nationalised industries and council houses. The post-Thatcher Labour Party bore a closer resemblance to the SDP of 10 years previously than partisans of either cared to acknowledge.
>
> (*Hope and Glory Britain 1900–1990* by Peter Clarke, 1996)

This continuity between Thatcherism and New Labour was a point emphasised by historian John Keegan:

> It is [Mrs Thatcher's] financial and industrial regime that prevails, and her mode of government also – centralist at home, Atlanticist in strategic affairs, cautiously co-operative in its relations with the European Community.
>
> (*The British Century* by John Keegan, 1999)

Problems abroad

Blair had certainly made a strong impression abroad. EU ministers and officials had warmed to him in personal meetings (see page 194), and the Clinton administration in the USA (1992–2000) was impressed. Indeed, President Bill Clinton had personal reason to be grateful to Tony Blair for offering his moral support in 1999 when impeachment proceedings were instituted against the President over alleged sexual misdemeanours. But at the close of the century the new government faced two particularly difficult problems in foreign affairs: the continuing war in former Yugoslavia where the Dayton agreement had broken down (see page 167) and Iraq.

Soon after becoming Foreign Secretary in Tony Blair's government, Robin Cook had declared that New Labour would pursue an 'ethical foreign policy'. The dilemma that this created was evident in the way the government handled these issues.

Key date

NATO intervention in Kosovo: 1999

NATO and Serbia

Blair took an important initiative in the complex struggle that had broken out again in former Yugoslavia (see page 167). In 1999, he persuaded both NATO and President Clinton's USA to intervene militarily by relaunching air strikes against the Serbian forces under Slobodan Milŏsević. Blair's justification was that the Serbs had been engaging in the genocide of the Albanian people of Kosovo. However, there were critics who argued that the NATO action had led the Serbs to intensify their mistreatment of the Kosovans. There were also voices raised against the manner in which NATO bombing raids, carried out principally by the USAAF and the RAF, had been conducted. To minimise the chance of casualties amongst themselves, the bomber crews had flown above 15,000 feet; this meant that, even with the sophisticated guidance systems available, bombs might well strike wrongly identified non-military targets. The Serbs produced evidence to show that this, indeed, had happened.

Initially Blair had also wanted to send in ground troops. In a speech in Chicago in 1999 he spoke of this as an act of necessary humanitarian intervention. Clinton, however, was not prepared to go that far. Nevertheless, the combined air strikes did eventually achieve their objective; Milošević withdrew his forces. Later events were to show that this success in Kosovo had convinced Blair that it could be used as a precedent for legitimate intervention elsewhere (see page 215).

Iraq

The accusation of indiscriminate bombing was also at the centre of the dispute in another area: Iraq. In 1998, as part of a programme to make Saddam Hussein, the Iraqi leader (see page 163), comply with UN resolutions requiring him to open up his country to weapons inspection, Blair's government again joined with the USA in imposing sanctions. Observers reported that the effect of sanctions was not to hurt the Saddam regime but to deprive ordinary Iraqis of vital supplies such as medicines. It was also charged that the frequent nightly bombing raids that the allies carried out against military installations had in fact caused the death of many innocent civilians. Iraq was to become the single biggest problem for Tony Blair in all his 10 years in office.

Key question

How had the Labour Party changed its attitude on the European question?

New Labour and Europe

Until the 1970s the Labour Party had been far from pro-European and it was not until 1983 that it officially dropped its commitment to withdraw Britain from the European Community. Thereafter, as part of its reformation as New Labour, the party began to warm towards Europe. In part this was opportunistic. Labour was swift to exploit Thatcher's ambiguous European attitude and it made the most of Major's embarrassments over Maastricht and the ERM. But there was a more positive aspect to it. The party's earlier fears that Europe was essentially a club for capitalists had diminished. Labour could see, for example, the gains that workers could now derive from the generous European employment laws contained in the '**Social Chapter**'. The party declared its commitment to the European ideal. Blair strove to impress the other European leaders with his sincerity.

The question that confronted him and his government at the beginning of the new century was how far they should lead Britain down the path of European integration. The critical test would be whether the government would abandon the pound sterling and enter fully into the single currency system, a step which all the other EU members, apart from Denmark, had taken by 1999. Labour's interim answer was that it would prepare the ground for entry but would make a final commitment only if and when it could be established that entry was in Britain's economic interests. Its decision would then be put to a referendum of the people.

There was an interesting personal aspect to this. Brown was far from being a Eurosceptic, but he was more cautious than Blair in this approach to further British integration. Left to himself Blair might well have been willing to accept the euro at this stage. It was the Chancellor who insisted that five economic tests had to be met before that could happen (see page 196).

Social Chapter
Sometimes referred to as the Social Charter, part of the Maastricht Treaty, which committed EU member states to introduce extensive welfare schemes.

Key term

Summary diagram: New Labour 1994–9

New Labour's approach
- Abandoning Clause IV and nationalisation
- Playing down of socialism
- Seeking partnership with the financial and business world
- Keeping trade unions at arm's length
- Accepting that the class war was over

Blair's style of leadership
- Essentially personal
- Presidential
- Presentation an essential characteristic

New Labour's buzz words
- Inclusiveness
- Stakeholder society
- Forces of conservatism

New Labour's economic policies
- Limited government spending
- Anti-inflationary
- Prudence the watch word

New Labour's constitutional issues
- Devolution
- House of Lords reform

Continuity between New Labour and Thatcherism
- Maintained restrictions on trade unions
- Same industrial policies
- Little effort to undo privatisation
- Insistence on accountability in the public services

New Labour's foreign policy
- Use of NATO to resolve international crisis: Kosovo
- Closer ties with Europe
- Special relationship with USA: Iraq
- 'Humanitarian interventionism'

Study Guide: AS Questions

In the style of Edexcel

Source 1

From: John Cole, As It Seemed To Me, *political memoirs published in 1995. Cole was political editor for the BBC in 1990. Here he is writing about 21 November 1990.*

At 1.00 pm her [Thatcher's] situation was desperate but she emerged from Number 10 on her way to the House of Commons and told the waiting cameras: 'I fight on, I fight to win.' Her defiant remark caused them to ask me at *Six O'clock* [TV news] 'John what went wrong in the rumour factory?' Doubtless this was not intended personally but it showed scant regard for the reports of trends I had been giving for the past 24 hours.

Source 2

From: The Benn Diaries, *published in 1994. Tony Benn was leading member of the Labour Party in 1990.*

Wednesday 21 November 1990
The rumour going round at the moment is that the men in grey suits* went round to see Mrs Thatcher to say 'time to go'. But according to the rumours she just absolutely refused to have anything to do with that advice, so then the Cabinet, whatever they thought individually, take a common line to support her. Actually, if you look around, there isn't a dominant alternative figure. In terms of stamina and persistence, you have to admit Margaret Thatcher is an extraordinary woman. She came out of Number 10, saying 'I fight on, I fight to win.'
[*Leading members of the Conservative Party]

Source 3

From: Margaret Thatcher's memoirs, The Downing Street Years, *published 1993. Here Thatcher is writing about 21 November 1990.*

I saw members of my cabinet one by one. The message, even from those urging me to fight on, was demoralising since my strongest supporters doubted I could win. In retrospect I can see that my resolve was weakened by these meetings but as yet I was still inclined to fight on. But I felt the decision would really be made at the meetings with my cabinet colleagues that evening. Before then I had to make a statement in the House.

Leaving Number 10, I called out to the assembled journalists in Downing St: 'I fight on, I fight to win,' and was interested to see later on the news that I looked a great deal more confident than I felt.

Study Sources 1, 2 and 3.

How far do these sources suggest that John Cole was right to say about Margaret Thatcher: 'At 1.00 pm her situation was desperate'? Explain your answer, using the evidence of Sources 1, 2 and 3.   (20 marks)

Exam tips

The cross-references are intended to take you straight to the material that will help you to answer the question.

Re-read the section on page 154. John Cole himself suggested that he was confident about his judgement (how does he do this?), but Source 1 also suggests that his colleagues on the *Six O'clock News* had doubts (what is the evidence for this?). However, Cole also says that it was Thatcher's 'defiant performance' which caused his colleagues to doubt him – and this can be cross-referred with Sources 2 and 3. Tony Benn comments on her 'stamina and persistence' in relation to her statement and Margaret Thatcher herself notes that she looked more confident than she felt.

Tony Benn clearly felt that Margaret Thatcher was still in a strong position on the afternoon of 21 November (what is the evidence for this?): what comment will you make about such evidence coming from a leading member of the opposition party? However, Thatcher's own evidence points in both directions. What weight will you give ultimately to her comments about her own feelings and reactions?

Remember, as you come to your overall decision, that you are asked to come to a judgement on the basis of these sources. You are not being asked about Margaret Thatcher's eventual resignation, you are being asked what this evidence suggests about her position at that point in time.

In the style of OCR A

Was the poll tax or Europe the more important factor in
bringing down Margaret Thatcher in 1990? Explain your answer.

(50 marks)

> ### Exam tips
>
> *The cross-references are intended to take you straight to the material
> that will help you to answer the question.*
>
> This question type is a little different from most because it gives you
> two possibilities and asks you to weigh the importance of one
> against the other in explaining something (here, Mrs Thatcher's
> downfall) (pages 149–54). Don't wander off to consider other factors
> that you think were as, if not more, important – that is not what you
> have been asked to do, although your conclusion could argue *briefly*
> that 'x' was as important as, if not more, important than either or
> both of the given factors. Link poll tax unpopularity with unrest in
> Conservative ranks – the question is about the impact of the tax, not
> the tax itself. The tax had always been opposed within the party by
> 'one-nation Conservatives'. When introduced, the unexpected size of
> many bills meant that MPs everywhere faced angry middle-class
> voters. Electoral defeat was possible, but Mrs Thatcher would not
> back down.
>
> Was the same true over Europe? No. The population was probably
> Eurosceptic and her earlier success over budget payments had been
> highly popular. Conservative MPs were not going to lose their seats
> in the next election because Britain had joined the ERM or Mrs
> Thatcher was fighting Delors. The Euro issue was a problem within
> the government because it brought to a head (and Howe's
> devastating resignation speech brought into the open) long-standing
> unease at her style of leadership – that had already caused the
> resignation of another two Cabinet ministers (Heseltine, Lawson).
> Europe was important in Mrs Thatcher's fall because, with her party
> so low in the polls, it led to a leadership contest. So, in the end, both
> came down to Conservative MPs facing the prospect of defeat for
> the first time since 1974. Your job is to decide which had the greater
> impact, and justify your choice with hard evidence.

In the style of OCR B

Answer **both** parts of your chosen question.

(a) How is the struggle over the Maastricht Treaty best explained?
[Explaining motives and events]   (25 marks)

(b) Why did Labour win the 1997 general election?
[Explaining events and circumstances]   (25 marks)

Exam tips

The cross-references are intended to take you straight to the material that will help you to answer the questions.

Revise the general introduction at the start of the Exam tips in Chapter 1 (page 33).

(a) Your circles of explanation must include behaviour on both sides of the argument; do not just examine the Eurosceptics. Your initial circle of explanation could include the growing divisions within the Conservative Party over EU membership during the 1980s. By the time Mrs Thatcher fell, the EU was a subject liable to rip the party apart. From that point, your next circle might contrast fevered Conservative opposition to Maastricht with support for the Single European Act. What had changed? Part of the answer lies in the humiliation of withdrawal from the ERM. In part, the opposition was the product of the anti-EU hysteria whipped up by Mrs Thatcher and certain newspapers. In part, however, the Maastricht battle was an aspect of the wider struggle for the soul of the Conservative Party, with the Eurorebels prominent on the pro-Thatcherite right. Your next circle should turn to the government. For Major, the Treaty was a central feature of his policy agenda. Maastricht became a test of strength that he could not afford to lose, hence his turning of parliamentary ratification into a vote of confidence in the government itself. In showing how motives and events fed each other, you will be explaining how both sides saw this as a vital struggle. (See pages 163–4 and 166–7.)

(b) The prompt tells you that you need to give a causal explanation. You will need to construct two sets of circles of explanation: one dealing with positive reasons why Labour won and the other with negative reasons why the Conservatives lost, but keep the focus primarily on Labour. At the end, you will need to decide which was the more important. In the circles of explanation on Labour, give due credit to the modernisation under Kinnock and Smith that prepared so much of the ground for Blair. Do not miss out either the careful work Labour did to woo the City and business (claiming that it was a friend of capitalism and no longer socialist) while keeping the unions and 'traditional' Labour supporters loyal. And make space for image: the powerful contrast between 'youthful' energetic Blair and 'tired' Major that made such an impression on some voters. That point relates to Major's difficulties. Chief among Conservative problems was the loss of reputation for economic competence after ERM withdrawal. When combined with the reputation for sleaze that the Conservatives simultaneously acquired, the defeat of a deeply unpopular government looked more and more likely.

In your final circle, consider one 'what if?' The scale of Labour's victory was created by the electoral system, but might Major have limped home again (as in 1992) had Labour not succeeded in reforming itself? (See pages 168–70.)

Study Guide: A2 Question

In the style of AQA

To what extent were John Major's difficulties as Prime Minister of his own making, in the period 1990–7?   (45 marks)

Exam tips

The cross-references are intended to take you straight to the material that will help you to answer the question.

You will need to consider a range of factors affecting Major's position and should balance those 'of his own making' against those which you feel were beyond his control in order to reach a well-supported conclusion in response to the question (pages 163–70). Try to follow a single line of argument throughout your answer and support all your ideas with specific evidence.

   Problems of his own making might include issues that suggested 'uninspiring leadership':

- failure to 'ditch' the Thatcher legacy
- economic incompetence
- failure to heal rifts over Europe (and his attitude to and relationship with his Cabinet)
- problems over foreign affairs
- failure to control the sleaze allegations.

But against these can be set:

- the problem of the Thatcher legacy
- broader economic difficulties
- problems created by his ministers rather than himself
- the small government majority and its reliance on the Ulster Unionists
- the recovery of the Labour Party and Blair's leadership.

6 New Labour in the New Century

POINTS TO CONSIDER

Tony Blair's New Labour government entered the twenty-first century with considerable confidence. Its early years in power had gone well, particularly on the economic front. But there were problems that still needed resolution; Northern Ireland and the UK's relations with Europe were prominent among these. In 2002, however, a problem arose in foreign affairs that was to dominate the remainder of Blair's premiership: Iraq. This issue was to test Britain's special relationship with the USA and lead to Blair's taking Britain into a war on terror.

The opportunity is also taken in this final chapter to examine a number of social issues that confronted Blair's government that had been building over the whole period covered by this book. The chapter begins with a listing of the critical developments that occurred between the end of the Second World War and the first decade of the new millennium, then goes on to examine the following themes:

- New Labour and the economy
- The elections of 2001 and 2005
- Blair and Europe
- Britain's relations with Ireland 1969–2007
- Blair and Britain's special relationship with the USA
- Social issues in Britain in the new century

Key dates

1993	Downing Street Declaration
1998	Good Friday Agreement
1999–2002	UK sold off half of its gold reserves
2000	Blair argued for a 'third way' on the European issue
2001	Labour won second successive election
	9/11 Terrorist attacks on USA
2002	The euro adopted by EU
2003	Anglo-American invasion of Iraq
2004	Blair argued for reform of CAP
	Signing of the 'Treaty establishing a Constitution for Europe'
2005	Labour won third successive election
	7/7 London bombings

2006   St Andrews Agreement
        Blair gave in over rebate and CAP reform
2007   Northern Ireland Executive formed
        Brown succeeded Blair as Prime Minister
        Treaty of Lisbon

A number of critical developments gave shape to Britain between 1945 and the first decade of the twentieth-first century. It is helpful to list these. They are numbered for clarity, but this is not meant to suggest their order of importance:

1. the adoption of the welfare state
2. a significant rise in the standard of living of the people
3. continuing heavy defence commitments and expenditure
4. the shift from a manufacturing to a service economy
5. a decrease in the number of industrial workers in the staple industries
6. a decline in trade union membership and influence
7. inflation and recession as recurring features of the economy
8. population increase and distribution, including significant levels of immigration which changed Britain into a multiracial society
9. the weakening of Parliament as an institution, in the face of the growth of power of central government
10. class shifts and political realignments that altered electoral voting patterns
11. the retreat from Empire and the abandonment of Britain's economic ties with the Commonwealth
12. the loss of sovereignty entailed by Britain's entry into the European Community.

1 | New Labour and the Economy

Income and expenditure

Key question
What were the distinctive features of the Blair government's handling of the economy?

During Tony Blair's first period in office from 1997 to 2001, the economy appeared to flourish and his government reaped the benefit politically with another sweeping election victory in 2001. Gordon Brown gained an enviable reputation for restricting inflation and building up Britain's financial reserves. But, as later became evident, the ground was already prepared when he took over as Chancellor. When the Conservatives went out of office in 1997, the inflation rate was 2.6 per cent. Ten years later when Brown became Prime Minister, it was 4.8 per cent. The basic explanation for the rise was that after three years of tightly controlled spending, Brown relaxed his prudent approach and engaged in large-scale government expenditure. Large amounts were pumped into the public sector, particularly into the NHS. While there was an obvious argument for this on social grounds, the effect financially was to increase inflation.

Pensions

There was another aspect of Brown's policy which created more lingering bitterness among the population than perhaps any other government finance measure. In order to build up the reserves of money which he later spent, the Chancellor began what in effect was a sustained raid on people's pension provisions. He did this by taxing the dividend payments which companies made to their investors. Since the purpose of having a pension is for holders to see a return in the form of interest on the money they pay in premiums, the taxing of dividends meant that the value of pensions rapidly fell. By 2007, the amount lost was over £8 billion.

The British pensions industry, which had been one of the world's best funded and highest paying financial concerns, was sunk in despondency by 2007. Individuals and companies no longer looked on pensions as a worthwhile form of investment. One statistic that illustrates this is that the **savings ratio**, which stood at 9.7 per cent in 1997 had declined to 3.7 per cent 10 years later.

An additional effect of the pensions raid was that since share prices are dependent on dividend values, the cutting of dividend payments meant that total UK share values were some £120 billion lower than they would have been without government interference. The raid on the pension funds was an example of what has been call 'stealth tax'. In the elections of 1997 and 2001 the Labour Party had promised a low taxation policy. In order not to appear to break that commitment, financial adjustments were made which, while not technically classed as taxation, were so in practice. Among these were:

- raising National Insurance contributions
- removing the marriage tax allowance for couples under the age of 65 years
- removing the tax relief on mortgage payments
- reducing the level of tax-free savings that could be made each year under such schemes as **TESSAs**, **PEPs** and **ISAs** (e.g. in 1999 the untaxed amount an individual could save was £12,000; by 2007 that had been reduced to £7000).

Employment

One of the government's proud claims was that the number of people in employment in Britain grew during the Blair years. This is certainly true in overall terms; by 2007 there were 29.1 million people in work, 2.5 million more than in 1997. However, while there had been a growth in jobs this had not been in the areas where it was most needed, among the unskilled and the young. In 2007 there were 5.4 million people of working age, many of them between the ages of 16 and 30, who had never had a job, and lived on unemployment benefit.

Another consideration that rather diminished Labour's achievement was that 37 per cent of the increase in jobs were in the public sector, which by 2007 was employing seven million people, an increase of some 900,000 during Blair's 10 years. Britain had become a **client state** in which a quarter of the workforce were employed in the public sector; that is, workers did jobs which were paid for by the government out of public funds. This could be faulted on a number of counts:

Key term

Client state
A society in which a significant number of the population work directly for the government or its agencies.

- It undermined democracy since public workers were hardly likely to vote against a government on whom their jobs depended.
- It was economically unsound since it undermined incentive; public sector workers whose guaranteed wages and pensions came from state funds were unlikely to make efficiency and productivity their main goals.
- Many of the positions in the public sector were in fact non-jobs in the sense that they had no productive value. This resurrected the situation which both James Callaghan and Margaret Thatcher had tried to end. Callaghan in 1978 had told the Labour Party conference, 'we are paying ourselves with money we have not earned'.

Any government of whatever political colour can, of course, use its power to bribe an electorate, but the particular charge against New Labour was that its eagerness to create an ever-expanding public sector derived from its antipathy towards small businesses and the self-employed; the workers in these independent areas were not as easy to manipulate and control.

Borrowing
The government's justification for expanding the public sector was that it was a way of improving public services. However, the costs incurred tended to outrun the revenue received. The increase in government expenditure on the public sector, in areas such as the NHS, welfare services and education, could not be met entirely from taxation revenues. Over the period of Gordon Brown's Chancellorship £100 million had to be borrowed from foreign bankers. The reason why this did not hit the headlines was that the 10 years after New Labour came to power in 1997 were a period of relative stability and growth in the international economy. However, the ominous signs by the end of 2007 were that this period was coming to an end and that there was a likelihood of a serious world economic recession. In a period of decline a country that has borrowed heavily has real problems, since its growth and revenues fall at the very time it needs them to rise so that it can meet its debts.

Judged by how much people spent, the decade after 1997 was in many ways a boom time in Britain. House buying and retail sales increased markedly. Mass buying of new technology, such as personal computers and mobile phones, showed great willingness among consumers to spend, spend, spend. However, the commodities and goods were paid for not by money earned but by money borrowed. Encouraged by banks and loan companies, ordinary people took out credit. The plastic card was a symbol of the times. The criticism made of this consumer boom by economists is that the government allowed it to run on too long in order to mask the difficulties it had created for itself and the nation through its own borrowing.

This was a recipe for recession. By 2008 the recession had arrived.

'Golden Brown'

One of Gordon Brown's highly significant actions, which went largely unnoticed at the time, was his decision to sell off gold. Between 1999 and 2002 when the price of gold fell on the international markets, the British government sold off 13 million ounces, which amounted to nearly half of its of gold reserves. In the same period the Republic of China bought up nearly seven million ounces. With the subsequent recovery of gold prices by 2005 Britain found it had lost some £3 billion, equivalent to a penny on the basic tax rate. China in contrast had doubled its money. *The Scotsman* newspaper condemned what it called 'Brown's disastrous foray into international asset management', while one of the tabloids cuttingly referred to the Chancellor as 'Golden Brown'.

It is interesting to note that China also proved far sharper at using the **WTO** system to its advantage than Britain. In 2006, the British government woke up to the fact that China was selling much more to Britain than it was buying and that Britain's European competitors had taken advantage. In 2005 Britain's exports to China were worth only £5 billion compared to Germany's £31 billion. In an effort to redress the balance, Britain embarked on a major campaign to increase its influence and trade with China. The effect diplomatically of this eagerness to develop commercial contact was that the government took care not to be too critical of China on other issues, such as abuse of human rights; it did not wish to risk losing trade with China's vast market of 1.4 billion people.

Key date

UK sold off half its gold reserves: 1999–2002

Key term

WTO
World Trade Organisation, the international body responsible for negotiating and monitoring trade agreements between countries.

Summary diagram: New Labour and the economy

Income and expenditure

Policy: from 2001 the prudence of the earlier Blair–Brown years gave way to high public spending

Result
• Rising inflation

Pensions

Policy: government raid on pensions funds

Results
• Rapid £8 billion fall in pension values
• Decline of British pensions industry
• Savings ratio fell

Employment

Policy: to reduce unemployment

Results
• 2.5 million more in work by 2007 than in 1997
• 5.4 million people of working age still living on unemployment benefit
• 37 per cent of the increase in jobs were in the unproductive public sector which made Britain increasingly a client state

Borrowing

Policy: to borrow in order to fund the expansion of public services

Results
• Costs of services outran revenue returns leading to increased borrowing
• Government borrowing encouraged a consumer credit boom
• Britain not well prepared for the international economic downturn that had set in by the end of 2007

Gold

Policy: to sell off half of Britain's gold reserves since gold prices were falling

Result
• Subsequent recovery of gold market meant Britain had sold at a heavy loss amounting to £3 billion

2 | The Elections of 2001 and 2005

The 2001 election

In 2001, Labour maintained the massive majority it had gained in 1997, suggesting that the electorate considered the government had performed well over its four years in office. In terms of seats it was the status quo, Labour losing only five with the Conservatives down just one. There was a fall of 3.7 per cent in Labour's aggregate vote, but this had minimal effect on its overall strength. It is true that there was a leaking of nearly three million voters from Labour, but commentators put this down to a general apathy among the electorate which led to a turnout of 59 per cent compared with 71 per cent in 1997. The apathy was largely explained by the opinion polls giving the government such a clear lead that neither supporters nor opponents had an incentive to vote since the outcome was a foregone conclusion.

Table 6.1: Election results 2001

Political party	No. of votes	No. of seats	Percentage of vote
Labour	10,724,895	413	40.7
Conservative	8,357,622	166	31.7
Liberal Democrats	4,812,833	52	18.3
Northern Irish parties	544,108	15	2.3
Scottish Nationalists	464,314	5	1.5
Plaid Cymru	195,893	4	0.6

Blair's personal popularity was a major factor in Labour's success. Although William Hague, who had been elected as the Conservative leader in 1997, was a skilled opponent in the House of Commons, being particularly formidable at Prime Minister's Questions, his qualities did not translate into popularity in the country at large. The same was true of his party, which found it difficult to encroach on Labour's lead. The Conservatives at this stage lacked a distinct enough image to make them an attractive alternative in the eyes of the voters. Although, as is the nature of party politics, they sniped at the government, they found it difficult to score a palpable hit. Britain's finances seemed secure in the hands of Gordon Brown as the Chancellor of the Exchequer and the economy was growing. In regard to Northern Ireland, Blair had taken a number of important initiatives (see page 199), leaving little room for the opposition to attack him. In foreign affairs the government's record was sound and while there was some uncertainty about its dealings with Europe there was even more about the attitude of the Conservatives.

Reasons for Labour's victory in 2001 included the following:

- Blair's continued personal popularity with voters
- Blair laid stress on the improvements in the public services
- Hague's inability to present himself as a better alternative to Blair

Key question

Why was Labour able to win both the elections called by Blair?

Key date

Labour won second successive election: 2001

- the perception that the government was handling the economy and foreign affairs effectively
- trust in Brown as a prudent Chancellor of the Exchequer
- the Conservatives ran a poor campaign as they lacked a clear set of targets on which they could attack the government. Their main line was opposition to adopting the euro, which failed to attract floating voters
- the opinion polls had concurred in forecasting a Labour victory, thus decreasing the incentive to vote.

The 2005 election

In May 2005 Tony Blair achieved a remarkable first for a Labour Prime Minister; he won his third straight election victory in a row. The number of seats achieved by Labour was 57 fewer than the 2001 figure, 356 compared to 413, and its aggregate vote fell by more than five per cent. The Conservatives gained 32 more seats than four years earlier, while the Liberal Democrats did better in proportional terms than either of the two main parties. However, the Liberal Democrats' aggregate of nearly six million votes, approaching two-thirds of Labour's total, was not reflected in the number of seats they acquired. The proportion of seats won against votes cast for the three parties again makes instructive reading (see page 170):

- for each seat Labour Party won, it polled an average of 26,872
- for each seat the Conservative Party won, it polled an average of 44,373
- for each seat the Liberal Democrat Party won, it polled an average of 96,538.

Despite losing some ground in the election, Blair's government had retained a comfortable overall majority. There was no reason for thinking it could not run another full term if it chose.

Table 6.2: Election results 2005

Political party	No. of votes	No. of seats	Percentage of vote
Labour	9,566,618	356	35.3
Conservative	8,785,941	198	32.3
Liberal Democrats	5,985,414	62	22.1
Northern Irish parties	544,108	18	2.3
Scottish Nationalists	412,267	6	1.5
Plaid Cymru	174,838	3	0.6

Reasons for Labour's victory in 2005 included the following:

- Although Blair's involvement in the Iraq war lost him some popularity (see page 216), he was still regarded by the electorate as the outstanding choice among party leaders.
- Since the Conservatives had supported the government's decision to go into Iraq, they were unable to gain from the mounting criticism of the war.

Key date — Labour won third successive election: 2005

- Knowledge of the economic and financial difficulties that were beginning to face Britain had not become sufficiently widespread for it to count as a factor against the government.
- Despite the Conservatives' maintaining their vote and slightly increasing their aggregate support, they were still not able to make significant inroads into Labour's lead.
- The Conservative Party had had three different leaders within two years. William Hague had been replaced with Iain Duncan Smith after the 2001 election defeat and then in 2003 Duncan Smith, having proved less than charismatic in leading the party, was in turn replaced by Michael Howard. All this did not sit well with the general public who regarded the Conservatives as a divided party lacking in confidence and unlikely to be able to govern well.
- Backed by a wily team of spin doctors, Blair by 2005 was an experienced political operator who knew how to project his image. Howard was a competent leader but he was no real match for Blair in the presidential-style campaign that the Prime Minister conducted.
- Howard made a bad choice of issues on which to fight the election. His emphasis on immigration and law and order, concerns on which his own record when dealing with them as Home Secretary in Major's government was not impressive, proved something of an embarrassment. As early as 1997, a fellow Conservative, Ann Widdecombe, had described Howard as having 'something of the night about him'. He tried to make light of her description, but it proved a handicap thereafter. He was never quite able to get rid of the sinister image that one of his own side had given him.

3 | Blair and Europe

In 2008, on its official website, the Labour Party listed the government's 'top 50 achievements since being elected in 1997'. Surprisingly, Europe did not feature in the list. Yet it had been one of Tony Blair's preoccupations. One of the first comments he made after becoming Labour Party leader in 1994 referred to Europe. He declared: 'Under my leadership I will never allow this country to be isolated or left behind.' He showed none of the uncertainties that he himself and the Labour Party had had previously about Europe. On becoming Prime Minister three years later, he kept his promise by immediately instructing British officials to withdraw the objections that the Major government had raised with Europe on a number of unresolved issues. These related to the extension of European authority over:

- the environment
- regional policies
- criminal justice
- the Social Chapter.

Blair's chief aim in purposefully withdrawing Britain's original objections was to show the goodwill of the new government

Key question
What were Blair's aims in his dealing with Europe?

towards Europe. Some commentators have suggested that even at this early stage Blair had dreams of eventually becoming president of the EU and so wished to impress European colleagues with his dedication to the European ideal. Within two years Blair had attended a series of EU summit meetings at which he made a number of major concessions:

- Amsterdam 1997: Britain abandoned its opt-out on EU employment and social policy.
- St Malo 1998: Britain withdrew its objection to a common European defence policy which would operate independently of NATO. The French under President Chirac were delighted since it had long been a French aim to have a European force separate from the USA.

Key dates

Blair argued for a 'third way' on the European issue: 2000

The euro adopted by EU: 2002

To appease those in Britain, including many in the Labour ranks, who might have thought he had gone too far, too soon, Blair in 2000 tried to perform a balancing act. In a speech in Warsaw, he said that attitudes towards Europe could be divided into two main types. On one side were those still totally committed to the nation state and the free market, who wanted the EU to have the minimum of power; opposite them were the 'superstaters', those who wanted the EU to supersede the nation state and have maximum powers of control. Blair argued for a **third way**. He spoke of an EU made up of friendly states, retaining their individual sovereignty, but collaborating on matters of common economic and political interest.

Key terms

Third way
A term, relating to the avoidance of extremes, often associated with Blair and New Labour's policies in general.

Majority voting
A system that attracted federalists since it enabled contentious resolutions to be passed without being blocked by a member state using its individual veto.

The 'third way' notion was intended mainly for home consumption. It certainly made little impression on EU ministers and officials who felt no compulsion to make concessions to Britain simply because Britain had made concessions to them. For them, there was no room for a third way within the EU. As an organisation it was intent on greater integration and federation. That indeed was its basic purpose; it was no longer really a matter for discussion. Major's talk of Britain's 'being at the heart of Europe', which Blair repeated, was unrealistic. The EU was simply waiting for Britain to catch up and start conforming to the rules already drawn up.

Blair was made aware of this when he tried to push for a reform of the notorious Common Agricultural Policy (CAP) (see page 61). As a *quid pro quo* he spoke of his willingness to accept **majority voting** and drop the veto principle. Anticipating that he would do this, the French and German governments had previously got together to block any attempts to alter CAP whose purpose from the beginning had been to protect French agriculture and was not negotiable. For France, CAP was the purpose of the EU.

The euro

The merits and disadvantages of Britain's membership of the EU again became a matter for public debate in 2002 over the issue of whether the UK should give up the pound sterling and join the euro. On New Year's Day, 2002, the euro became the common currency of all but three of the members (Denmark, Sweden and the UK). Whether and when Britain should join were questions that divided Blair from Gordon Brown, his Chancellor of the Exchequer. Blair was less concerned with the financial aspects of the case and more with the political implications. He calculated that to join the **euro zone** would help put the UK at the heart of Europe and enhance his own standing as a European statesman.

Brown's approach was more guarded and practical. He defined the problem in the form of a question: would joining the euro 'serve the long-term national economic interest?' He laid down five economic tests that the euro would have to pass before it could be adopted. These included judgements about its effect on jobs, inflation and trade.

Blair even suggested a national referendum. He knew that opinion polls showed the British people currently to be against the euro but he believed that, as had happened in 1975 (see page 105), the people could be educated into saying 'yes'. Clare Short, a Cabinet minister at the time, later suggested that Blair at this point was even willing to step down as Prime Minister in favour of Brown, if Brown would commit himself to the euro. Whatever the truth of that suggestion, the fact was that in June 2003 Brown declared that the euro came nowhere near meeting the five tests and so there was no need for a referendum. He had economic and political logic on his side: the economy was performing well under his stewardship, so there was no point in putting it at possible risk by adopting the euro.

Key terms

Euro zone
Those countries that gave up their individual currencies for the euro.

Rebate
The return to the UK of a proportion of its budgetary payment to the EU.

The rebate issue

A concern that had clouded Britain's relations with Europe since 1973 was the size of the annual budget paid by member states to Europe. Britain felt that it had been discriminated against from the beginning by being obliged to pay a disproportionately higher amount. In 1984 Mrs Thatcher had swung her handbag to some effect and had won an annual **rebate** for Britain. But there were strong complaints among many members states, including most prominently, France, which argued that rebates offended the various treaty obligations which members had signed. In 2004 this issue forced itself to the foreground when the EU was enlarged to include the states of Eastern Europe.

Tony Blair told Europe that Britain was prepared to pay its 'fair share of the costs of enlargement', but he added that it could not give up its rebate and that he would use Britain's veto to block any EU attempt to force the UK to do so. One of Britain's strongest arguments was that the UK never actually received its full rebate because, in accordance with European regulations, 66 per cent of any EU funding that it was granted was deducted from the rebate. The result was that in net terms the UK since joining in 1973 had never received any funding from the EEC/EU. It had always paid out greatly more than it got back.

Key dates

Blair argued for
reform of CAP: 2004

Blair gave in over
rebate and CAP
reform: 2006

In 2004, Blair further stated that 'the rebate and the Common
Agricultural Policy are inextricably linked and there cannot be
fundamental change in one unless there is fundamental change in
the other'. He was on strong grounds. CAP had never worked in
Britain's favour. In 2004, as the pie chart in Figure 6.1 shows,
Britain received less from CAP than any of the major nations of
Western Europe.

Blair had used fighting words in 2004, but these were not
matched by actions. Apart from vague promises, he did not get
the reform of CAP that he had asked for. When Europe closed
ranks against Britain in 2005 and demanded that it increase its
budget contributions, he gave in and complied. One of Blair's last
acts as Prime Minister on the European stage was in December
2006 when he negotiated away the UK's rebate, as a result of
which Britain's annual contribution rose to £7 billion. As one
German newspaper remarked, the British Prime Minister 'began
as a tiger and has ended up a doormat'. As one caller to a radio
phone-in pointedly put it, 'Think of how many schools and
hospitals Britain could build with £7 billion.'

European directives

There is an interesting cultural dimension to Blair's eventually
giving in to European pressure. Arguably, he took it all too
seriously and legalistically. Most other European governments
tend to ignore EU regulations that they do not like. France, for
example, by 2004 had over 400 outstanding complaints against it
regarding its refusal to comply with directives. This seemed not to
worry the French unduly and it certainly did not embarrass them
in their relations with the EU. The French have a capacity for
taking from the EU what they want by way of advantages and

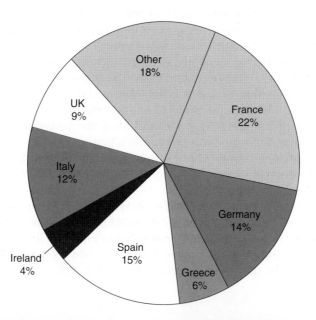

Figure 6.1: CAP
beneficiaries in 2004.
Why was Tony Blair
keen to reform the
CAP?

simply ignoring the restrictions they find irksome. Britain has never been able to develop this relaxed attitude. British officials rush to carry out European directives with a speed and commitment that bemuses and amuses their French counterparts. Despite its odd-man-out image, Britain is the most compliant of all the member states. During 2006, the EU imposed over 3000 regulations and directives on Britain. None of these was discussed, let alone modified, by the Westminster Parliament. Eighty per cent of the new laws that came into force in Britain during Blair's years as Prime Minister were laid down by the EU.

The European constitution

Running parallel with the debate over CAP was the equally important and divisive issue of the adoption of a European constitution. In October 2004, the 27 EU members met in Rome to sign the '**Treaty establishing a Constitution for Europe**' (TCE). The Treaty was scheduled to come into force in November 2006, provided it was ratified by each of the member states. Blair's government promised that, before the TCE was ratified by the UK, the question whether it should be accepted would be put to the British electorate in a referendum. However, when in 2005, in separate referendums in France and Denmark, the electors there rejected the Treaty, the British government declared that ratification was now a dead issue, which made a referendum no longer necessary. This did not satisfy those who asked why the British people were to be denied a referendum which other member states had chosen to hold. Eurosceptics claimed that the government had reneged on its promise because it knew the TCE would be rejected in Britain, an outcome strongly suggested by the opinion polls.

Undeterred by the failure to achieve ratification, the EU adjusted its approach and in June 2007 produced a replacement for the TCE. Technically, the new document was termed a 'reform treaty', a linguistic subtlety which meant that, although the new treaty was in every major respect precisely the same as the TCE, it was not formally a constitution. As a consequence when the reform treaty was subsequently accepted and signed by the EU members in Lisbon in December 2007, the British government (now led by Gordon Brown as Prime Minister) declared there was no need for a referendum on it. Claiming that its promise to hold a referendum applied only to a constitution, the government asserted that ratification was now solely a matter for parliamentary approval. This was duly granted in March 2008, when the government used its majority to push through ratification.

It was all very reminiscent of the way John Major's government had resorted to undemocratic means to achieve parliamentary acceptance of the Maastricht Treaty (see page 166). It left many in Britain feeling that the people had once again been ignored and cheated by their own government over Europe.

Key dates

Signing of the 'Treaty establishing a Constitution for Europe': 2004

Brown succeeded Blair as Prime Minister: 2007

Treaty of Lisbon: 2007

Key term

Treaty establishing a Constitution for Europe
Brought together the existing EU treaties into one formal binding document.

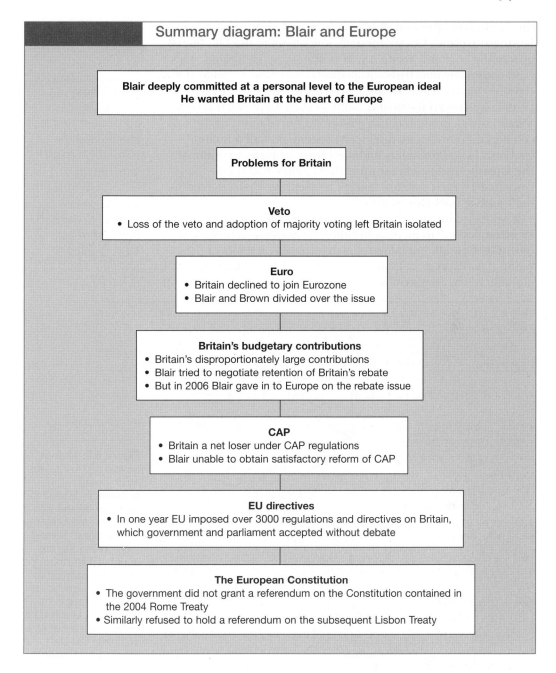

Summary diagram: Blair and Europe

**Blair deeply committed at a personal level to the European ideal
He wanted Britain at the heart of Europe**

Problems for Britain

Veto
• Loss of the veto and adoption of majority voting left Britain isolated

Euro
• Britain declined to join Eurozone
• Blair and Brown divided over the issue

Britain's budgetary contributions
• Britain's disproportionately large contributions
• Blair tried to negotiate retention of Britain's rebate
• But in 2006 Blair gave in to Europe on the rebate issue

CAP
• Britain a net loser under CAP regulations
• Blair unable to obtain satisfactory reform of CAP

EU directives
• In one year EU imposed over 3000 regulations and directives on Britain, which government and parliament accepted without debate

The European Constitution
• The government did not grant a referendum on the Constitution contained in the 2004 Rome Treaty
• Similarly refused to hold a referendum on the subsequent Lisbon Treaty

Key question
Why did it take so long to resolve the problems of Northern Ireland?

4 | Britain's Relations with Northern Ireland 1969–2007

One of the achievements in which Blair could take the greatest pride was his contribution to the peaceful settlement of the tragic Northern Irish issue. To put his role in perspective, it is necessary to trace the problem that had confronted every government and Prime Minister since the late 1960s.

Britain's formal links with the south of Ireland had finally ended in 1949 when the Irish Free State became the sovereign Republic of Ireland. This seemed to have finally put an end to the Anglo-Irish question. But one great problem remained: Northern Ireland. Constitutionally it was part of the UK, but its geography obviously made it part of the island of Ireland. This was an anomaly that Irish nationalists found objectionable. They claimed that the **1921 Treaty** had deliberately drawn the boundary between north and south so as to leave Northern Ireland with a predominantly Protestant population. In the six counties there were one million Protestants to half a million Catholics. The Protestants had used their majority to dominate the separate Parliament set up in 1921. They had then consolidated their political control by securing rights denied to the Catholic minority.

It was certainly the case that over the decades after partition Protestants came to monopolise the best housing, schools and jobs. The Catholic complaint was that this was a result of the political corruption in Ulster, which allowed Protestant councillors and officials to operate a system of favouritism and patronage. It

Key term

1921 Treaty
The Anglo-Irish agreement that had partitioned the island of Ireland between an independent south and Northern Ireland (loosely referred to as Ulster) which remained part of the UK.

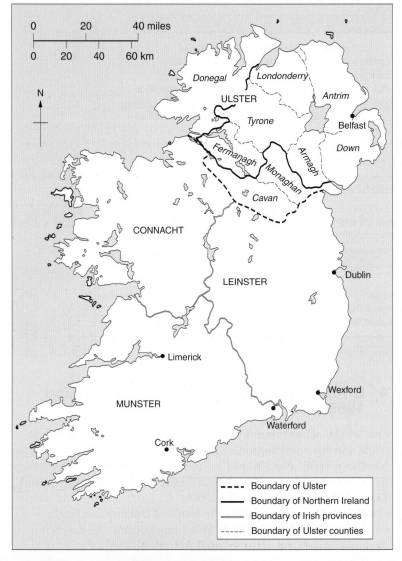

Figure 6.2: Map of Ireland 1914–22. The 1921 Treaty settlement divided the island of Ireland into the Irish Free State and Northern Ireland (comprising the six counties). Northern Ireland is sometimes loosely referred to as Ulster, although historically Ulster had been made up of nine counties: the six shown plus Donegal, Cavan and Monaghan. The fact that Northern Ireland did not include these last three was of immense importance since it left the Protestants in a majority in the north. Why did the Treaty not provide a permanent settlement of the Ulster question?

Key terms

Gerrymandering
Manipulating constituency boundaries so as to leave Protestants in control.

B Specials
A wholly Protestant part of Northern Ireland's reserve police force, seen by many as a Protestant army.

Londonderry
A disputed place name; republicans called it Derry.

RUC
The Royal Ulster Constabulary. An almost exclusively Protestant armed police force. The Catholic population came to regard the RUC as a sectarian force whose main task was to coerce them and protect the Protestant political establishment.

IRA
The Irish Republican Army. Dedicated to the creation through violence of an all-Ireland republic. Its political front was Sinn Féin, a legitimate political party. At the end of 1969 the movement split into the Official IRA and the Provisional IRA.

was even said that constituency and ward boundaries were deliberately adjusted so as to maintain permanent Protestant majorities.

One area where local politicians could not control things was admission to higher education, since this was administered directly from London. By the end of the 1960s nearly a third of the students at Queen's University, Belfast, came from the Catholic minority. It was from among such students that the Northern Ireland Civil Rights Association (NICRA) developed. Founded in 1967, NICRA condemned the **gerrymandering** of elections in Ulster and demanded the disbanding of the **B Specials** and a fair distribution of social and financial resources across the whole population. NICRA took as its model the black civil rights movement in the USA.

NICRA's first major public protest occurred in Dungannon in August 1968. In October of the same year a second demonstration, this time in **Londonderry**, Northern Ireland's most depressed economic area, ended in violence when the **RUC** baton charged the marchers to break up what the authorities had declared to be an illegal march. This incident is often taken as marking the beginning of 'the troubles'.

'The troubles'

'The troubles' refers to the cycle of violence dating from the 1960s to the 1990s whose main feature was terrorist conflict between the republicans and the unionists, with British troops caught in the middle trying to preserve the peace. It should be stressed that mainstream nationalists and unionists always condemned the violence. It was the extremist groups within the two movements which resorted to terrorism.

Rival demonstrations showed the depth of Catholic–Protestant sectarian (religious) divide. In 1969, disorder grew as protest and counterprotest invariably resulted in violence. The Reverend Ian Paisley emerged as the leader of unyielding, anti-Catholic unionism which exploited Protestant bitterness. In the summer of 1969, the season of the traditional Protestant marches in Ulster, the first deaths occurred. Responsible politicians on both sides of the border and in London appealed for calm but both communities, Catholic and Protestant, were liable to be attacked by terrorists from the other side.

British troops sent to Northern Ireland 1969

In August 1969, James Callaghan, Labour's Foreign Secretary, took the momentous decision to send the British army to Northern Ireland to keep the peace. At first the troops were welcomed by the Catholic community. Residents cheered and clapped as the soldiers encircled the Catholic Bogside area in Londonderry with protective barbed wire. This happy relationship was not to last. The **IRA**, which had been dormant, reorganised itself and took the lead in the struggle. However, not only did it resolve to attack unionism and head the Catholic nationalist protest movement, it also targeted the troops in

Northern Ireland as representatives of the hated British imperialist government, which was the root cause of Ireland's problems.

For the next 38 years the continued presence of the British army in Ulster indicated that the province's problems had not been solved. But amid the violence and disruption one aspect did become clear. The tide was running against the unionists and with the nationalists. Reasonable opinion in every quarter found it hard to justify the continuation of a Protestant political and economic monopoly. Genuine power sharing was the only answer. The movement towards shared power is the basic story that can be detected through the pall of outrages and terror. Of course, it was not a simple story. Progress was never smooth. The path was littered with failed initiatives and disappointed hopes, but in the end all except those on the very extremes of the question had accepted that some form of compromise was the only acceptable and workable solution. Optimists could say in 2007 that prospects for a peaceful Northern Ireland were brighter than at any point in the previous 40 years. How things came to reach the position they had by 2007 is best studied chronologically.

Internment introduced, August 1971
The continuing violent disruptions convinced Edward Heath's government that the situation could be contained only by internment. This was essentially a policy of arresting suspected troublemakers and holding them without trial. The aim was to remove the violent men from their communities and so reduce sectarian tensions. It had the opposite effect. Internment had the following results:

- There was an increase in tension in Northern Ireland.
- It made the Catholic population feel persecuted.
- Relations between the Irish government in Dublin and the British government in London were harmed.
- The shared understanding between the parties in Westminster over the Northern Ireland question was broken since many Labour opposition MPs opposed internment and called for the British troops to be withdrawn.

Bloody Sunday, January 1972
How little internment had improved matters became evident in 1972 when a prohibited civil rights march in the Bogside area in Londonderry ended in carnage with 14 demonstrators being shot and killed by British troops. The exact details of what happened and who was responsible remain disputed to this day. Over the years, there have been a number of official inquiries but none of their balanced findings have been acceptable to republican sympathisers who want the British army to be condemned outright. The first inquiry, conducted by Lord Widgery, concluded that it was 'the shots that had been fired at the soldiers before they started the firing that led to the casualties'. This was seen by republicans as an attempt to whitewash the British army and

condone its actions. 'Instead of justice we got Widgery.' The publication of the Widgery Report in May 1972 may be said to have made the situation worse:

- It further convinced the Catholic population that the British government was hostile.
- There were tightened tensions between the London and Dublin governments.
- The gap between the IRA and the non-violent Social Democratic Labour Party (SDLP) widened.
- The gap between the moderate official Unionist Party and the **DUP** led by Ian Paisley also widened.

Before the report appeared, Heath's government had taken the step of suspending the Unionist-dominated **Stormont** Parliament and imposing direct rule of Northern Ireland from Westminster. A year later, in an effort to produce a workable governing arrangement, Willie Whitelaw, Heath's Northern Ireland Minister, managed to persuade the rival parties to consider co-operating in a power-sharing experiment. In the Sunningdale Agreement of December 1973, backed by the London and Dublin governments, the SDLP, led by Gerry Fitt, and the Official Unionists, led by Brian Faulkner, agreed to form an executive which would govern Northern Ireland on behalf of both the Catholic and Protestant communities.

It was the first time since 1921 that Catholics had been offered a share in government, and for that very reason it frightened the majority of unionists. The general situation deteriorated; violence continued on the streets, usually involving the IRA and **loyalist** groups, with frequent IRA attacks on the police and army. The province became a highly dangerous place. Catholics continued to feel aggrieved by the following:

- the high level of unemployment, which always affected them the most
- the continued presence of the British army
- slow progress in gaining full civil rights
- the way the law seemed tilted against them, as in the **Diplock Courts**.

The Protestant community felt no less aggrieved. They feared that such moves as the Sunningdale Agreement between London and Dublin were a cover for a sell-out of Unionist Ireland. Their fears led to the creation of the Ulster Defence Force, drawn from loyalist extremists, the mirror image of the Provisional IRA.

The Labour government and Northern Ireland 1974–9

It was Harold Wilson's great misfortune to be in power during one of the worst periods of the Ulster story. In May 1974, only three months after he had taken office, the province was paralysed by a massive 15-day strike organised by the pro-Paisley Ulster Workers Council (UWC) in protest against the Sunningdale Agreement. Merlyn Rees, the Northern Ireland Minister, tried to

---

Key terms

DUP
Democratic Unionist Party, which had broken away from the Official Unionist Party in 1971.

Stormont
The building in Belfast which housed the Northern Ireland Parliament.

Loyalist
Anti-republican, pro-unionist.

Diplock Courts
Set up in Northern Ireland in 1972 to hear cases without a jury, the aim being to avoid the problem of jury members being intimidated.

take a tough line, refusing to negotiate with the UWC. Wilson backed him, referring in a television interview to the Unionists as 'spongers'. It was no surprise when even the moderate Unionist Brian Faulkner, who had signed the Sunningdale Agreement for his party, declared that it was no longer workable and resigned from the Executive. Power sharing seemed dead in the water.

Yet, despite the deep divisions in the province, Wilson did not despair of finding a solution. A Northern Ireland Act was introduced in 1974, which created a Constitutional Convention, a way of reintroducing the power-sharing principle. The first elections to the Convention in 1975 saw a 66 per cent turnout, a sign that the majority of the population were still willing to follow a peaceful, political path. However, when the 83 Convention members met they soon adopted their partisan positions. The Ulster Unionists presented a resolution prepared by Ian Paisley, declaring that they did not accept the right of republicans to take part 'in any future cabinet in Northern Ireland'.

In the face of such inflexibility there was little the SDLP could do. When the resolution was passed by a majority of three, the Convention lost any real meaning and the British government's formal dissolution of it in 1976, after barely a year in existence, was a recognition of what had already happened. Tensions increased still further when, in an attempt to maintain its hard-line policy towards terrorism, the government withdrew the 'special status category' for prisoners serving sentences in Northern Ireland for terrorist acts. In future they would be treated not as political prisoners but as common criminals.

Wilson and his successor, James Callaghan, continued to talk of finding a settlement but there were a number of factors that made this unrealistic:

- The 1970s were an especially violent time in Northern Ireland. Since the IRA was the major culprit in the outrages and assassinations that occurred, including some notorious murders on mainland Britain, it was difficult to make political concessions to the legitimate nationalists without appearing to be giving in to terrorism. Indeed, in the face of a series of lethal IRA attacks in Britain in 1974, which included the **Birmingham pub bombings**, the government introduced a **Prevention of Terrorism Act**.
- There were suggestions that, since the Labour majority was so small in the Commons throughout the 1974–9 period, the government could not afford to antagonise the Ulster Unionists, whose support might be needed in critical Westminster votes.
- The presence on the Labour backbenches of a number of MPs who openly supported the republican cause in Northern Ireland and the 'Troops out' campaign compromised and inhibited the government.

Key terms

Birmingham pub bombings
On 21 November 1974, in separate explosions in two public houses in Birmingham's city centre, 21 people were killed and 180 seriously injured.

Prevention of Terrorism Act
Introduced in November 1974 to give the police and authorities considerably extended powers of search and arrest.

Margaret Thatcher and Ireland 1979–90

In 1979, the year she took office, Margaret Thatcher was made all too aware of the task facing her in Northern Ireland. In March, two months before she became Prime Minister, Airey Neave, the man whom she intended to make her Northern Ireland Minister, was killed when a bomb planted under the bonnet of his car exploded as he drove out of the House of Commons' car park. The killers were the **INLA**, an extreme breakaway group from the IRA, which gloatingly claimed responsibility in a statement:

Airey Neave, got a taste of his own medicine when an INLA unit pulled off the operation of the decade and blew him to bits inside the 'impregnable' Palace of Westminster. The nauseous Margaret Thatcher snivelled on television that he was an 'incalculable loss' – and so he was – to the British ruling class.
(Quoted in *INLA Deadly Divisions* by Jack Holland, 1996)

Key terms

INLA
The Irish National Liberation Army, whose republicanism was part of its programme for Marxist world revolution.

Taoiseach
Gaelic for Prime Minister.

Five months later, it was a member of the royal family who fell victim. At the end of August, Earl Mountbatten of Burma, uncle of the Prince of Wales, was killed by a bomb planted on board his holiday yacht, moored in Mullaghmore harbour in County Sligo. The explosion also killed the Earl's daughter and grandson, and two others in the holiday party. The murders were synchronised with the detonation of two remote-control bombs at Warrenpoint in Northern Ireland which killed 18 British soldiers of the parachute regiment. The troops were deliberately targeted because the IRA considered that particular regiment to have been responsible for 'Bloody Sunday' in 1972 when 14 protesters had been shot (see page 202). Soon after, a couplet was painted on a wall in a Catholic area of Belfast: '14 gone but not forgotten, We got 18 and Mountbatten'.

The INLA was right in thinking that Mrs Thatcher would take a tough stance over Northern Ireland. But her approach did not exclude negotiation and co-operation where these were thought possible. In 1980 she had a number of meetings with Charles Haughey, the Irish *Taoiseach*, with a view to establishing 'closer political co-operation' between Dublin and Westminster.

The death of Bobby Sands 1981

However, such gains as were made on that front were overshadowed by developments in Northern Ireland. In March 1981, in protest against the refusal of the authorities in the Maze prison to treat him as a political prisoner, Bobby Sands, a convicted bomber, went on hunger strike. Mrs Thatcher told the authorities to stand firm in the face of such coercive martyrdom. The result of the intransigence on both sides was that Sands died after refusing food for 66 days.

Sands became an iconic figure to the Catholic population of Northern Ireland. Yet, despite the intense anger towards the British government that his suicide aroused, there was a more positive consequence: Sinn Féin, the legitimate republican party, began to pick up votes in elections. Although Sinn Féin was the political wing of the IRA, the growing willingness of nationalists and republicans to use the ballot box was at least a sign that violence was not looked on as the only recourse.

However, a political solution was still a long way off. This was dramatically illustrated on 12 October 1984 when Margaret Thatcher narrowly escaped being assassinated in the IRA bombing of the Grand Hotel in Brighton. The bomb had been concealed in a bathroom wall three weeks before and was timed to go off in the early hours of the morning when most of the Cabinet, who were using the hotel as a base during the Conservative Party conference, were expected to be there. In the event, five people were killed, none of them ministers, and 30 others injured. Mrs Thatcher gave an impressive performance later that day, insisting that the conference must go on and declaring that democracy would never bow to terrorism.

The Anglo-Irish Agreement, August 1985

A major step towards democracy was made a year later with the signing of the Anglo-Irish Agreement by Margaret Thatcher and the Irish Premier, Garrett Fitzgerald. It contained three main provisions:

- The Irish Republic recognised Northern Ireland as being constitutionally a part of the UK.
- The British government gave an assurance that it supported full civil rights for all in Northern Ireland and acknowledged the strength of nationalist desires for a united Ireland.
- The two governments committed themselves to close co-operation over cross-border security matters.

With hindsight, the Agreement can be seen as an important stage in the advance towards a peaceful settlement. However, at the time, the Agreement was bitterly condemned by many of those it most closely concerned. Mrs Thatcher, who had genuinely intended it to be a basis for reconciliation in Ulster, was shocked at the vehemence of the response; she recorded that it was 'worse than anyone had predicted.' The reasons for opposition to the Agreement were:

- Unionists objected to the involvement of the Irish government in Northern Ireland's affairs, fearing that it gave encouragement to the notion of a united Ireland under the rule of Dublin. At a massive unionist rally in Belfast a few days after the signing of the Agreement, Ian Paisley cried out emotionally 'Mrs Thatcher tells us that the Republic must have some say in our province. We say never, never, never, never.' The Unionist MPs showed their bitterness by resolving not to attend Westminster, copying a tactic that Sinn Féin had used continually.
- The republicans rejected the Agreement for a similar but opposite reason; its terms confirmed the very thing they were fighting against: Northern Ireland's continuation as a part of the UK. They pledged themselves to continue 'the armed struggle'.

- Some members of Mrs Thatcher's government were unhappy with the Agreement on the grounds that it might be wrongly interpreted as a concession towards the men of violence in Northern Ireland. Ian Gow, the Housing Minister, resigned, although he continued to be on good terms with the Prime Minister. In 1990, he paid the ultimate price for his tough line on Ulster when he was blown up outside his home in Sussex by an IRA car bomb.

Massacre at Enniskillen 1987

The IRA's commitment to 'armed struggle' was murderously expressed in November 1987 when it exploded a bomb at a Remembrance Day service in Enniskillen in Northern Ireland. Eleven people were killed and 60 others, including women and children, maimed. So poignantly tragic was the fate of these innocent victims that there were many in both the Catholic and Protestant communities who openly doubted that any cause, no matter how just, could ever justify such suffering. The IRA, however, stated that the carnage would not deter it from its mission. Its official terse comment was 'The British army did not leave Ireland after Bloody Sunday.'

Death on the Rock 1988

The undeclared war continued. In March 1988, in the British colony of Gibraltar, the **SAS** shot and killed three IRA agents before they had time to detonate a car bomb intended to decimate British troops at a changing of the guard ceremony. There was official disquiet, although little public sympathy for the victims, when eyewitness accounts suggested that they had been shot without warning. At the funeral of the three a week later in Belfast, a crowd of some 5000 attenders were fired on by Michael Stone, a deranged, loyalist gunman; three died and another 50 were injured. Three days later two off-duty British soldiers inadvertently drove into an area where an IRA parade was being held. They were dragged from their car by the crowd and beaten. Later they were shot and killed by IRA men.

In October 1988, in an effort to deny the terrorists 'the oxygen of publicity', Mrs Thatcher's government imposed a broadcasting ban on the IRA. This involved blanking out the voices of terrorists and their supporters, and substituting actors' voices. As even the government later reluctantly admitted, it was all rather pointless since the IRA personnel could still be seen and their message heard.

Although the catalogue of death made bitter reading, behind the violence that obviously caught the headlines, efforts continued to be made to bring stability to Ulster. In the final years of Margaret Thatcher's administration, her government introduced the following measures:

- 1987: the Central Community Relations Unit was established to foster greater contact and understanding between Catholics and Protestants.

Key term

SAS
Special Air Service, the crack anti-terrorist unit of the British armed services.

- 1989: the Fair Employment Act required employers who had more than 25 workers on their books not to discriminate when allocating jobs and opportunities for promotion.
- 1990: the Northern Ireland Community Relations Council extended the support and resources granted to the Community Relations Unit three years earlier.

These were perhaps small advances but at least they kept alive the idea that the government was not totally consumed with the fight against terrorism; it had time for the smaller things. But as the number of outrages and the death toll mounted, it was evident to all that only a political solution could end Northern Ireland's agonies.

John Major and Ireland 1990–7

Northern Ireland was the bitter chalice that was passed to Major as Prime Minister at the end of 1990. He had been in office for only two months when, in its most audacious act yet, the IRA lobbed mortar shells at 10 Downing Street from a parked van. This was the prelude to a sustained IRA bombing campaign in Britain. In March 1993, a boy of three and one of 12 years were killed and 50 people injured by bombs left in litter bins in a shopping mall in Warrington, Cheshire. In April, one person was killed and 40 were injured by a bomb planted in a lorry in Bishopsgate in the City of London. The bomb also caused over a billion pounds worth of damage to a number of bank premises, including the NatWest tower.

The anger among ordinary people at these brutalities led to large peace rallies in London, Belfast and Dublin. Aware how public opinion was turning against them on both sides of the Irish Sea, the IRA put out disclaimers saying that the deaths had not been intended and that it was the fault of the British police who had failed to act on the detailed warnings that the IRA had given them about the location of the bombs.

The Downing Street Declaration, December 1993

Although the times did not seem propitious for a new political initiative, the Irish Republic and the UK had as premiers at this point two men with very similar characters and temperaments. Albert Reynolds and John Major shared an unflappable, practical attitude which enabled them quickly to agree on a common approach towards improving the chances of peace. The outcome of their agreement was the Downing Street Declaration whose chief features were:

Key date

Downing Street Declaration: December 1993

- The British government announced that it had 'no selfish, strategic interest in Northern Ireland'; its sole concern was to accede to the democratically expressed wishes of the people there.
- It also accepted that it was 'for the people of the island of Ireland alone, north and south, to bring about a united Ireland, if that is their wish.'

- Reynolds declared that the Irish Republic accepted the right of the majority in Northern Ireland to decide its future and that, if a democratic settlement could be achieved there, the south was prepared to drop its traditional claim that Northern Ireland was part of the Republic.

The ceasefire 1994

Unofficial contacts between the British government and Sinn Féin eventually convinced the IRA that the Declaration had indeed recognised the key republican and nationalist positions on the status of Northern Ireland and that Britain was not committed to indefinite control of the province. This was sufficient for the IRA to declare a ceasefire in August 1994.

The big question was whether the loyalist paramilitary units could be persuaded to do the same. Everybody knew the IRA would not keep the ceasefire for long if it remained a one-sided affair. The government's fear was that the precise point that had temporarily pacified the IRA, Britain's willingness eventually to allow Northern Ireland to determine its own status, might be seen by the Unionists as a sell-out. Major took the step of assuring them that the British government had no intention of forcing the North into a united Ireland. This proved sufficient for the time being to quell Unionist fears. In October the loyalist units announced that they would be observing their own ceasefire.

For the first time since the troubles reignited in 1969 Northern Ireland was at peace. Given all the bitterness that had preceded it, it could be only a fragile peace and how long it would hold depended on how long the IRA and the loyalist paramilitaries considered it served their individual interests.

The Mitchell Report, January 1996

The ceasefire did not hold; between 1996 and 1998, there were frequent outbursts of renewed violence. The basic fact was that the two sets of paramilitaries did not trust each other. However, a more encouraging development was the involvement of the USA. In 1995, President Clinton made rapturously received visits to both Dublin and Belfast and, in the following year, Senator George Mitchell chaired an international commission set up to consider the Irish issue. Major showed a generous breadth of mind in accepting the American move. Rather than see it as an outside interference in a British problem, he welcomed the commission as offering a way forward.

Mitchell, in a report he presented in January 1996, laid down a set of principles on which a peace process might be developed. The major ones were:

- the total disarmament of all paramilitary organisations and their renunciation of force
- the agreement by all parties concerned to accept as binding any agreement reached in an all-party negotiation.

Mitchell's central conclusion was that real progress towards a settlement was ultimately impossible without **decommissioning**. Yet, to achieve this, both sides would have to be assured that laying down arms could achieve the same results as using them. Peace had to be seen as politically profitable as violence.

Decommissioning
The giving up of weapons.

Key term

Tony Blair and Ireland 1997–2007
The Good Friday Agreement, April 1998
When Tony Blair became Prime Minister in 1997 he was the heir to the benefits that Major's quiet, accommodating diplomacy had brought, a fact that Blair willingly acknowledged. It was on the basis of the Mitchell principles that Blair, through his Northern Ireland team of ministers, gained Sinn Féin's agreement to persuade the IRA to accept decommissioning. A Sinn Féin delegation, including the party's leader Gerry Adams, was invited to talks with the Prime Minister at 10 Downing Street. That such a meeting took place at all showed how far things had progressed and it eased the path towards the Good Friday Agreement, April 1998, the biggest constitutional advance since 1969.

Good Friday
Agreement: 1998

Key date

The Agreement owed much to the persistence of Blair and his Irish counterpart, Bertie Ahern. Refusing to accept that the cycle of violence was unbreakable, both leaders used a mixture of charm and determination to bring the parties to the table. The Agreement was accepted by the Ulster Unionists, the SDLP and Sinn Féin. Of the major parties only Ian Paisley's DUP rejected it. Under the Agreement:

- Northern Ireland's union with Britain was guaranteed for as long as the majority of the people of the province wanted it.
- The Irish Republic withdrew its territorial claim to Northern Ireland.
- A Northern Ireland Assembly with a new power-sharing executive government was created.
- As an act of goodwill, all terrorist prisoners would be released within two years.

The terms of the Agreement were then put to the electorate in an all-Ireland referendum on the future of Northern Ireland. David Trimble, leader of the Ulster Unionists, and Gerry Adams of Sinn Féin urged their respective supporters to vote for it. The result was a large majority in favour of acceptance. In the Irish Republic there was a 95 per cent yes vote, in Northern Ireland a 71 per cent yes vote. So, in return for their chance to share in government, the nationalists and republicans had given up their demand for a united Ireland. For their part, the official Unionists had agreed to the end their power to control Northern Irish politics and public affairs.

It was a remarkable study in direct democracy and gave renewed hope that peace could be achieved. The troubles did not immediately end. Republican and loyalist extremists rejected the Agreement and violence continued, the worst instance being a car bomb explosion in Omagh in August 1998, which killed 28 people and injured 200. Yet it was evident that the perpetrators of such outrages were becoming isolated. Gerry Adams made a striking statement condemning the atrocity in which he said that 'violence must be a thing of the past, over, done with and gone'. International recognition of the progress being made in Northern Ireland came with the awarding in October 1998 of the Nobel Peace Prize jointly to David Trimble and John Hume, the SDLP leader.

Although the troubles continued for a number of years into the new century, there was a growing sense among all but a few on the extremes that a political solution was the only answer. This sense of the futility of violence was quickened by the events of 11 September 2001 in the USA (see page 213). Many Irish-Americans who had previously given moral and financial support to the IRA campaigns in Northern Ireland now had a graphic example in their own homeland of what terrorism actually meant in practice. It was no coincidence that thereafter all the talk by responsible Americans, politicians and people, was of the need for a peaceful resolution of Northern Ireland's ills.

In a similar way, the death and mutilation caused by the London bombings in July 2005 (see page 216) re-emphasised the illegitimacy in a civilised society of violent means being used to achieve political ends. In Northern Ireland itself the main obstacle to peace remained the issue of decommissioning. Could the paramilitaries be brought genuinely to abandon their arms? On 28 July 2005, responding to a number of appeals by Sinn Féin, the IRA announced that, while it would remain in being as a force pledged to defend nationalist Ulster, it was giving up its weapons and pledging itself to the use of 'exclusively peaceful means'.

The question now was whether the loyalist paramilitaries, such as the Ulster Volunteer Force (UVF), would do the same. The UVF's claim had always been that they could not trust the IRA declarations of intent and therefore, could not themselves disarm. Yet the ultra-Unionists were also undergoing a form of conversion. Ian Paisley, although never an advocate of violence, had always proved a major obstacle to constitutional advance. His DUP had rejected the Downing Street Declaration and the Good Friday Agreement. As long as he held out, loyalist paramilitaries were unlikely to budge.

However, the Unionists were also undergoing a form of conversion. It was a matter of accepting reality. **Demography** was the key. Protestant Unionists were fast becoming a minority in Northern Ireland. As Table 6.3 shows, the Catholic proportion of the population was growing, with a higher birth rate in the Catholic community than in the Protestant.

Unless they adapted to these irreversible changes, Ulster Unionists would become an increasingly embattled enclave. With few sympathisers anywhere beyond their own ranks, they could expect little help from outside. History was not on their side. It was such thinking that played a part in persuading Paisley and the DUP that it was far better to accommodate themselves to the situation, while they still had the chance to be part of a power-

Key term

Demography
Population analysis.

Table 6.3: Religious affiliations in Northern Ireland (as a percentage of population) 1961–2001

Religion	1961	1991	2001
Roman Catholic	34.9	38.4	40.3
Protestant	62.5	50.6	45.2

sharing government, than to continue with a resistance that might ultimately destroy their power altogether. The result was that in May 2006 the UVF renounced 'violence' and pledged itself to give up its weapons. This opened the way for the St Andrews Agreement between the British and Irish governments.

St Andrews Agreement, October 2006

The terms of the St Andrews Agreement included:

- the Northern Ireland Assembly was to be restored
- the DUP agreed to share power with republicans and nationalists in the Northern Ireland Executive
- Sinn Féin accepted the authority of the Police Service of Northern Ireland (PSNI), which had replaced the RUC.

St Andrews Agreement: 2006

Northern Ireland Executive formed: 2007

Key dates

Northern Ireland Executive 2007

Elections were held in March 2007 under the terms of the Agreement. The number of seats gained by the main parties were:

- DUP   36
- Sinn Féin   28
- Official Unionists 18
- SDLP   16.

In May 2007, the new executive came into being with Ian Paisley, leader of the largest party, appointed First Minister, and Martin McGuinness, deputy leader of Sinn Féin, the second largest party, the Deputy First Minister. In July 2007, the British army announced the end of its mission in Northern Ireland which it had been operating since 1969.

This was an extraordinary climax to nearly 40 years of bitterness, which had cost the lives of thousands. It was a tribute to those on both sides of the Irish Sea, most notably John Major, Bertie Ahern and Tony Blair, who had stayed committed to the peace process no matter how many times it faltered. Perhaps most extraordinary of all was the amicable relations that developed in government between Paisley and McGuinness. At the end of 2007, McGuinness remarked, 'Up until the 26 March this year, Ian Paisley and I never had a conversation about anything – not even about the weather – and now we have worked very closely together over the last seven months and there's been no angry words between us. This shows we are set for a new course.'

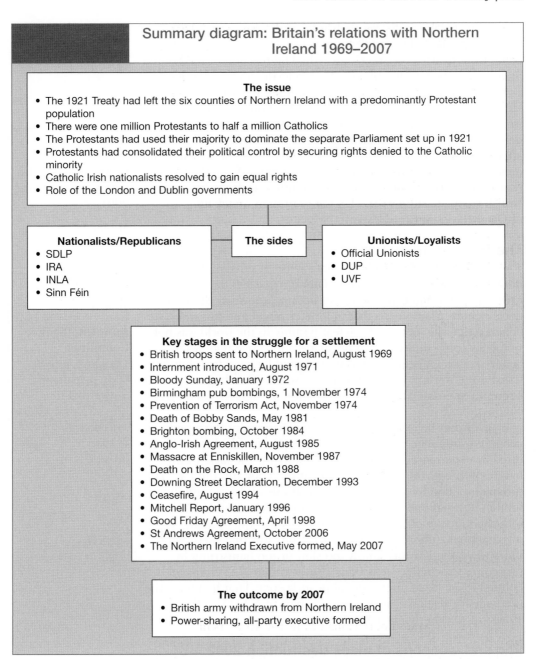

Summary diagram: Britain's relations with Northern Ireland 1969–2007

The issue
- The 1921 Treaty had left the six counties of Northern Ireland with a predominantly Protestant population
- There were one million Protestants to half a million Catholics
- The Protestants had used their majority to dominate the separate Parliament set up in 1921
- Protestants had consolidated their political control by securing rights denied to the Catholic minority
- Catholic Irish nationalists resolved to gain equal rights
- Role of the London and Dublin governments

The sides

Nationalists/Republicans
- SDLP
- IRA
- INLA
- Sinn Féin

Unionists/Loyalists
- Official Unionists
- DUP
- UVF

Key stages in the struggle for a settlement
- British troops sent to Northern Ireland, August 1969
- Internment introduced, August 1971
- Bloody Sunday, January 1972
- Birmingham pub bombings, 1 November 1974
- Prevention of Terrorism Act, November 1974
- Death of Bobby Sands, May 1981
- Brighton bombing, October 1984
- Anglo-Irish Agreement, August 1985
- Massacre at Enniskillen, November 1987
- Death on the Rock, March 1988
- Downing Street Declaration, December 1993
- Ceasefire, August 1994
- Mitchell Report, January 1996
- Good Friday Agreement, April 1998
- St Andrews Agreement, October 2006
- The Northern Ireland Executive formed, May 2007

The outcome by 2007
- British army withdrawn from Northern Ireland
- Power-sharing, all-party executive formed

Key question
How did 'the special relationship' develop between Tony Blair and George W. Bush?

Key date
9/11 Terrorist attacks on USA: 2001

5 | Blair and Britain's Special Relationship with the USA

9/11

On 11 September 2001, the USA was subjected to the deadliest act of terror it had ever experienced in its own homeland. Islamic terrorists hijacked four commercial aircraft. Two of the planes were flown into the twin towers of the World Trade Centre in New York, causing both to collapse. The third plane was piloted into the Pentagon building in Washington DC, while the fourth crashed near Pittsburgh, Pennsylvania, as the passengers fought with the hijackers. The death toll was nearly 3000, the victims being from nearly every race on earth. The reaction of the United States was to begin what became known as the 'war on terror'.

Tony Blair immediately committed himself to that war. He announced that Britain 'stood shoulder to shoulder with our American friends' in the struggle 'between the free and democratic world and terrorism'. The attacks of **9/11** and their aftermath turned him into president George W. Bush's closest and most dependable ally, a relationship that was to shape the remainder of Blair's premiership. A month after 9/11, Blair sent British troops to support the US forces in their attack upon the **al-Qaeda** bases in Afghanistan.

The Blair doctrine

The attacks of 9/11 intensified Blair's sense of mission, but did not create it. In a speech given in Chicago in 1999 the British Prime Minister had expressed what became known as the Blair doctrine. His position was that of a determined anti-appeaser; he believed that the best way to defeat tyranny in the world was not simply by using diplomacy to persuade oppressive regimes to behave better. Of course, diplomacy should be tried first, but, if this did not work, it was legitimate to use force to oblige aggressor states to conform to internationally agreed standards of conduct.

Blair further believed that international action of the type he proposed should be carried out by those powers which were best fitted by experience and military capability for the task. In the nature of things, this necessarily meant the USA and the UK. The two major allies, therefore, had a special role and responsibility to fulfil in international affairs. Whenever possible they should act with the sanction of the UN, since the UN was the ultimate international authority. But the hard reality was that there were times when the UN was simply too slow or too hamstrung by procedure to act effectively. Blair also held that NATO was entitled to act as an international peacekeeper. That had been the rationale for Britain's involvement, as part of NATO, in the attacks against Serbia in 1999 (see page 167).

Iraq and weapons of mass destruction 2002

It was in keeping with this doctrine that, in September 2002, addressing a specially convened House of Commons, the Prime Minister set out to explain why it was essential that Saddam Hussein, still leader of Iraq 11 years after being defeated in the Gulf War (see page 163), be brought down. Blair quoted from a dossier (later referred to in the popular press as the 'dodgy dossier') passed to him by the **Joint Intelligence Committee** (JIC), which claimed to have evidence that 'Saddam's weapons of mass destruction (WMD) programme is active, detailed and growing.' It was this that would provide the justification for invading Iraq. However, at this stage Blair denied that an invasion was inevitable; he said it was the aim of the USA and

Key terms

9/11
The American formulation for the date 11 September 2001.

al-Qaeda
The Islamic terrorist organisation which organised the 9/11 attacks.

Joint Intelligence Committee
The government body principally responsible for providing ministers with national security information.

Britain to work through the UN to bring about regime change in Iraq.

Anxious not to lose support at home, particularly among his own party, Blair was initially insistent that Bush should take no action until the UN had formally resolved to back the Western allies. There had already been a first resolution (No. 1441, passed in November 2002) requiring Saddam Hussein to prove to UN inspectors that he had abandoned all his WMD as he was required to do by the peace settlement that followed the Gulf War in 1991. Resolution 1441, however, did not authorise the armed invasion of Iraq; to achieve this there would have to be a second UN resolution.

The possibility of gaining this rapidly disappeared when Russia and China made it clear that they would block any attempt to push this through the Security Council. Bush, feeling that the opposition of those two countries arose from mischievous power politics rather than being a principled objection, decided to go ahead with the invasion plan. At a third key meeting between President and Prime Minister, Bush, aware of the difficulty Blair would have in convincing his Cabinet and party, offered the Prime Minister the chance to withdraw. But Blair, describing the fight against tyranny as 'the most fundamental issue of our time', declined to back out. He tried to gain support from Europe but failed; most significantly, France and Germany found the grounds for military intervention unconvincing. If Britain and the USA went ahead, they would be acting alone.

Anglo-American invasion of Iraq 2003

Key date

Anglo-American invasion of Iraq: 2003

So it was that on 20 March 2003 American and British forces began the invasion of Iraq without formal UN sanction and, in Britain's case, in the face of fierce opposition at home. Mass peace demonstrations were held in London and other cities, and Robin Cook, the former Foreign Secretary, resigned from the Cabinet in protest at the invasion, declaring in his Commons' resignation speech that the war had 'neither international agreement nor domestic support'.

Blair and Bush

Key term

Respect
Founded on 25 January 2004 in London as a socialist breakaway group from the Labour Party, its name represents the words Respect, Equality, Socialism, Peace, Environmentalism, Community, and Trade Unionism.

The charge was made at the time, and has often been repeated since, that Blair was Bush's 'poodle', that he allowed himself to be dragged into the war. But this overlooks the driving sense of conviction and mission that inspired Tony Blair. His judgement may be faulted but it should not be denied that throughout he was his own man. Indeed, George Galloway, the rebel Labour MP who resigned to set up his own anti-war party, **Respect**, believed that the Prime Minister was the initiator rather than the follower in his relations with the President. The special relationship that bound them was one of equals.

The military operation in Iraq proved highly and rapidly successful. By the middle of April 2003 Saddam's forces were broken and the allies declared that the 'major combat' was over. It was then that the problems really started. In the rush to war, insufficient time had been devoted to planning what would follow victory. The toppling of Saddam may have removed a vicious oppressor of his people but it did not lead to peace. Indeed, it could be said that civil war followed, with rival Muslim and regional factions fighting each other. The final capture of the fugitive Saddam Hussein in December 2003 brought rejoicing among Iraqis who had been victims of his brutal regime, but it did nothing to end the internal strife. The victorious Allied forces that had been intended to liberate Iraq were obliged perforce to become its occupiers.

On 31 January 2006, in one of the saddest coincidences of the war in Iraq, the 100th British serviceman to be killed there was Corporal Gordon Prichard, who a month earlier had been photographed smiling with Tony Blair during one of the Prime Minister's visits to the troops. Eighteen months later when Blair stood down as Prime Minister, US and British forces were still in Iraq with no prospect of their leaving soon.

The WMD issue

The political problems that the war created for Blair were intensified by the failure to discover any evidence of WMD in Iraq. The suicide in July 2003 of Dr David Kelly, a WMD expert working for the Ministry of Defence, deepened the gloom and stimulated the furore relating to the Iraq affair. Two months before his death Kelly had confided to a BBC journalist his concerns that the government had exaggerated the findings in the JIC dossier on which Blair had based his reasons for going to war. The journalist, Andrew Gilligan, then went public on radio and in the press, accusing the government of having 'sexed up' the report largely at the promptings of Alistair Campbell, the Prime Minister's chief spin doctor. It was after being revealed as Gilligan's source that Dr Kelly had taken his own life.

The government immediately set up an inquiry, which, under the chairmanship of Lord Hutton, examined the circumstances of David Kelly's death. Among the 70 witnesses were the Prime Minister himself and Alistair Campbell. When the inquiry published its findings in January 2004, it cleared the government of any direct involvement in Kelly's tragic end. But what the Hutton report did not, and could not, do was lift the thickening cloud of doubt about the legality and morality of the Blair government's original decision to go to war.

The London bombings, July 2005

On 7 July 2005 the reality of the war on terror was brought home to Britain in a particularly fearful way, when four co-ordinated bomb explosions in London killed 56 people and injured another 700. The dead included the suicide bombers, all of them young British Islamists. Two weeks later, a similar bomb plot was foiled at the last minute when police arrested the intended assassins, who were again all crazed Islamists. Responsible Muslim leaders were quick to condemn the assassins and plotters and to distance

7/7 London bombings: 2005

Key date

their faith from the mad perversion of it that the killers represented.

Some critics saw the bombings as a direct consequence of the Iraq War and the foreign policies of Bush and Blair. It was argued that:

- The removal of Saddam Hussein was not enough to justify the war. Britain and the USA had invaded Iraq for wholly inadequate reasons. Rather than being a war on terror, the allied actions in Iraq had encouraged the spread of terror. The West had lost the moral high ground.
- By declaring war on terror and selecting particular targets to attack, as with Afghanistan and Iraq, the two leaders had in fact created or encouraged the very forces of terrorism that they were trying to defeat.
- The Anglo-American hostility to Islam which the war revealed led to retaliation by Muslim extremists who became **jihadists** in order to defend their faith against the West.

The counter-response to such arguments by those sympathetic to the Bush–Blair alliance was to point to the fact that:

- Jihadist terrorism, as in the case of 9/11, pre-dated the Iraq war.
- The Anglo-American military campaigns fought since the 1990s had been undertaken largely to protect Muslim people and interests, e.g. Kuwait in 1991, Bosnia in 1995 and Kosovo in 1999.
- By far the greater number of Muslim deaths were caused by other Muslims.
- Even though Iraq had not developed WMD, its leader, Saddam Hussein, had had the money and the will to produce such weapons. Had he not been brought down by the Anglo-American invasion in 2003, the world at some point might well have had to deal with a nuclear-armed Iraq.

Yet whatever the arguments for and against Blair's actions and policies towards Iraq and the war on terror, there is little doubt that they conditioned the character of his government after 2003. Notwithstanding his achievements on the domestic front, it was his foreign policy that defined his years in office. For good or bad, it had been his seriousness and sincerity of purpose in pursuing what he judged to be a moral cause that had created the perception of Britain's position in the world in 2007.

Key term

Jihadists
Self-proclaimed warriors in the defence of Islam.

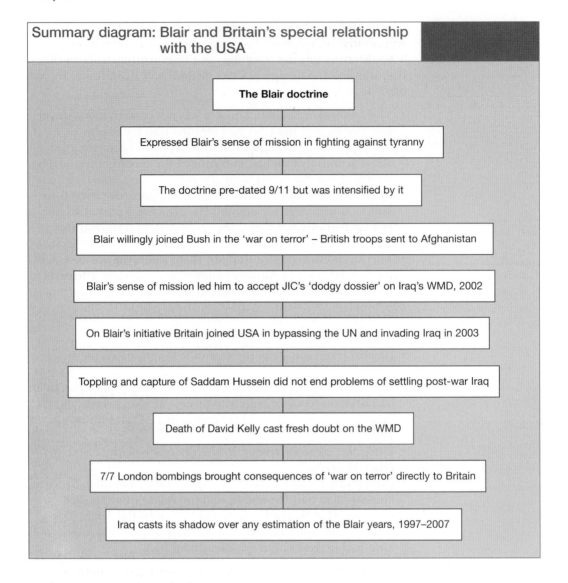

Summary diagram: Blair and Britain's special relationship with the USA

The Blair doctrine

Expressed Blair's sense of mission in fighting against tyranny

The doctrine pre-dated 9/11 but was intensified by it

Blair willingly joined Bush in the 'war on terror' – British troops sent to Afghanistan

Blair's sense of mission led him to accept JIC's 'dodgy dossier' on Iraq's WMD, 2002

On Blair's initiative Britain joined USA in bypassing the UN and invading Iraq in 2003

Toppling and capture of Saddam Hussein did not end problems of settling post-war Iraq

Death of David Kelly cast fresh doubt on the WMD

7/7 London bombings brought consequences of 'war on terror' directly to Britain

Iraq casts its shadow over any estimation of the Blair years, 1997–2007

6 | Population Change and Social Issues

Population change

A dominant social feature of Britain in the first decade of the twenty-first century is the size and age distribution of its population. As to size, Table 6.4 shows the figures for 2006.

Key question
What problems have the growth and changing composition of the population created in Britain?

Table 6.4: Population of Britain in 2006 (to nearest 100 people)

Country	Population	Percentage of UK total
England	50,762,900	83.8
Scotland	5,116,900	8.4
Wales	2,965,900	4.9
Northern Ireland	1,741,600	2.9
Total	60,587,300	100.0

The growth in total figures over the previous half-century is shown in Table 6.5.

Table 6.5: Total UK population 1951–2006 (to nearest 1000 people)

Year	Population
1951	50,225,000
1961	52,709,000
1971	55,515,000
1981	56,337,000
1991	57,808,000
2001	58,789,000
2006	60,587,000

Life expectancy The remaining number of years an individual is likely to live after a given age.

The total of 60.5 million marked a growth in population of around five million since 1971 and towards two million since 2001. More significant than the simple aggregate increase was the rise in the average age of the population, going up from 34 in 1971 to 39 in 2006. Five years may not seem a big difference, but it pointed to a disturbing trend: Britain had a rapidly ageing population. The number of young people under 16 was shrinking in proportion to those over 65. By 2006, 10 million people, one-sixth of the population, were over 65, while one million were over 85. This was a result of the increase in **life expectancy** over the previous century, as shown in Table 6.6.

The social impact of the population shift

One result of these population changes was that there were twice as many 'senior citizens' in 2006 as there had been 50 years earlier (when they were known as 'old-age pensioners'). This tendency has been referred to as the 'demographic time-bomb'. The problem this dramatic expression describes has these components:

- Welfare services are funded by revenue raised in taxation from those in work. As the older, retired section of the population grows in number it makes increasing demands on those services, which it no longer contributes as much money for in taxes.
- The amount people paid in taxes and National Insurance while they were working seemed high at the time, but because of inflation and the ever-rising cost of medical technology, their original payments are inadequate to pay for their welfare needs after retirement.
- It follows that to sustain welfare services at the expected level, the working population which is in relative decline in numbers will have to pay an ever-increasing burden in taxation.
- This threatens to give rise to social injustice. As the ageing part of the population grows disproportionately larger, its sheer numbers render it a powerful voting bloc, which no political party can afford to ignore or upset. The result may be that the legitimate voice of the working revenue payers may be drowned out by that of the non-contributing retired members of society.

Table 6.6: Life expectancy in Britain 1901–2001

	1901		1931		1961		2001	
	Male	Female	Male	Female	Male	Female	Male	Female
At birth	45.5	49.0	58.4	62.5	67.9	73.8	74.5	79.9
At age 1	53.6	55.8	62.1	65.1	68.6	74.2	74.0	79.3
At age 10	50.4	52.7	55.6	58.6	60.0	65.6	65.2	70.5
At age 20	41.7	44.1	46.7	49.6	50.4	55.7	55.4	60.6
At age 40	26.1	28.3	29.5	32.4	31.5	36.5	36.2	41.0
At age 60	13.3	14.6	14.4	16.4	15.0	19.0	18.7	22.7
At age 80	4.9	5.3	4.9	5.4	5.2	6.3	7.0	8.8

There have even been suggestions, perhaps not entirely serious in intention, that to correct the democratic imbalance, the franchise should be withdrawn from those aged over 65. The more sober reflection is that the growth and shift in the population means that the state has the impossible task of meeting ever-growing demands from ever-diminishing resources. How serious the trend is can be judged from Figure 6.3, which shows the projected rise in the population by 2050.

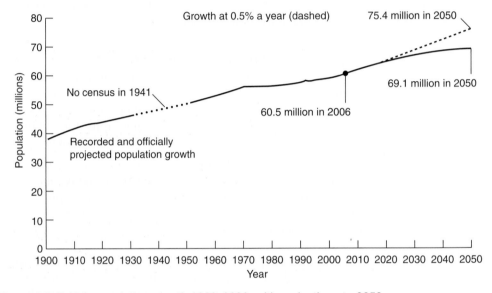

Figure 6.3: British population growth 1900–2006, with projections to 2050.

Immigration

The increase in population was not only a result of greater longevity; immigration was also a contributory factor. Figure 6.4 shows both the **natural change** that occurred and the impact of **net migration** in the years 1991–2006, which accounted for an increase of some three million people in that period.

Immigration had been a factor in population growth throughout the twentieth century. Significant numbers from the West Indies and India had arrived in the 1950s and 1960s, in response to the government's appeal for workers in the public services (see page 54). Another important contingent were the ethnic Asians who came to Britain in the 1960s and 1970s after being driven from where they had settled in such African countries as Kenya and Uganda. The **census** of 2001 revealed the following details:

- Indians were the largest single ethnic group in Britain with 984,000 people.
- People of Caribbean or African descent numbered 969,000.
- Pakistanis and Bangladeshis numbered 932,000.

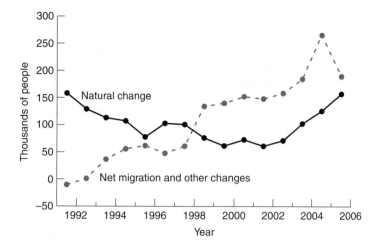

Figure 6.4: Natural change and net immigration 1991–2006.

- Ethnic minority groups represent just over seven per cent, much less than one in 10, of Britain's population.
- The 2001 census was the first time that religious affiliation had been measured. One of the findings was that there were 1.6 million Muslims in Britain, making them the largest British non-Christian faith group.

Of course, overall numbers are not the only pertinent factor. Where there is racist reaction to the presence of immigrants it is not usually in regard to aggregate numbers, but to their concentration in particular urban areas where there are poor or limited resources (see page 54).

An interesting development in the pattern of immigration came after a number of countries of Eastern Europe joined the EU in 2004. Their workers now had the right to come to Britain. Official government figures recorded that in 2006 approximately half a million Poles had registered for work in Britain. However, Polish sources suggested that the actual number who had gone to Britain was over twice that figure. What the discrepancy highlighted was something that embarrassed the Blair government during its decade in office: it had only partial or inexact figures on a range of immigration issues, such as how many refugees and asylum seekers had either settled in Britain or had returned to their country of origin. Such uncertainties led sceptics to suggest that the government did not have an immigration policy at all. One of the government responses to the charge was to point to the number of immigrants who entered illegally and who in the nature of things could not easily be counted or monitored. It was this that makes the collection of exact figures extremely problematical.

As to the role that recent immigrants played in the life of the country there were two main and opposed views:

- It was argued that immigrants played a vital role in the economy by taking unpleasant, but essential, low-paid jobs that the indigenous workers would not consider. By working and paying taxes they contributed to the nation's revenue and gave an object lesson in hard work and responsibility.

- A counterclaim was that while the first point about filling vacant positions might be true, it could only be a stop-gap measure since once immigrants became settled they would begin to demand the better wages and conditions enjoyed by host workers. As to taxation, ran the argument, since immigrant workers did low-paid jobs the revenue they contributed was smaller than the added costs of providing them and their families with health welfare and educational services.

Multiculturalism

The big social question that Britain faced in the early twenty-first century was no longer about race. The argument for racial equality had won the day. None but a bigot could claim that one race was superior to another and that a person's worth and rights were to be determined by the ethnic group to which he or she belonged. The issue that remained to be resolved was not a racial but a cultural one. Were all cultures to be regarded as morally equivalent? Was there such an identifiable concept as British culture? If there was, what were its main features? And if, for example, these included the principle of fair play, freedom of speech, religious tolerance, and race and gender equality, how were other cultures to be treated that did not accept or practise these values? Could a liberal society accept, for example, the persecution of homosexuals as perverts and the genital mutilation of infant girls, practices to be found occurring among extreme religious groups in Britain?

Riots in Bradford, Manchester and Oldham in 2001 in which black, white and Asian groups clashed were a disturbing sign that integration had not taken place in the more deprived urban areas. Significantly, Trevor Phillips, the Chairman of the **EHRC**, acknowledged that the multicultural policies which successive governments had followed had largely failed and that integration was not taking place in the way that had been hoped.

In 2005, Phillips expressed fears that multiculturalism could cause Britain to 'sleepwalk towards segregation' and argued that a key way of preventing segregation hardening was not to allow it in British education in the form of exclusive faith schools. He had in mind particularly the madrassas, exclusively Muslim schools where children were trained in an Islamic way of life. Not unnaturally, the supporters of the madrassas responded by pointing out that:

- Catholic and Jewish faith schools had long been established in Britain.
- The teaching of Islamic values was wholly compatible with preparing young Muslims to become responsible British citizens.

Phillips' comments aroused anger on the left. Ken Livingstone, the Labour Mayor of London, attacked him for giving currency to racist ideas by 'pandering to the right'. Phillips replied by saying

Key question
Why did multiculturalism become such a disputed issue?

EHRC
The Equality and Human Rights Commission, successor to the Commission for Racial Equality.

Key term

it was essential 'to ask hard questions about multicultural Britain', adding in a memorable phrase that the basis of free speech was the right 'to allow people to offend each other'. Interestingly, Phillips was supported in principle by two prominent Christian clerics, Michael Nazir-Ali, the Pakistani-born Bishop of Rochester, and John Sentamu, the Ugandan-born Archbishop of York, both of whom expressed strong doubts about multiculturalism, arguing that, whatever its intentions, in practice it created social division not social harmony.

Religious Hatred Act 2006

That people of such obvious goodwill and informed experience as those mentioned in the previous paragraph should be so concerned over the effect of multiculturalism indicates that during the Blair government it had become one of the most demanding and contentious of issues. The government's awareness of this and its desire to give the right example led to the introduction in 2006 of a religious hatred bill intended to protect people from being abused and attacked for their religious beliefs. It was undoubtedly intended to give assurance and comfort to British Muslims who felt they were under suspicion and attack in the current atmosphere created by religious terrorists.

The bill met stiff criticism from both believers and non-believers who suggested that religious hatred was too imprecise an attitude to give definition to it and that existing laws against incitement already gave adequate protection. There was no justification, therefore, for giving a privileged place in law to religious belief. In the end the bill went through in a very watered-down form, adding little to existing laws on incitement.

The Danish cartoons

What had pushed the government into introducing the Religious Hatred Act had been the wish to calm the tensions created by two events that had illustrated in tragic and dramatic form that far from being integrated into society there were religious groups in Britain who felt deeply alienated from the mainstream culture. The first was the London bombings of July 2005 (see page 216). The second was the violent reaction to the publication of the Danish cartoons. In 2005 a Danish magazine had published a set of satirical cartoons, which, according to many Muslims, defamed and insulted the prophet Mohammed, the sacred founder of the Islamic faith. In London in February 2006, some 300 Muslims demonstrated against this publication. Four of the demonstrators were arrested and subsequently tried and imprisoned for incitement to violence and murder. One of the convicted four had whipped up the crowd by leading a repeated chant containing the words: 'Bomb, bomb the UK' and 'Annihilate those who insult Islam'.

The most disturbing aspect was that the four convicted demonstrators, like the London suicide bombers, had all been bought up in average households in the UK.

Extraparliamentary movements

An important development that began in the last quarter of the twentieth century was the growth of **extraparliamentary** groups and campaigns which sought to achieve their ends by direct action rather than through party politics.

Environmentalism

At its best, environmentalism was an idealistic attempt to preserve the world from the harmful effects of unplanned and uncontrolled economic growth. Courageous protests were made by groups and individuals to preserve valuable cultural treasures and conserve threatened natural habitats. Through the work and propaganda of such movements as **Friends of the Earth**, founded in 1969, and **Greenpeace**, founded in 1971, the attention of the public was drawn to a range of issues such as climate change. There were also important developments in the popularising of aspects of science that previously had been a closed book to those not trained in such areas.

But there was also a less attractive side to environmentalism. Some commentators saw in it a patronising attempt by self-appointment moralists to thrust their views on the working class and make them change their traditional habits. On the basis of dubious scientific findings, an attempt was made to preach to people and make them feel guilty. The danger for all movements that challenge establishment values is that they tend to attract extremists and oddballs. Environmentalism attracted the sort of people who love imposing their ideas on others. It recalled the social reformers of the Victorian and Edwardian periods who, while their intentions were no doubt good, tended to act as if they knew best when it came to morality and social behaviour. Some saw it as resurgence of **puritanism**, a trend that has been recurrent in British life.

Although people of any political persuasion could and did join the movement, environmentalism naturally attracted those on the left. This became particularly evident after the collapse of Communism in the USSR and Eastern Europe in the 1990s. Disappointed socialists who had seen their great experiment fail turned to environmentalism as a way in which they could still further their ideas of a controlled, collective society committed to a particular ideal. Destroying the bourgeoisie was replaced by saving the planet. Environmentalism appealed to the collective mentality.

The environmental lobby became a faith rather than a scientific viewpoint. Its campaign was based on the belief that it could tell the future. The only evidence it accepted was those models and projections that supported its case that current industrial trends were leading the world to disaster. It rejected contrary evidence and doubted the integrity of those who offered alternative theories of climate change. But there was no doubting its influence. Dubious and disputed though its arguments may have been, it succeeded in frightening Western governments, including Britain's, into introducing a range of measures which threatened

Key question
Why was there a significant turning to non-parliamentary ways to achieving political ends?

Extraparliamentary
Not relying on conventional party politics.

Friends of the Earth and **Greenpeace**
Similar movements, which originated in North America, but quickly spread to Europe. They believed in direct action as a way of spreading their beliefs about the threat to the planet.

Puritanism
An attitude that has religious roots but has become secularised. It is the view among certain people that because they find some forms of social behaviour distasteful they are entitled to prohibit others from engaging in them, even to the point of making the behaviour illegal.

Key terms

'So it wasn't the H-Bomb that finished off the earth people, after all!' A newspaper cartoon from November 1969 drawing attention to the pollution that followed from a number of accidents in which damaged tankers had leaked their cargo of oil; the most disturbing case for Britain had occurred two years earlier when the tanker *Torrey Canyon* hit a reef off the coast of Cornwall and discharged over 100,000 tonnes of crude oil into the sea, resulting in over 100 miles of Cornish coastline being seriously polluted. How might this depiction have helped stimulate the environmental movement?

to damage British industry while doing little to tackle the world's real economic problems.

Authoritarianism

The growth of a new form of non-parliamentary politics may also be seen as a reaction against the permissiveness that had come in since the 1960s (see page 90). But it was never as clearcut as that. Some of those who had been the strongest advocates of the abolition of censorship, for example, were among the foremost in demanding that restrictions be placed on social conduct and political actions of which they disapproved, such as smoking and the **BNP**. It is a dilemma that has always troubled the liberal mind; how to reconcile freedom and conviction. It tested the limits of how far liberals would allow others to go in expressing ideas of which they disapproved.

There is also a case for interpreting the spread of environmentalism and related movements as being an aspect of the decline of organised religion in Britain in the second half of the twentieth century. Figures for all the major faiths and denominations showed a fall in formal worshippers until the

Key term

BNP
British National Party, an extremist, racist party that appeals largely to people with personality disorders. Whether it should be described as a left- or right-wing movement has excited considerable debate.

1990s when increasing numbers of immigrants (e.g. Polish Catholics and Pakistani Muslims) saw the decline reverse. As the number of church attenders decreased there was an inclination for many people to turn to modern causes to fill the gap. It may not be entirely accidental that the fervour with which environmentalists hold their views is reminiscent of the passion of some religious believers. The downside of that has been that genuine debate has been sometimes stifled with committed environmentalists regarding those who questions their assertions as being little better than '**holocaust deniers**'.

The Countryside Alliance

An interesting extraparliamentary group that appeared on the right rather than the left of politics was the **Countryside Alliance**. Angered by the Labour government's declared intention to outlaw fox hunting with hounds, the Alliance resolved to fight back. It argued that New Labour was fighting a class war not on a significant issue, but in a vindictively petty way. Knowing that the 'toffs' who took part in country sports were never likely to vote Labour in large numbers, the government could afford to attack them safe in the knowledge that it would not suffer electorally. This exposed New Labour as an urban party that had no understanding of the true nature of the land or of the people who worked on it; hence its willingness to ban hunting without thinking through the harmful effects this would have on the livelihoods of those who depended on it.

At a demonstration in London in September 2002, the Alliance was able to amass 400,000 supporters. This was nearly half the number of those who in February 2003 protested against the war in Iraq (see page 215). Tony Blair has the dubious distinction of presiding over the biggest ever anti-government protests in British history. Nevertheless, the Alliance failed. In September 2004 the government pushed its ban on fox hunting through the Commons and it became law two years later.

Focus groups

The government's ignoring of the massive protests against the Iraq War and the outlawing of fox hunting suggested that popular direct democracy had little effect if it contradicted government plans. Much more influence was exerted by **focus groups** and lobbies, which said things that government wanted to hear. This was one of the undemocratic results that sceptics had warned against when payment for MPs was introduced at the beginning of the twentieth century. This was expressed in the notion of an elective tyranny. Once a government is in power with a comfortable Commons majority there is little the ordinary citizen can do. It is true that at a general election the people can defeat a government, but only at the price of installing in office another party which will have access to the same undemocratic powers as its predecessor.

Defenders of the existing system counter this argument by acknowledging the **democratic deficit**, but pointing out the sheer

Holocaust deniers Those who dispute that the Nazi murder of the Jews took place.

Countryside Alliance An amalgam of landowners, land workers, vets, riding schools and those involved in the commercial side of fox hunting.

Focus groups Representatives of a particular viewpoint who advise government on the policies it should follow. Such groups often represent only themselves rather than the wider public. An example is the lobby group ASH (Action on Smoking and Health) which, although small in number, was able to exert a disproportionate influence.

Democratic deficit The gap between democratic intentions and their realisation.

impracticability of trying to operate direct democracy in a modern state as complex in its structures as Britain. No modern state is in a position to run such a system. The everyday demands of administration prevent it. The best that can be expected is that parties will offer in their manifestos a set of commitments to which they can then be held to account by the electorate.

Scepticism about traditional politics

A further possible explanation for the spread of extraparliamentary activity was the loss of faith in traditional politics, which, by the end of the twentieth century, could be regarded as having become stale and self-satisfied.

Peter Hennessy, the distinguished political analyst, wrote in 2003 of the cult of 'celebocracy' affecting politics as much as popular culture. This referred to a lack of substance in the new generations of MPs who made politics a career but had no experience of life and work. Many went straight from university into politics without ever having done a proper job. Largely gone were the days of workers and trade unionists with their real knowledge of the world of work or of business people who had run enterprises successfully, making money for themselves and providing jobs for others in the process.

What added to the irony was that Parliament had declined significantly in power. Decision-making was made in Brussels or by the government. That was why MPs were desperate to obtain government posts. Opinion polls suggested that MPs were not held in high esteem by the general public. One reason was that they were seen to be earning easy money; MPs were well paid, their salaries being well above the national average income, with many perks in the form of generous expenses and copper-bottomed pension rights. A more telling reason, however, for their unpopularity was that they were no longer regarded as being particularly useful.

This had been another of the warnings sounded against the introduction in 1911 of payment for MPs. It had been suggested then that to create a class of professional politicians, as MPs would necessarily become, would undermine the concept of selfless public service. Independence of thought would disappear since all MPs would become lobby fodder, casting their votes as dictated by their parties.

Yet the system had its defenders. It was arguable that lobby fodder was exactly what was wanted. Since the parties represented broad blocks of public opinion, it was appropriate that MPs elected on a party label should see it as their primary duty to vote in accordance with their party's wishes. That was the form modern democracy had taken. Politics does not stand still, so it was of little value to bemoan the passing of a system that was only ever transitory.

The decline in standards of public behaviour

There is a case for saying that despite its good intentions and undoubted achievements in many areas, the Blair government presided over a decline in social standards. It was certainly true that between 1997 and 2007 crime and social disorder grew and the streets became less safe. In Blair's final year in office there were:

- 2,731,000 cases of criminal damage in England and Wales
- 2,420,000 cases of violent offences against the person, including gun and knife crime
- 733,000 cases of burglary.

Some commentators stressed that these were merely the official figures. If to these were added the crimes that were committed but not reported to the police, or were not proceeded with because witnesses were frightened to give testimony, matters would look even worse. Every major city had its sink estates with high crime rates, widespread drug abuse and dysfunctional families. In 2007, 27 young people were stabbed to death in various cities. One journal wrote of 'a broken society of feral youths dependent on state handouts'. Britain appeared to be a truly lawless society.

Yet there was also a sense in which there was too much law. During the Blair decade, over 3000 new restrictive laws were introduced curtailing the freedoms of the individual. Some observers explained this as '**displacement theory**'. Unable to control the flourishing vandalism and violent crime that turned many parts of Britain's inner cities into **no-go areas** and made life a constant misery for the ordinary people living in them, the authorities instead got tough with easy targets. This was particularly evident in relation to motoring offences. In the year 2006–7, the use of speed cameras raised £120 million in fines. This did little to advance road safety; figures showed that speed was a contributory factor in only 10 per cent of fatal road accidents. But it outraged motorists who, guilty though they were of a technical offence, felt they were the victims of a racket run by the authorities to raise money.

Reasons for social breakdown

Pundits from left and right offered various explanations:

- Some blamed it on the progressive thinking that infected the educational and legal systems in which the experts appeared to be on the side of the disruptive pupil and the destructive young criminal.
- Some blamed it on poverty, claiming that there were still significant areas where people felt deprived and saw their only outlet in law-breaking. Others saw lawlessness as a consequence of affluence; in a get-rich-quick, celebrity consciousness age with its demand for instant gratification, enough was never enough.

Key question
Why did the Blair government become tainted by suggestions of corruption by 2007?

Key terms

Displacement theory
The process by which the inability to act successfully in one area is compensated for by overzealous action in another.

No-go areas
Regions in which the police are reluctant to pursue enquiries because of the hostility and wall of silence they will meet.

- Others put it down to the decline in religion, arguing that, whatever the rights or wrongs of religious belief, it had provided a sense of personal responsibility. Its erosion had led, therefore, to unchecked selfishness and the disregard of traditional social values based on the distinction between right and wrong.

Education

A particular explanation for declining standards that was put forward was that Tony Blair had failed in the very task that he had declared to be his priority in 1997: 'Education, Education, Education.' While it was true that there more teachers in schools by 2007 and that exam results had improved each year, there was still an underlying feeling that the system had let its pupils and the nation down.

There were repeated suggestions that the comprehensive system had largely failed in its social objective of providing equal education for all because in the end the quality of a school was largely determined by the quality of the area in which it was located. The poorest schools educationally were invariably to be found in the most socially deprived areas. Nor was it simply a matter of money. Some of the worst under-achieving schools in Britain were to be found in the London boroughs whose per capita expenditure on school pupils was among the highest in the land.

Perhaps it was all a plot, some said, to destroy quality and achievement since such concepts implied competition and elitism which undermined the egalitarian notion of the social engineers who did not care how grim things were as long as they were equally grim for everybody. It was one of the consequences of liberalism, not of the party political sort, but of the mindset that assumed that because some people had benefited unfairly under previous systems nobody at all should now be allowed to benefit.

One of the arguments was that the widespread adoption of comprehensive education had coincided with the swinging sixties when progressive educational ideas were taken up. In the training colleges and university education departments, trainee teachers were encouraged to regard deference and discipline as oppressive. Progressive theory had it that children should be encouraged in free expression. By the turn of the century, therefore, swathes of pupils in the worst areas had become ungovernable and unteachable.

Not everyone was convinced this was truly progressive. By the early twenty-first century there were signs of a significant reaction against many of the ideas that had taken hold. The Blair government, worried by drug misuse and binge drinking among the young, including those of school age, violent behaviour on the streets and a general disregard of traditional manners and civilities, introduced various initiatives in an attempt to return to the tried and tested ways of doing things. The government's plan to introduce **city academies** was a tacit admission that the

Key term

City academies
A plan, started in 2004, to create by 2010 over 200 special schools to replace the failed comprehensives in urban areas.

comprehensives had not met the expectations that had
accompanied their introduction.

Privilege

The government did not always help its own cause of ending
privilege in education. Among the leading figures in the Labour
Party, Diane Abbot, Harriet Harman and Tony Blair himself sent
their children to private schools, and other Labour MPs used
their high incomes to move house so as to be able to send their
children to a reputable school. The complaint, here, was not that
it was wrong for them to do so – it was natural for parents to wish
to do the best for their children – but that it was improper for
them to follow educational policies that denied the same right to
others.

Corruption

It never helps to create confidence in the people when their
leaders in public life fall short of the expected standards of
integrity and truthfulness. The Major government had became
mired in accusations of sleaze, the buying and selling of influence
(see page 168). The Labour opposition had been quick to taunt
and condemn the Conservatives over this. But the difficulty for
any party adopting a moral stance is that it is likely to be let down
by its own members. Human nature being what it is, scandal and
impropriety are always just around the corner. While it had been
fun for Labour in opposition to mock or grow indignant over the
follies and scandals of Conservatives, it was to find in office that it
was just as open to the charge of impropriety. Sleeze was matched
by the **cash for honours** scandal that appeared to implicate the
Prime Minister himself.

It was not simply a matter of some behaving illegally. MPs
generally seemed willing to take advantage of their access to
privilege. In 2006, there was a sense of public dismay at
Parliament's voting itself copper-bottomed pensions at a time
when ordinary pensioners were seeing a sharp decline in the
value of their contributions. Official figures also revealed that, in
2007, £337,000 of public money had been claimed by MPs in
travelling expenses.

The Conservatives during the Blair years

It could not be said that the opposition distinguished itself during
the Blair years. After a series of leaders, William Hague, Iain
Duncan Smith and Michael Howard, had failed the grab the
attention of the country or the full support of party members, the
Conservatives elected David Cameron as their leader in 2005. He
made it his task to become more Blairite than Blair. His main line
of approach was to offer more of the same. No new policies
emerged; on health, welfare, European integration, education
and the economy, Cameron promised to do the same as Labour
only better. It many ways it was a striking reversal of the way New
Labour had transformed itself by becoming more Thatcherite.
The Conservatives now planned to win the next election by

becoming Blairite. Just as Labour's left wing had complained that by shifting its ground to the centre New Labour had lost its soul, the Conservative right complained that Cameron was depriving the party of its distinctive character. Mrs Thatcher's warning on the weakness of consensus politics (see page 117) had come back to haunt both parties: 'There are dangers in consensus: it could be an attempt to satisfy people holding no particular views about anything.'

Summary diagram: Population change and social issues

Phenomenon:
- Increase in size and distribution of British population through natural increase and immigration

Problem:
- Ageing population makes increasing demands on diminishing revenue sources

Phenomenon:
- Growth in extra-parliamentary politics

Problem:
- Pressure from unrepresentative lobbies creates a democratic deficit

Phenomenon:
- Multiculturalism

Problems:
- Segregation
- Racism
- Religious tensions
- Terrorism
- Challenge to liberal values

Phenomenon:
- Decline in social values

Problems:
- Feral youths in a disordered society
- A failed education system
- Displacement theory
- Maintenance of privilege
- Low standards in public life

Study Guide: AS Question

In the style of OCR A

Assess the claim that the Downing Street Declaration was the **most** significant step towards a settlement for Northern Ireland during the period 1969–94. (50 marks)

Exam tips

The cross-references are intended to take you straight to the material that will help you to answer the question.

This question picks out one event during a 25-year period so your task is to assess its significance by comparison with other initiatives and events during the period that might have contributed to a settlement (pages 199–213). Look at it seriously, even if you are going to reject it as being less significant than another event or initiative. Equally, you must look seriously at other possibilities: 'assess' requires you to weigh events/factors/influences against each other and put them in order of significance.

Start by considering the 1993 Declaration. It was not the first agreement between the British and Irish governments, but it went further than the 1985 Anglo-Irish Agreement when, for example, Dublin accepted Ulster as part of Britain: a political fact that undermined a key IRA aim. What was new was the acceptance that the people of Ireland (north and south) had the exclusive right to solve the problems of Ireland. Further, it opened the way to the 1994 ceasefire by Republicans (Loyalists followed quickly) and was the high-profile act in the quiet but effective policy of the Major government.

Alternative tipping-points must next be considered. You might consider tough measures (e.g. sending troops to Ulster in 1969, the introduction of internment in 1971) as well as initiatives to bring both sides together (e.g. the Constitutional Convention in 1975, the Anglo-Irish Agreement in 1985). Equally, the impact of, say, the Enniskillen bombing in 1987 in turning opinion towards peace or the Fair Employment Act 1989 in tackling institutionalised prejudice might be considered. Alternatively, you might argue that the constant demographic shift against the Unionists was the underlying reason for all steps forward in the latter years. Wherever you take your argument, your answer must be clear and your analysis justified with hard evidence.

Study Guide: A2 Question

In the style of AQA

'Between 1997 and 2007, the Labour governments' economic policies were extremely successful.' Assess the validity of this view. (45 marks)

Exam tips

The cross-references are intended to take you straight to the material that will help you to answer the question.

This essay question is seeking an analytical answer that will balance the strengths and weaknesses of the Labour governments' economic policies (pages 174–5, 187–91 and 194–6). Before beginning, it would be wise to make a list of what these strengths and weaknesses were and to consider which line to argue. It is unlikely you will want to agree with the quotation in its entirety (although you might try to do so), so you should decide whether you mainly agree/disagree and for what reasons. Your paragraphs should present a clear and logical argument in support of your viewpoint.

Successes are likely to include the apparent strength of the economy in contrast to what had gone before, the lack of (or low levels of) inflation; the development of economic reserves; low levels of direct taxation; high levels of employment and the consumer boom. Weaknesses are likely to include the gradual return of inflation; the use of stealth taxes; the failure to increase employment among the young and unskilled and over-concentration on the public sector; the depletion of pension funds; the sale of gold and the extent of borrowing.

You might also like to consider whether the apparent economic success of Labour's early years had already been anticipated under the Conservatives and was more the result of international developments than Labour's own initiatives.

Glossary

1921 Treaty   The Anglo-Irish agreement that had partitioned the island of Ireland between an independent south and Northern Ireland (loosely referred to as Ulster) which remained part of the UK.

9/11   The American formulation for the date 11 September 2001.

Adam Smith Institute   A Conservative 'think-tank', which challenged the idea that the state should redistribute resources in society by taxing the rich and providing for the poor; it argued that the free play of market forces was the best way of fulfilling people's needs.

Aeneid   An epic poem by the Roman writer Virgil (70–19BC).

al-Qaeda   The Islamic terrorist organisation which organised the 9/11 attacks.

Apartheid   In theory, the notion of separate and equal development for different racial groups in South Africa; in practice, the subjection of other races to white rule.

Appeasement   The policy followed by the British government between 1935 and 1939 of trying to avoid war by accepting German and Italian territorial demands.

Arms race   In 1983 US President Reagan announced the development of a strategic defence initiative (popularly known as 'Star Wars') which when fully operational would give the USA complete protection against missile attack. This may have been exaggeration but it convinced the USSR that it could no longer keep pace with the West.

Aswan Dam   A dam on the Nile river that was intended to modernise Egypt by providing a huge supply of hydroelectric power.

Austerity   Describes the hard times the British experienced in the late 1940s. In addition to the restrictions and rationing imposed on them, people had to endure a particularly severe winter in 1946–7 which exhausted coal stocks and led to fuel shortages and regular and dispiriting cuts in domestic and industrial electricity supplies.

B Specials   A wholly Protestant part of Northern Ireland's reserve police force, seen by many as a Protestant army.

Balance of payments   The equilibrium between the cost of imports and the profits from exports. When the cost of imports outweighs the income from exports, financial crisis follows.

Battle of Orgreave   In 1984, strikers tried to prevent coke lorries leaving a British Steel coking plant in Orgreave, South Yorkshire. An estimated 6000 pickets struggled for hours against some 5000–8000 police before finally being overcome. Ninety-three arrests were made, and 51 strikers and 72 policemen were injured.

Bevanites   Followers of Aneurin Bevan, a hero of the left. Interestingly, Bevan was not always as radical as his followers. For example, at the 1957 Labour Party conference, he rejected unilateralism as a policy, describing it as an 'emotional spasm'.

Birmingham pub bombings   On 21 November 1974, in separate explosions in two public houses in Birmingham's city centre, 21 people were killed and 180 seriously injured.

Block vote   Labour Party procedures allowed individual trade union leaders to cast their conference votes on behalf of all the members of their union, which could number millions.

BNP   British National Party. An extremist, racist party that appeals largely to people with personality disorders. Whether it should be described as a left- or right-wing movement has excited considerable debate.

Broad church   Containing many conflicting viewpoints.

Capitalism   The predominant economic system in the Western world by which individuals and companies trade and invest for private profit.

Cash for honours   There were various accusations during the Blair years that the government was engaged in giving out honours and peerages to wealthy donors in return for cash donations to the Labour Party. A long police inquiry eventually concluded in 2007 that there was insufficient evidence to warrant prosecutions.

CBI   Confederation of British Industry. Represented Britain's leading manufacturers and industrialists. Officially it was politically neutral, but it tended to side with the Conservatives.

CDS   Campaign for Democratic Socialism. A number of CDS members went on to break from Labour in 1981 and form a new political party, the Social Democratic Party.

Census   An official recording of population figures, held every 10 years in the first year of the decade.

City academies   A plan, started in 2004, to create by 2010 over 200 special schools to replace the failed comprehensives in urban areas.

City-orientated   Relating to the money markets in London's international financial centre, known as 'the City'.

Client state   A society in which a significant number of the population work directly for the government or its agencies.

CND   Campaign for Nuclear Disarmament. Founded in 1958 to agitate for unilateral nuclear disarmament, it was dominated from the first by left wingers.

COHSE   Confederation of Health Service Employees.

Cold War   The period of strained relations over the period 1945–91 between the Soviet Union and its allies and the Western nations led by the USA.

Collectivism   The people and the state acting together with a common sense of purpose, which necessarily meant a restriction on individual rights.

Common market   A trading system between equal states with the minimum of regulation.

Commonwealth Immigrants Act Attempted to limit immigration by creating a voucher scheme which restricted the right of entry to those who actually had jobs to go to.

Consensus   Common agreement between the parties on major issues.

Conviction politician   Someone with strong opinions who acts out of principle rather than political expediency.

Countryside Alliance   An amalgam of landowners, land workers, vets, riding schools and those involved in the commercial side of fox hunting.

Cuban missile crisis   In October 1962, the USA, having discovered that Soviet nuclear missiles were being installed on the island of Cuba, ordered their removal. After days of acute tension, the Soviet Union gave way and ordered their dismantling and withdrawal.

Decommissioning   The giving up of weapons.

Deficit budgets   Occur when a government spends more than it raises in revenue.

Democratic deficit   The gap between democratic intentions and their realisation.

Demography   Population analysis.

Depression   The period of industrial decline that had witnessed high unemployment and social distress in many areas of Britain in the 1930s.

Devaluation   Reducing the value of the pound against the dollar with the principal aim of making it easier to sell British goods abroad since they would be cheaper in real terms.

Devolution   Granting to Wales and Scotland a considerable degree of control over their own affairs by the creation of a separate Parliament or national assembly. This form of home rule stopped short of complete independence from the UK.

Diplock Courts   Set up in Northern Ireland in 1972 to hear cases without a jury, the aim being to avoid the problem of jury members being intimidated.

Displacement theory   The process by which the inability to act successfully in one area is compensated for by overzealous action in another.

Dollar gap   Since the pound was weaker than the dollar, the goods that Britain desperately needed from North America had to be paid for in dollars.

DUP   Democratic Unionist Party, which had broken away from the Official Unionist Party in 1971.

East of Suez   A traditional shorthand way of referring to Britain's military and naval bases and commitments in the Middle East and Asia.

EFTA   The European Free Trade Association formed by Britain, Norway, Sweden, Austria, Portugal, Switzerland and Denmark.

EHRC   The Equality and Human Rights Commission, successor to the Commission for Racial Equality.

ERM   Exchange rate mechanism. A precursor to monetary union within the EU.

Euro zone   Those countries that gave up their individual currencies for the euro.

European dictators   As Foreign Secretary between 1935 and 1938, Eden had developed a deep distrust of Germany's Adolf Hitler and Italy's Benito Mussolini.

Eurorebels   A large group of Conservative MPs, openly led by Bill Cash, and supported by most of the party's Eurosceptics, who fought against the ratification of the Maastricht Treaty.

Eurosceptics   Those who doubted that the UK's closer integration into Europe would serve British interests.

Extraparliamentary   Not relying on conventional party politics.

Federation   The essence of a federation is that the member states forgo a significant degree of individual sovereignty in order for the union of states to have effective executive power.

'Fellow travellers' Crypto-Communists and Soviet sympathisers.

First past the post system The candidate with more votes than his nearest rival wins the seat, irrespective of whether he has an overall majority of the votes cast.

'Five giants' A representation of the major ills afflicting post-war Britain. *Want*, to be ended by national insurance. *Disease*, to be ended by a comprehensive health service. *Ignorance*, to be ended by an effective education system. *Squalor*, to be ended by slum clearance and rehousing. *Idleness*, to be ended by full employment.

Flying pickets Groups of union members ready to rush to areas where strikes had been called to add their weight in persuading workers not to go through the factory gates.

Focus groups Representatives of a particular viewpoint who advise government on the policies it should follow. Such groups often represent only themselves rather than the wider public. An example is the lobby group ASH (Action on Smoking and Health) which, although small in number, was able to exert a disproportionate influence.

Free market An economic system in which the forces of supply and demand are allowed to operate naturally without regulation by the government.

French Algeria Algeria, part of the French empire, had a large Arab population most of whom supported the Algerian independence movement.

Friends of the Earth and **Greenpeace** Similar movements, which originated in North America, but quickly spread to Europe. They believed in direct action as a way of spreading their beliefs about the threat to the planet.

GDP Gross domestic product. The annual total value of goods produced and services provided in Britain.

Genocide The planned extermination of a people or a race.

Gerrymandering Manipulating constituency boundaries so as to leave Protestants in control.

Gestapo The notorious Nazi secret police that had terrorised Germany under Adolf Hitler, between 1933 and 1945.

GNP Gross national product. The annual total value of goods and services provided by Britain at home and in trade with other countries.

GPs General practitioners, family doctors.

Greenham Common Became the site of a women's peace camp which picketed the US base from 1981 to 2000, a graphic example of the extraparliamentary protests against government policy that were a feature of late twentieth-century politics.

Holocaust The murdering of six million Jews in Nazi-occupied Europe.

Holocaust deniers Those who dispute that the Nazi murder of the Jews took place.

Hubris Punishment for arrogance.

Humiliation of France In a six-week period in May and June 1940, France had been totally overwhelmed by German forces and forced to surrender and accept occupation.

IMF The International Monetary Fund. A scheme intended to prevent countries going bankrupt. It began operating in

1947 and by 1990 had been joined by over 150 countries. Each of the member states deposited into a central fund from which it could then draw in time of need.

Imperial guilt   The feeling among the ex-colonial powers that their previous possession of colonies disqualified them from taking direct action in African affairs.

Independent nuclear deterrent   In 1947, to the anger of its left wing, the Labour government initiated a research programme that led to the detonation of a British atom bomb in 1952 and a hydrogen bomb in 1957.

Inflation   A decline in the purchasing power of money, which meant Britain had to spend more dollars to buy its imports.

Infrastructure   The interlocking systems and installations which enable a nation's industrial economy to operate, e.g. transport, power supply, sewerage and communications.

INLA   The Irish National Liberation Army, whose republicanism was part of its programme for Marxist world revolution.

Interest rates   Used to raise or lower the cost of borrowing money, thus retarding or stimulating economic activity.

Invisible exports   The sale of financial and insurance services to foreign buyers, traditionally one of Britain's major sources of income from abroad.

IRA   The Irish Republican Army. Dedicated to the creation through violence of an all-Ireland republic. Its political front was Sinn Féin, a legitimate political party. At the end of 1969 the movement split into the Official IRA and the Provisional IRA.

ISA   Individual Savings Account.

Israel   In 1948, in the face of the undying hatred of its Arab neighbours, Israel became a sovereign Jewish state, taking most of the territory known as Palestine.

Jihadists   Self-proclaimed warriors in the defence of Islam.

Joint Intelligence Committee   The government body principally responsible for providing ministers with national security information.

Kenya   Between 1952 and 1960 clashes between British forces and Kenyan nationalists resulted in the death of 13,000 native Kenyans and 100 Europeans.

King's Speech   The formal address delivered by the monarch at the beginning of each parliamentary year setting out the government's policies.

Korean War   US-dominated UN armies resisted the takeover of South Korea by the Chinese-backed Communists of North Korea from 1950 to 1953. Britain suffered the loss of 1788 servicemen, with another 2498 being wounded.

Labour left   A significant number of Labour MPs, some of whom were Marxists, were strongly sympathetic towards the Soviet Union. At this stage, the full horrors of Stalin's regime had yet to be revealed, so it was still possible to believe that the USSR was a model socialist state.

'Land fit for heroes'   Term used by Lloyd George's wartime government of 1916–18 when promising to reward the British people for their heroic efforts.

Lib–Lab pact   A deal made by James Callaghan and David Steel in March 1977, committing the Liberals to vote with the government in the Commons in return for the government's agreement to consult the Liberals on key issues. The pact lapsed in the autumn of 1978.

Life expectancy The remaining number of years an individual is likely to live after a given age.

Londonderry A disputed place name; republicans called it Derry.

Loyalist Anti-republican, pro-unionist.

Mahatma Great soul.

Majority voting A system that attracted federalists since it enabled contentious resolutions to be passed without being blocked by a member state using its individual veto.

Market forces The natural laws of supply and demand operating without interference by government.

Means test In the pre-war period, to qualify for dole or relief, individuals or families had to give precise details of all the money they had coming in.

Militant Tendency A Marxist group founded in 1964 with the aim of infiltrating Labour and forcing revolutionary policies on it. It had considerable success at local level, becoming a dominant force in the 1970s and 1980s in the councils of Merseyside.

Mod cons Short for modern conveniences, e.g. central heating, and household accessories such as vacuum cleaners, refrigerators, radios and TVs.

Mods and rockers Mods drove motor scooters and were rather more smartly dressed than rockers, who rode proper motorbikes; their pre-arranged fights usually took place in seaside resorts on bank holidays.

Mons and Dunkirk Celebrated occasions in the First and Second World Wars when British forces recovered from initial defeats to win the final military struggle.

Nationalisation Clause IV of the Labour Party's constitution committed it to achieving 'the common ownership of the means of production, distribution and exchange'. In practice, common ownership or public control meant government control.

NATO The North Atlantic Treaty Organisation. A defensive alliance formed in 1949 by 10 Western European countries as a safeguard against Soviet expansion. The USA eagerly accepted the invitation to join.

Natural change The net difference between the number of deaths and the number of births.

NCB The National Coal Board, the body with overall responsibility for running the industry.

Net migration The net difference between the number who left Britain and those who entered it.

New Commonwealth Largely West Indians, Indians, Pakistanis and Bangladeshis.

New Labour Began as a slogan at the 1994 Labour Party conference, the first held with Tony Blair as leader, and became the title by which the party was known from then on.

New right A broad conservative movement in the USA and Britain in the 1980s which combined an attack on Keynesian economics and growing state power with an emphasis on the need to maintain traditional social values.

Night of the Long Knives A deliberate over-dramatisation used by the press to compare Macmillan's reshuffle with Hitler's massacre of his leading supporters in Germany in 1934.

No-go areas   Regions in which the police are reluctant to pursue enquiries because of the hostility and wall of silence they will meet.

North Sea oil   This resource had come on tap in the late 1970s and turned Britain from a net importer to a net exporter of oil.

NUPE   National Union of Public Employees.

Old Commonwealth   Largely Australians, New Zealanders, Canadians and South Africans.

OPEC   Organisation of Petroleum Exporting Countries. Formed in 1961, this body came to represent all the leading oil-producing nations, including the strategically important Arab states of Bahrain, Iraq, Kuwait, Libya and Saudi Arabia.

Parliamentary Reform Act of 1949   First introduced in 1947, this measure, which became law in 1949, reduced the delaying power of the House of Lords over a Commons' bill to two sessions and one year.

PEP   Personal Equity Plan.

Poll tax   A flat-rate levy to fund local services, to be paid by all the adults resident in the local area, not just owners of property; introduced into Scotland in 1989 and into England and Wales in 1990.

Populist   A way of appealing directly to ordinary people that bypasses normal party politics.

Poverty trap   The dilemma facing the low paid; if they continued working they were penalised by being taxed, which reduced their net income to a level little higher than if they simply drew unemployment benefit.

Prevention of Terrorism Act   Introduced in November 1974 to give the police and authorities considerably extended powers of search and arrest.

Prime Minister's Questions   A weekly session when selected members of the House of Commons put direct questions to the Prime Minister.

Print workers   Until the 1980s, among the highest paid workers in British industry, they were reluctant to accept new work practices based on new technology since this would threaten their job security and high earnings.

Privatisation   The selling of nationalised (government-owned) concerns fully or in part to private buyers and investors.

Property-owning democracy   A society in which as many people as possible are encouraged to become homeowners, an extension of the principle that the ownership of property is an essential component of democracy.

Proportional representation   The allocation of seats to parties according to the number of votes they gain overall.

Protectionist   Making non-common market goods uncompetitive by denying them entry or placing tariffs on them.

PSBR   Public Sector Borrowing Requirement. The public sector includes the whole of national and local government activity and the nationalised industries. The cost of running these has to be met from government revenue. If the revenue is insufficient the difference is made up by borrowing. The gap between government revenue and government needs is known as the PSBR.

Psephologist   An expert on election trends and voting patterns.

Puritanism   An attitude that has religious roots but has become secularised. It is the view among certain people that because they find some forms of social behaviour distasteful they are entitled to prohibit others from engaging in them, even to the point of making the behaviour illegal.

R&D   Research and development. Economic research and development provide the means of industrial growth.

Reagan's America   Ronald Reagan and Margaret Thatcher shared a great respect and liking for each other. Reagan's presidency from 1980 to 1988 saw the USA follow economic policies which were very similar to Mrs Thatcher's.

Real wages   The purchasing power of earnings when set against prices. When prices are high money will buy less; when prices are low the same amount of money will buy more.

Rebate   The return to the UK of a proportion of its budgetary payment to the EU.

Respect   Founded on 25 January 2004 in London as a socialist breakaway group from the Labour Party, its name represents the words Respect, Equality, Socialism, Peace, Environmentalism, Community, and Trade Unionism.

RUC   Royal Ulster Constabulary. An almost exclusively Protestant armed police force. The Catholic population came to regard the RUC as a sectarian force whose main task was to coerce them and protect the Protestant political establishment.

Run on sterling   A catastrophic fall in Britain's currency reserves caused by large withdrawals of deposits by international investors.

SAS   Special Air Service, the crack anti-terrorist unit of the British armed services.

Savings ratio   The annual percentage of an individual's disposable income that is saved rather than spent.

Schuman Plan   A scheme by which the European nations pooled their most productive resources – coal and steel – in a European Coal and Steel Community (ECSC).

Scottish Parliament   Created in 1998 following a referendum in Scotland the previous year, in which, in a turnout of 60 per cent, three-quarters of the voters opted for a system in which Scotland, while remaining within the UK, would have its affairs run by a Scottish Parliament and a Scottish Executive with tax-raising powers.

Selsdon man   An imaginary anti-Keynesian, pro-market individual.

Shareholders   Investors in companies or public utilities, such as electricity and gas.

Sleaze   The term covered such activities as 'cash for questions', the practice whereby, in return for payment, MPs asked questions in the Commons that were intended to promote the interests of particular commercial companies.

Smack of firm government   Eden had an unfortunate habit, when emphasising a point, of smacking the palm of one hand with the back of the other. It was this that the press were mocking when they accused him of being irresolute as Prime Minister.

Social Chapter   Sometimes referred to as the Social Charter, part of the Maastricht Treaty, which committed EU member states to introduce extensive welfare schemes.

Social contract   An agreement in 1972 between Wilson and Vic Feather, the TUC General Secretary, to the effect that when Labour was returned to power the unions would follow a wage restraint policy in return for the adoption of pro-worker industrial policies by the government.

Social reconstruction   Shaping society so as to provide protection and opportunity for all its citizens.

Soviet bloc   The countries of Eastern Europe, which were dominated by the Soviet Union.

Special relationship   The term coined by Churchill in 1946 to describe the common values and perceptions that, he believed, made the USA and Britain natural allies.

Stagflation   A compound word of stagnation and inflation. It referred to the situation in which industry declined but inflation still persisted, with the result that the economy suffered the worst of both worlds.

Stop–go   When consumption and prices rose too quickly, the government put on the 'brake' by increasing taxes and raising interest rates, thus making it more difficult to borrow money. When production and exports declined, the government pressed the 'accelerator' by cutting taxes and lowering interest rates, thus making it easier to borrow money.

Stormont   The building in Belfast which housed the Northern Ireland Parliament.

Subsidiarity   The principle that in matters of special concern to a particular member state, that state should have the right to bypass European decisions.

Swinging sixties   The 1960s saw the relaxing of many of the old taboos in regard to lifestyle and social behaviour; the music of the Beatles and the Rolling Stones, and the fashions of London's Carnaby Street typified the youthful character of the age.

Taoiseach   Gaelic for Prime Minister.

Teddy boys   Young men of the 1950s with a strong tendency to violence when gathered in numbers; they took their name from their style of dress which recalled the fashions of King Edward (Teddy) VII.

TESSA   Tax-Exempt Special Savings Account.

TGWU   Transport and General Workers Union.

'The six'   France, Germany, Italy, Belgium, the Netherlands and Luxembourg.

Third way   A term, relating to the avoidance of extremes, often associated with Blair and New Labour's policies in general.

Treaty establishing a Constitution for Europe   Brought together the existing EU treaties into one formal binding document.

UDI   Unilateral Declaration of Independence.

UN Security Council   The body set up to resolve international disputes; its permanent members were the USSR, the USA, Britain, France and China.

Unilateralists   Those who believed that Britain should give up its atomic weapons without waiting for a multilateral agreement between the nuclear powers to do so.

Velvet revolution   In the face of popular nationalist opposition, the USSR abandoned its authority over the countries of Eastern Europe without a fight; this culminated in the collapse of the USSR itself in 1991.

Veto   Each individual member of the UN Security Council had the right to cancel out the collective or majority decision of the others.

Wage freeze   An undertaking not to press for higher wages until Britain's economy had improved.

Welsh Assembly   Created in 1998 following a referendum the previous year which gave the pro-devolution voters a mere 0.6 per cent victory; initially the Assembly was simply a revising chamber examining UK measures that related to Wales, but later legislation gave Wales governmental powers, similar to those enjoyed in Scotland.

'Wets'   Used during the Thatcher years as a description of those in the government and Conservative Party who opposed or were uncertain about the tough measures that Mrs Thatcher adopted.

White Paper   A preliminary parliamentary statement of the government's plans in regard to a bill that it intends to introduce.

Winter of discontent   The term comes from the familiar first line of Shakespeare's *Richard III*: 'Now is the winter of our discontent'.

WTO   World Trade Organisation, the international body responsible for negotiating and monitoring trade agreements between countries.

Yuppy (or yuppie)   Young upwardly mobile professional person.

Zeitgeist   Spirit of the times, i.e. the dominant prevailing attitude.

Index